"*Losing the Garden* tells the story of two remarkable lives and one remarkable death. But what makes this memoir so unusual—and so valuable—in the literature of suicide is that in trying to understand why her beloved husband of twenty-seven years chose to freeze to death on a mountaintop, and why she supported that choice, the author comes to understand her own life better as well. In the process, we learn as much about life and love—and love's limitations—as we do about despair and self-destruction. Written with astonishing candor, uncommon grace, and, I think, real courage, *Losing the Garden* is a book I will not soon forget."

— George Howe Colt, author of *The November of the Soul: The Enigma of Suicide*

"*Losing the Garden* is a beautiful book, full of detail that I am amazed the author amassed, and wise, ruminative insight. The book was painful to read, yet wondrous in its lyricism and truth."

— Alison Osius, senior editor, *Outside*

"*Losing the Garden* is much more than a story of a marriage. It is a story of a complicated man who found solace in mountains. Guy Waterman, a much adored, charismatic leader in protecting wilderness lands, needed wild places. I have read this book perhaps ten times. Each time I find a deeper layer of art, truth, and courage. Many of us are obsessed with wilderness. I suspect we go there for more than just beauty and fun—and dare not explore why. *Losing the Garden* shows that we can explore the unexplored in ourselves. That we must know our own demons. Waterman shows that there is nothing 'bad' in mental illness when it joins with joy, intelligence, and caring to make a fascinating and complicated person."

— Christine Woodside, author of *Going Over the Mountain*

"I've written three books on the memoir as a genre, but I have never read a more powerful one than Laura Waterman's *Losing the Garden*. Waterman has traveled far out of her comfort zone here, and the honesty and insights of her writing are astonishing. I have many favorite passages, but my favorite is this one: 'Shortly before his suicide, Guy told me that he had accomplished all he wanted. In a way, he was saying that he had come to the end of learning—that is, all he was interested in learning. There is always more to learn.' I will remember this passage, and the entire memoir, for a long time."

— Jeffrey Berman, author of *Dying to Teach:*
A Memoir of Love, Loss, and Learning

"*Losing the Garden* is a beautifully written, detailed chronicle of thirty years of a marriage that included mountain climbing, wilderness living, and collaborative writing. Guy and Laura Waterman shared a seemingly idyllic life, but there was a tragic dimension, revealed here with thoughtful compassion and remarkable honesty. This is a complex, courageous, and quietly stunning book."

— Reeve Lindbergh, author of *Two Lives*

"Laura and Guy Waterman set the wilderness ethics' bar high, not just for themselves, but for the rest of us who spend time in wild places. Learning that Guy was besieged by his own demons does not diminish the power of their message to live lightly on the land, but rather it gives it depth and humanity."

— Mary Margaret Sloan, former president, American Hiking Society

"A compelling memoir demands a precarious dance between the universal and the unusual. . . . The result is a very slow waltz during which the dancers hardly touch."

— *Boston Globe*, Editor's Pick

"Like the treasured books the Watermans read aloud every evening for solace, instruction, and delight, through times of enchantment and times of great pain, here is a book that proves again that whatever life's catastrophes, the garden surrounds us."

— *Northern Woodlands*

Losing the Garden

Losing the Garden

The Story of a Marriage, a Suicide, and a
New Life of Self-Discovery

Laura Waterman

Foreword by Charles Johnson

AN IMPRINT OF STATE UNIVERSITY OF NEW YORK PRESS
www.sunypress.edu

Cover Credit: Ned Therrien

Published by State University of New York Press, Albany

Printed in the United States of America

Excelsior Editions is an imprint of State University of New York Press

For information, contact State University of New York Press, Albany, NY
www.sunypress.edu

Library of Congress Cataloging-in-Publication Data

Names: Waterman, Laura, author.
Title: Losing the garden : the story of a marriage / Laura Waterman.
Description: Albany : State University of New York Press, [2025]
Identifiers: LCCN 2024009234 | ISBN 9781438499925 (paperback) | ISBN
    9781438499918 (ebook)
Subjects: LCSH: Wives of suicide victims. | Suicide. | Suicide
    victims—Family relationships.
Classification: LCC HV6545 .W38 2024 | DDC 362.28—dc23/eng/20240916
LC record available at https://lccn.loc.gov/2024009234

10 9 8 7 6 5 4 3 2 1

ALSO BY LAURA WATERMAN

Starvation Shore: A Novel

Calling Wild Places Home: A Memoir in Essays

ALSO BY LAURA AND GUY WATERMAN

The Green Guide to Low-Impact Hiking and Camping,
    previous editions published as *Backwoods Ethics: A Guide to Low-*
    Impact Camping and Hiking

Forest and Crag: A History of Hiking, Trail Blazing, and
    Adventure in the Northeast Mountains

Wilderness Ethics: Preserving the Spirit of Wildness

Yankee Rock & Ice: A History of Climbing in the
    Northeastern United States

A Fine Kind of Madness: Mountain Adventures Tall and True

Barra: The Waterman Homestead.
The Waterman Collection.

For Guy

[The Mole] had patiently hunted through the wood for an hour or more, when at last to his joy he heard a little answering cry. . . . "Ratty! Is that really you?"

— Kenneth Grahame, The Wind in the Willows

It is those we live with and love and should know who elude us.

— Norman Maclean, A River Runs through It

It is hard for me to say what is precisely true. Memory distorts. Psychology, emotions, good health or bad — all drag their feet across events. The details that I might remember one day are not those that I might remember on another day. And certainly my memory has its own agenda — to show me off this way or that. My subjectivity is the smudgy window through which I squint.

— Stephen Dobyns, contributor's note,
Best American Short Stories 1999

FOREWORD

Charles Johnson

We are called "survivors," those of us who have lost a loved one to suicide. We are so named because suicide is not a solitary act, affecting only the victim. As with soldiers killed in combat, such deaths profoundly and eternally impact those who fought alongside, but lived. Survivors are forever bound to one another in a perplexing and tenacious grief. But they are also united in trying to make sense of what happened, while struggling to recover their own lives from the emotional rubble, and put the pieces back into some kind of coherent whole, however different it may be from what it was.

Laura Waterman and I knew of each other for decades, through like interests, mutual friends, outdoor activities, and writing. She, often coauthoring with her husband, has written several classic books on hiking and climbing the mountains of New England and the Northeast (*Forest and Crag, Yankee Rock & Ice, Wilderness Ethics*, and others), while I have focused on natural history of the same region (*The Nature of Vermont, Bogs of the Northeast, In Season*, etc.). Each has published a book related to polar exploration, particularly during the "golden era" of the nineteenth and early twentieth centuries: her *Starvation Shore*, a historical novel based on the ill-fated Greely Expedition of 1881, my *Ice Ship*, a "biography" of the famous Norwegian ship *Fram*, 1892 to 1912.

But we did not get to know each other until we shared our experiences with suicide, she of her husband, I of my son. We read each other's memoirs — hers already published, mine in manuscript form — and discovered the same current coursing through our separate stories. Laura's memoir *Losing the Garden: The Story of a Marriage* has a deceptively straightforward title that embraces much: the foretelling of Guy's suicide, the enfolding of the paradoxes of a complex relationship. She recounts her life with enigmatic, charismatic, obsessive, and highly principled Guy Waterman, like Laura a noted writer and devotee of high mountain areas of Northeastern United States. The subtitle refers to the life they lived together for thirty years: deep in the backwoods of Vermont, in a house they built themselves, a mile and a half from the nearest road, without electricity, plumbing, or phone, heated with wood, nourished by food they grew and stored. This was their "garden," their Eden, their physical and spiritual sustenance, the nucleus of their bond, the point from which they ventured out into the mountains they loved and would write about.

Yet, there was another part of this garden, the hidden side of this Eden. Guy was burdened in body and soul: by depression (which he either did not recognize or refused to acknowledge), by the deaths of two sons from his previous marriage, by an increasing frustration — almost anger — with the physical losses of aging. He meticulously planned his suicide for over a year and a half, with Laura's knowledge and reluctant, dismayed acceptance. On the appointed day in February 2000, Guy said goodbye, walked out of the house, and disappeared into the forest. Honoring his wishes, she waited three days before notifying authorities. His frozen body was found near the summit of Mt. Lafayette in New Hampshire's White Mountains.

As her story evolves, it becomes much more than a documentary of Guy's life and death, something well beyond a eulogy. Through unflinching eyes, by writing that carries all the more power for being understated and unsentimental, Laura widens her field of vision. By degrees, she becomes aware of her own complex, buried feelings about the tormented man she loved, even in his fatal obsession, and begins examining what was behind her acquiescence in the face of his long-wished-for dramatic demise.

At its core, this stirring memoir is about discovering one's inner self through the loss of what is most precious in life. It is also about coming to understand, then accept, love in all its contradictory dimensions — the fulfilling and comforting aspects, but also the painful, the maddening, even the incomprehensible.

In the biblical story of Eden, Adam and Eve are cast out of paradise for their sins. In *Losing the Garden*, no one is cast out, there is no sin, no one is at fault. Laura and Guy lose their Eden because they are only human. Do not all our Edens, created out of imagination and desire, eventually disappear, or grow into something else?

To me, a fellow survivor, her words ring pure and true, the tones passing directly to the heart, and to the heart of things, where deepest feelings lie. The reverberations, though fading over time, never completely end.

CHAPTER *one*

There is a land of the living and a land of the dead and the bridge is love, the only survival, the only meaning.

— Thornton Wilder, *The Bridge of San Luis Rey*

The morning Guy leaves would seem like any ordinary winter morning to someone looking in the window of our small cabin in the clearing.

I prepare our hot cereal of rolled oats, wheat germ, raisins, dried milk, and maple syrup on the woodstove. Guy dishes out applesauce, which I canned that fall. At the table he goes over his plans with me again: drive to Crawford Notch in New Hampshire's White Mountains to get the most accurate forecast from the Mount Washington Observatory, then drive to Franconia Notch, and if the weather holds cold and clear, start hiking up the Old Bridle Path by noon. If not, he'll wait it out in a motel. "I hope you won't have to go to a motel, Guy," I say. I picture the dismal bed, Guy sitting on it reading his copy of *Baseball Digest* while he waits for the weather to get cold.

Our voices are low as we sit at the table, the usual easy back-and-forth. The kettle on the stove hums, a background sound that steadies me. As Guy talks, I can't take my eyes off him.

He springs up, ever the fast eater. He wants to be off by eight. I sit at the table and finish my breakfast, continuing to watch him as he completes his packing with the same efficiency, almost enthusiasm, he always shows when preparing for a hike. He moves around our cabin, his energy focused. I've seen this so often. But today I see he is taking very little. Usually his pack bulges with winter gear, even for a day trip. I watch him slide in his two canteens: one with water, the other holding half alcohol and half water, "to make the job easier," as we have talked about. He wraps his sweater in a plastic bag and stuffs it in his pack.

I leave the table to set up the dishpan and drain board. Guy strides over to the ash log by the door and sits down to put on his gaiters and boots. The sight of him within touching distance on the ash log is so utterly familiar that I can't make it real that in a few minutes my husband is going to walk out the door for the last time. He finishes lacing the first boot and looks up at me with a half-smile. I feel his concern, and I imagine him saying: *I've changed my mind.* But he doesn't. And I know he isn't going to, even though these words keep hanging in my head. I watch my hands in the dishpan doing their job, not shaking much. I look at him again. His head is bent, knotting the second boot. "This time you won't be coming home to tell me the tale — how it all comes out," I say, and send him a small smile.

He looks up and grins back, and I feel the connection between us tighten. "I won't even be able to send you a postcard," he says, continuing the joke.

He bends over the boot, and when he looks up again the concerned look is back, and he says, "Make bread today, Laura."

I stare at him, thinking this is a strange thing to say. But in fact the old loaf is down to a few stale slices. We need bread, or rather, I will need bread.

He stands up, adjusting his tam to its usual jaunty angle. I know he's almost ready to leave. I reach for the dish towel. I don't feel tears, but I know I can't speak. Again I hear his voice saying: *I've changed my mind.* I have to lean with my back to the counter, the towel in my hand, a pose that looks casual but is keeping me upright. I'm watching him, trying to take in all of him, every bit forever at once. At the same time I'm studying what he does next so I can know what to do next, like meshed gears. One tooth following another. Mine is the following tooth.

"I'll always be with you," Guy says. He is leaning toward me, looking me full in the eyes, and as he speaks I feel his strong love.

"I know you will," I say. But I'm thinking: *How can you "be with me" if you're not actually with me?*

"I feel very close to you, Laura," he says.

I say I feel close to him. Though, again, his words surprise me. In that moment I feel, as always, an immense love, a desire to help him do what he needs to do. As to feeling close, I know that Guy has always held one part — the deepest part — separate from me. I watch his face as he speaks, and I know he is trying to leave me with the right words. My eyes drop to the familiar knobby shape of his hands. Woodsman's hands. Climber's hands. Muscled fingers with arthritic knuckles, yet when he plays his piano he never blurs the notes. And I find myself thinking the unthinkable: that if he changed his mind now, I would need to make an enormous adjustment. Guy has been heading toward this moment for years; I have known that he wanted to end his life for the past eighteen months. I've made plans for how I will live without him. We're on the same train, and though I want Guy to pull the whistle, I realize that I've been such a willing passenger that if he chose to cut the engine now, I would feel derailed. The script Guy has written calls for this final scene to end with him walking out the door. So submerged I can't acknowledge it, I know that I will feel relief after he is gone.

He says: "Be brave."

Then he says: "Please don't come out on the porch." I don't know why he doesn't want me to come out to see him off, as I often do, but I don't ask why. I just nod against his neck. It is hard to give him a good hug because he is wearing his pack and windbreaker. I concentrate on taking in his smell, his compact size, the breadth of his shoulders, the strength of his chest. I feel the wetness on his face. It's his tears. I'm still holding on to mine.

We break apart. He opens the door. I go into the bedroom and watch out the window as he kneels to strap on his snowshoes, first the right foot, then the left. He stands up and straightens his pack, gazing down toward the garden buried in snow. I see he's about to start down the path without his ice axe, as I thought he might, the one his father took up the Matterhorn more than seventy years ago.

"Guy!" I call as I walk out onto the porch. But he has remembered at the last moment and turns back toward the house.

"You saw?" he asks. All I can manage is a nod.

"Thank you," he says.

Our eyes meet and lock as I hand him his father's ice axe with the long wooden shaft. As I let go, he says, "Goodbye."

"Goodbye, Guy." My voice answering seems to hold him there a second longer.

Then he drops his eyes and turns in the same motion. I watch him snowshoe away, standing on the porch without my coat in the February cold. He comes to where the path meets the woods and turns, as I knew he would, because he wants to catch in his mind the last sight of the cabin in the clearing — and me, left behind in the life that we built together at Barra. He throws up his arm in a wave. I wave back.

CHAPTER two

I have full cause of weeping, but this heart

Shall break into a hundred thousand flaws

Or ere I'll weep. O Fool! I shall go mad.

— William Shakespeare, *King Lear*

I came back into the house and began to make bread as Guy had suggested. Now I was in tears. He would never eat this loaf with me. But measuring out the flour, mixing, and kneading the familiar dough, the routine of this calmed me. After I'd wedged the bowl between the rafters above the woodstove so the dough would rise, I sat down at our table and opened the folder of notes Guy had given me that morning at breakfast. "Please don't look at this until after I'm gone," he'd said, adding, would I mind seeing that these letters reached their proper destinations among our family and friends?

"Of course," I answered. He'd finished writing these the night before.

"Here's the last three pages of 'Prospero's Options,'" he said.

"The ending." I cracked a feeble joke, and he handed me the last pages of the memoir he'd started two winters earlier, all of which I had read except for this.

But first I read his note to me: "So much of my life fell short, but with you together we built something here, didn't we?"

I sat at the table holding his note in my hands and felt a crushing sadness that Guy felt his life fell short. I knew he lived with regret, but to put it in his last words showed me how this regret had shadowed his life.

The second half of the sentence told me what our homesteading life of the past twenty-seven years had meant to him. As did his final words, "Thanks for showing me the greatest love I've ever known."

Nearly thirty years earlier we had talked about how if our plan of living self-sufficiently on the land did not work, we could move back to the city. We had said this, but we had burned our bridges — we left our jobs and packed up our belongings — and we both knew we weren't going back. Just a few months before, Guy had told me that it was not in him to move to another kind of life. By then, I knew that. Here at the place Guy called Barra he had created a world apart. After a while it grew into the only world he could bear.

Before moving to Vermont, Guy Waterman had been a jazz pianist in Washington, DC, a political aide on Capitol Hill, and a corporate speechwriter in New York City. Diverse careers — or stabs at careers — that were mostly in his past before we met. On June 8, 1973, he stood in front of the General Electric headquarters at Fifty-Second Street and Lexington Avenue with his fellow executives who'd just taken him out to a farewell lunch. "Gentlemen," Guy announced, as he loosened his tie and stuffed it in his pocket, "I'm never coming back to Manhattan Island again." He never did. He was forty-one.

From reading what he had left for me, I took the first unsteady steps that would lead me to a new perspective on our life, that is, the role I had played in my life with Guy. This began within hours of his leaving. It grew in me — a kind of awakening — as the days, then the weeks, months, even years went by. Guy's dissatisfaction with his life filled him with a blackness he didn't want to talk about. Small things could trigger it. Take building a set of shelves — something tricky that took two people working together. If it began to go awry, Guy would bear down, hammering harder with a set jaw. I could feel him draw into himself, and my "How can I help?" didn't help. His hammer strokes pelted down like knockout blows crowding me backward as I held the saw, which dangled uselessly in my hand. As the years moved on, I avoided pushing him into conversations that made him unhappy and placed us at odds. I told myself that the decisions he made, even if they would not have worked for me, worked for him. After all, hadn't this move to our land been a good idea? I had schooled myself not to question Guy's choices, even when I did not understand them. So I raised no questions in his final decision to take his own life.

"I could keep going, Laura," he said. "But I don't want to let one day slide into another, then another and another, until I can't climb a mountain anymore."

"But," I said, "at the beginning you had said you wanted to grow old with me."

"I have," he said.

To me sixty-seven wasn't old.

Later I found that he had kept going far longer than I had ever imagined.

When I was cleaning out his cupboards in our bedroom about two weeks after he died, I found some pages torn out of a three-by-five-inch spiral-bound notepad. Eight years before, on April 13, 1992, Guy had begun a suicide note to me.

Dearest Laura,

I expect you may take this as a very selfish act. It is. I am getting out of a world which I find increasingly unbearable, but I leave you behind to cope by yourself, in a setting we designed for two. I am very very sorry.

But I don't think you've found me a pleasure to be around lately. I hope that you may create a good life without me and then may look back on earlier, good times, things we created together, or enjoyed together, and maybe a few kindnesses I used to do for you once in a while. I think I've been hung up too long on wondering how you could get along without me. . . . I am going on the assumption that I was just getting worse and worse, and becoming a drag on your life. I'm not trying to say I do this for you — of course not, I do it for myself. I guess I'm just trying to justify why it's probably as well for you once you work out a new life.

You have been wonderful to me, I know no one so constant to her loved ones, but the demons within have taken over. Barra was a wonderful dream, and we pulled it off, we made it work, we created something. Didn't we? We also stood for something in this world, though others often articulated it better than we.

But, Laura, it's just too hard. It's just too sad. Everything fades, everything sours. Barra doesn't, but I can't shut out the rest of the world.

Please remember me from when I was kinder to you, in days now long gone, not the poisoned spirit I have become.

Please remember the good and forgive the bad.

This note wasn't signed. As I stood in the bedroom and turned the pages, I found another note dated a few weeks later, May 2, 1992. This was written the day after Guy's sixtieth birthday, and it read more like a meditation or stocktaking in a note to himself.

As I turn 60, it seems to me that life holds no further pleasure adequate to offset the disagreeableness. As of now, I would like to see the Spring '93 book projects to completion, because of the income which they will assure to Laura — and, admittedly, in hopes of seeing how they look when done. So it may be that after next sugar season — in late April '93 — might be a good time to conclude.

The trick probably is to get thoroughly in mind that life holds no further interest; that physical ailments are beginning to accumulate to the point of being a significant determent to enjoying life; and that the pain of unavoidable conflicts and repressed hostilities will persist from now on, so that there is less pain to leaving life than to holding on to it. Oddly enough the chief attraction to remaining on earth for now is curiosity to do more baseball research and writing, and to continue with the

elaborate fantasy baseball which has occupied my leisure hours
for so many years now.

Otherwise, I'm quite prepared to accept 60 years as a sufficient lifetime; and
my intermittent glories as piano player, politician, father, homesteader, and
mountain environmental advocate and activist as concluded.

Was Guy trying to talk himself into taking his own life? This note read more
like an account of debits and credits, even rationalization. There was so much
distance between what he seemed to feel and words like "unavoidable conflicts
and repressed hostilities." I was not even sure what he meant by them.

Next followed a list of seventeen ailments, any one of which struck me as triv-
ial — fallen arches, a nagging bowel complaint — but the accumulation, I knew,
was overwhelming to Guy, who had a tendency to project worst-case scenarios.

The note continued with ideas (for me?) to include in the books we were currently working on, and it ended as follows:

> Having thought a great deal about setting up a Living Will has
> prompted an extension of that principle.
> The Living Will essentially premises that each individual has
> a right to conclude life sooner rather than later, in situations
> where that makes sense.
> Having turned 60, I'm at a point of recognizing that the
> remaining years are limited from now on anyway. So is not each
> individual entitled to make a decision to conclude life when that
> makes sense?

Before 60, to end one's life may be viewed as destructive, or a failure to face
and solve problems. But after 60, may a decision to conclude life not simply be
a sensible option to take?

Why select the age of sixty? I found this note deeply disturbing. Down in the
subbasement of my consciousness, which I was very far from reaching then, I
felt the faint stirrings of anger at Guy — that he had had these thoughts and kept
them so secret from me.

I was aware that Guy had felt "down" at the time of his sixtieth birthday, but
I had no idea that he was looking for a way out of life. Around that time Guy
suggested we join the Hemlock Society. We had both drawn up living wills. Guy
had read Final Exit, the book the Hemlock Society offers about ways to end
one's life. He had talked then about how disagreeable death by hanging sounded,
how messy shooting oneself would be, and how risky and difficult it seemed to
acquire the medications needed to do the job properly. We had quite a conversation about this, but I never thought to ask him, "Are you thinking about suicide
anytime soon?" I took his interest as an intellectual curiosity that he might think

about turning into reality years down the pike. I didn't read that book, though I had no argument with suicide as a way out if things become bad enough. But what I meant by "bad enough" was evidently very different from what it meant to Guy.

Spring had been Guy's difficult season ever since he had received word of his son John's death on Mount McKinley in April 1981. Guy's birthday was May 1. In the years immediately following Johnny's death, when Guy was sad on his birthday, I told myself that he was still in grief. But as time passed I began to feel resentment, even flashes of anger, that he could not forget about being sad and enjoy this special day. I myself loved birthdays! I anticipated giving him his presents at breakfast — a pair of mittens I had made, a book on baseball or on his beloved Milton's Paradise Lost. While he was fetching water from the stream and checking the 7:00 a.m. temperatures, I had just time enough to scurry out and snip daffodils — the first blooms sure to open by May 1. If he walked into the cabin and didn't look at me, his gifts sitting by his place, or at the vase of daffodils in the middle of the table glowing like little suns, well, I just swallowed my disappointment. Those daffodils had thrilled me. I wanted Guy to feel this too. Instead, he had suddenly sucked away the joy from this day. It made me both mad and sad — full of despair — since there seemed to be nothing I could do. And overriding all my anger was a great welling loving longing for him just to throw off this bad mood and be happy on his birthday.

Sometimes he was fine, taking delight in his presents, admiring the daffodils, and giving me a warm hug and a kiss before we sat down for breakfast. But as our years of married life piled up and Guy kept himself locked in a dark inner room to which I had no key and no hope of admittance, I trained myself to wait outside the door, doing other things, until he came out. I managed to ball all unpleasant feelings toward Guy into a dense and tiny wad that I kept stuffed deep down in a nest I made sure never to touch or even look at. This was how Guy was. To make being with him easier I taught myself to feel little at all, except sadness for what seemed to me to be his own overwhelming sadness.

"Please remember me from when I was kinder to you . . . ," he had written in his April 13, 1992, note. Immediately I thought, Guy has never been anything but kind to me. I knew his low moods had caused a barrier between us, but I was willing to cut him endless slack because of my desire not to cause him pain. Wasn't he in enough pain? Whenever I tried to get him to talk he turned away, his face acquiring a woebegone, withdrawn expression that made me sorry I'd said anything at all. He looked both vulnerable and sealed off — and sad in a way that always went right to my heart. His words "poisoned spirit I have become" leapt off the page. Was this how he saw himself? I hadn't seen him as a "poisoned spirit." I tried to imagine how he must have felt to turn those words on himself.

He called his low moods his "demons." He could have used the word depression, but that was the word he never mentioned, and neither did I. In fact, I knew Guy wasn't depressed. He was always up at 4:15 a.m., and was known by all our friends for being amazingly productive. This didn't fit my image of a depressed person, who I imagined had trouble getting out of bed and was too incapacitated to get much of anything done.

But his message, penned eight years before, began to crack open for me just how poisonous he felt to himself. As I stood in the bedroom, reading these notes in Guy's neat ballpoint pen, I felt my own acute blindness. Yet, I told myself, he had kept the shades so firmly pulled and was so resistant to all my entreaties to raise them.

What would have happened to me if he had committed suicide back then? I thought. I would have been taken by complete surprise. I would have felt real anger. Betrayal. His suicide then would have called into question our entire marriage. Did he love me? It would appear that he did not, if he could walk out the door without a hint of goodbye. But though he did not take his life at sixty, this note written in 1992 told me that he had already turned toward death. He never asked for my help to change that. After Johnny's death, I had asked him if talking to someone — I meant a psychiatrist — could help. No. No! He made it clear that talking to a professional wouldn't help. In fact, Guy engaged sparingly with the medical world. When a doctor suggested invasive diagnostic tests for that troublesome bowel complaint, Guy decided he wasn't going to go that route. He had told me many times how much he hated being poked at by doctors. I didn't think this was cancer; he'd had it far too long. Then there were the sixteen other items, like knee and foot problems, that barely slowed him down. Now I see that even with only these minor physical ailments, Guy saw himself as losing control. And that was something he couldn't bear — the last thing Guy Waterman was going to let happen.

I was glad he had waited those seven years. By 1999, even though he still chose death-by-suicide as a way out, at least I was prepared. More important, I knew what our marriage had meant to him.

Yet when I read these notes standing there in our bedroom, I was troubled by the contradictions. We did as much work at Barra during those seven years as ever before — we planted the same large garden, collected the same eight cords of firewood a year, made enough maple syrup to take us through the year. In the early nineties, we began work on Twin Firs Camp, a log cabin for our guests. We felled and peeled softwoods. We limbed and sawed the trunks. We carried many together to the building site, and since by that time my knees were not in great shape, Guy did the bulk of that heavy lifting alone. Many of these trees came from far down in our woods and made a stiff uphill carry. Guy joked that this was his "workout," telling me he was "going down to the weight room." It seemed to me then that Guy made sixty look not half as old as it sounded. Despite the rocky crossing, I felt he had taken this turn into his seventh decade admirably, providing me, at fifty-two, with an excellent example of how to cope with this milestone of aging. It wasn't until after he was gone that I understood that while he appeared to take sixty well on the outside, he took it harder on the inside than he was willing to show. I did see enough, however, to tell a friend who had expressed concern about Guy's melancholy — something few picked up on — that I did not think he would make seventy.

After Guy had died, another friend asked why I had not sought help myself. It would have been difficult, I explained, because of the work demands at our homestead. It would have cost money we didn't have. She looked at me in a way that let me know my reasons sounded like excuses. "I never thought of it," I said. Why not? she asked. Months later I answered that question. "I was living in Guy's world," I finally said. "If he couldn't ask for help, neither could I."

When Guy was gone, his friend Tom Simon told me of a baseball game Guy had played in his head using actual teams and players with the action somehow triggered by lines or words from Milton's *Paradise Lost*. Tom said that Guy had a game going at all times and kept a box score on an index card he carried in his breast pocket. He had begun with the 1880s and was working his way forward. He told Tom about it on a weekend visit to Barra in early December 1999, when I was away visiting friends in New York.

"Why didn't Guy tell me about this game?" I asked Tom. Why hadn't he said a word to me about the thing that was so important to him: Milton! Baseball!

Tom replied, "Well, he told me he didn't want you to feel he might be thinking about something else when you were talking to him."

"What?" I said. "Guy frequently seemed preoccupied when we were talking. I could always tell when his mind moved on to something else, sometimes when I was in midsentence." It made me feel shut out when that happened, a feeling I learned to just "get over," like jumping over a branch in the woods and getting your legs whipped. It stings, and the sting fades slowly.

Yet Tom was saying it had been important to Guy that I feel I had his full attention. I felt I would rather have known about his game, even if he had said, "I can't listen to you right now. I'm playing my game."

But I never said, "You're not listening to me." I thought it, but I never said it.

By the time Tom told me this, I had found Guy's note written in the spring of 1992, where he'd said he wanted to see how the fantasy baseball he'd played in his head for many years turned out. Now I understood. I asked Tom if he thought Guy had completed his game. Tom said, probably not. He believed Guy had gone through fifty years of games and was up to the 1930s.

I had known for a long time that Guy sought refuge in numbers. His research notes for his baseball articles showed long columns of players' names written in pen, small and close together, each with a number beside it. "Baseball had been, for me," he wrote once, "a world apart, a sanctuary where I constantly found excitement and interest unalloyed by petty negatives." Now it jumped out at me how he used baseball — the statistics — to occupy his mind so as to hold at bay all the dark disturbing thoughts.

We were together so much — the work, the writing, the climbs — that it didn't surprise me Guy needed a spot that was wholly his. But I think this game went far beyond that. I believe it had to do with his own pain. The pain he wasn't talking about. He needed a sunny island, a sanctuary he could sail off to that was as safe as the surrounding ocean was dangerous, chaotic, and tempest-tossed. And he needed to keep it hidden to the same degree he kept hidden the dark painful place.

What I kept hidden from Guy was how much he hurt me by not talking. When Tom told me about Guy's game, my thought was: He kept that hidden? It seemed so unimportant in comparison to the deeper thing he wouldn't talk about. I remembered him telling me he tried to drive out bad thoughts by deliberately inserting a pleasant thought. I remembered his humming or whistling through his teeth. I could track him around the garden, even the woods, reassuring myself he must be in a good mood if he was whistling. But once he told me, "Just because I hum or whistle doesn't mean I'm feeling good." I couldn't make myself believe that. How can he feel bad and hum at the same time? I wondered. Well, I guess he could if he was using humming to block out terrible thoughts.

And I remembered the quotation Guy had taken from Melville's Moby-Dick for the calendar he made for Barra: "For as this appalling ocean surrounds the verdant land, so in the soul of man there lies one insular Tahiti, full of peace and joy, but encompassed by all the horrors of the half-known life. God keep thee! Push not off from that isle, thou canst never return."

Baseball and Milton, humming and whistling, gave Guy his "insular Tahiti."

What was mine? I didn't have an "insular Tahiti" in the sense Guy did. I didn't have to block out terrible thoughts. My down moods were precipitated by Guy's and at their worst left me feeling angry at him because he wouldn't talk. I handled this by losing (or finding) myself in the work of our homestead, often sawing wood or weeding or doing other garden jobs that were productive and physical. One afternoon, as I walked back into the woodshed where Guy was splitting wood, he said, "I always know when my moods affect you, Laura. I see you working so hard in the garden. It makes me want to work harder too."

At the time I wondered what Guy meant. As I see it now, he was saying it was through our mutual hard work that we could come together. I needed to be in accord with him, and he needed to be in accord with me. It was through the hard physical work at Barra that we found each other in the comfortable spot in the sunlight.

When I decided to write this book I thought it was going to be about my life with Guy, the two of us working side by side as homesteaders on the land. The story would be about the practical aspects of how we lived. From that first summer in 1973, visitors had said, "You should write about this," even though we had yet to endure our first Vermont winter. We had nothing yet to say. Our house was not built, nor were any of our outbuildings. Our garden was still a hillside clearing grown up to blackberries, juniper, and a few scrubby white pines. We had planted no blueberry bushes, no strawberries, no raspberries, no fruit trees. No asparagus bed, no rhubarb patch. Our woodlot was full of down and dead trees, unharvested. We had not built our sugar shed, and we had yet to tap a single maple.

Over the years we had talked about writing such a book and had always decided against it. Barra was our private life, we told ourselves. Writing a book about it would open us up to hordes of visitors, as had happened to Helen and Scott Nearing, homesteading gurus who welcomed hundreds of visitors a year to their land on the coast of Maine. We weren't looking to be spokespeople in this way. The mountains — the issues related to them — that was our public life, and that was what we wrote about.

Shortly before Guy died, I mentioned that I might write about how we had lived at Barra.

"I hope you'll do that, Laura." The way he said this made me feel he actually wanted me to. But even then I knew I would have to tell the whole story, not just how we planted the beans, but how it ended.

After Guy died and I began working on the manuscript, I began telling friends who asked that I was writing a book about our life at Barra and "how I let Guy go." In an effort to state the theme, I wrote my friend Alice Tufel: "It's the story of a woman trying to discover what happened to her. . . . I think that by understanding what happened to me, I'll be able to more fully continue on."

Alice fired back: "Those words interested (and surprised) me because they imply passivity or victimization (for lack of a better word) on your part — and that is so contrary to the way I see you!" Alice let me off the hook by adding, "It just doesn't seem to me that something 'happened to you' so much as it happened to Guy (since he was both victim and perpetrator) — and, as his life partner, you were necessarily there when it did."

But Alice's words "passivity or victimization" had hit their mark, and I squirmed, even as I did my best to fend them off.

Finally, I showed a draft to my friend Annie Barry, who said, "Laura, you have to pull apart the 'we.'" What did I think? she asked me. "The way you use 'we,' it means Guy," she pointed out. "Surely your thoughts were not always identical. You're two different people," Annie insisted.

True. But I persisted in thinking that my thoughts were identical with Guy's, and that Annie couldn't see this because, well, how could even a good friend see into my marriage?

But Annie had proposed a writing problem, and I got interested in this notion of examining the "we." It seemed to go along with the part about finding out "what happened to me."

So I went through the manuscript, and every time I came across a "we" — and there were, it seemed, thousands — I asked myself: What was I thinking here? What was my reaction? Picking apart the "we" was surprisingly difficult.

"When I ask you a question, Laura," Annie had said, "you say, 'I don't know.'" Bringing to the surface what I did know — all buried fathoms deep — became my focus. The whole book changed as I began to write myself out of a life enmeshed in the "we" and into a frame of mind that allowed me to go digging for the thoughts I'd kept hidden not just from Guy but from myself. As I rewrote I could finally ask: How could I support my beloved husband in his plan to commit suicide? How did that happen? I could now write the word *suicide*. Before, I could only express what Guy had done by saying (or writing), "Guy had left," or, "Guy had walked out the door." When I reached this point the entire piece began to unravel — faster and faster — and I was left with an ungainly skein of words piled up around my typewriter. When I began to cast on again, I came to see this was the story of my own awakening. The whole process was terrifying, exhilarating, and profoundly liberating.

When I first began writing, I had posted a quotation from Joyce Carol Oates near my desk that read: "All memoirs are finally about loss. We don't write of the past except when we've been ejected from it. The only way back is through memory, haphazard and unreliable as we know it to be, and the only means by which memory is realized is through language." As I began the process of digging for my own submerged feelings attached to these memories, Oates's words took on more and more meaning.

Right from the beginning I fell into a routine of listening to music before I began work. Every morning I put on my old operas, recordings I'd brought with me from New York that had sat unplayed under the piano at Barra for nearly thirty years. So much of my life with Guy had taken place below the surface, at a deep emotional level that I found very hard to tease apart: it was difficult to separate what I instinctively shied away from, because of the pain, from what I had convinced myself was how I should be reacting toward Guy in difficult emotional situations. After I began playing one or two records over and over, I realized I was using the emotion in the voices to get in touch with my own emotions. In particular, I was playing a Maria Callas recording of Bellini's *Norma*. Callas was well along in her career. Her voice sounded frayed and was often harsh and wavery. The tenor, Franco Corelli, was young, his animalistic sound blazing and whole. The contrast was heartbreaking to me. But I saw that the impairment of Callas's voice only drove her deeper. This great singer knew her voice was wearing away, but this only impelled her to plunge into her own rich storehouse of emotion. I was greatly moved by Callas, by her fearlessness. I took to heart that she was more willing than ever to lay bare the core of human emotions by reaching into her own. And I learned that my story was a love story — an over-the-top love story. In my life with Guy I had loved blindly, plunging wholeheartedly into this irrational, joyous, painful, perplexing territory we call love. I had taken love to extremes.

CHAPTER three

Oh, the wild joys of living! the leaping

from rock up to rock . . .

— Robert Browning, "Saul"

We met rock climbing. I arrived at the Shawangunks, the premier cliff east of the Rockies, a rank beginner, in the fall of 1969.

From that first weekend I tumbled down the rabbit hole and landed in Wonderland. I crossed a threshold into another country where I found the meaning of life in the dance up the rock. I was irretrievably drawn to the high spirits of these climbers, who were like kids on Saturday with their silliness and their uproarious tales of hard moves and close calls. I discovered that what mattered was the breeze on my face, the cloud shadows playing across the cliff as I gained height, the trees grew smaller, and I left the world behind.

From my first climb, Easy Overhang, I was ignited by gripping rough edges, by the electric surge of connecting my physical strength and power of mind. My first experience of exposure — looking out over the peaceful valley of the Wallkill across to the Hudson Highlands, high high high above the treetops, my toes overlapping the edge of a belay ledge, my back flat against warm rock in a vertical world — was intoxicating. It took just one climb for me to fall in love with climbing.

It took just a moment — one conversation — for me to fall in love with Guy Waterman. That winter of 1969 to 70, I ruptured my Achilles tendon in a skiing accident, but despite cast and crutches I was back in "the Gunks" in early April. I couldn't climb. But I could be there under those cliffs that had the power to shoot lives off like stars in new directions.

That sunny April weekend Guy Waterman was in charge of the beginners who had come to learn from the more experienced climbers with the Appalachian Mountain Club. Since Guy's managerial position kept him grounded, I could ask unlimited questions about climbs like the Arrow, which had everyone talking about a high thin top move on clean white rock. Guy grinned, extended way up with two right-hand fingers, and lifted his right foot up near his left hand positioned at waist level. He hopped around, trying to maintain his balance as he pushed down on an invisible hold the size of his thumb. "You're two hundred feet up doing this," he grinned. I couldn't imagine it. I was dying to get good enough to climb the Arrow. He resettled his tam and began telling me how he'd driven up from New York City every weekend to climb on snowshoes in the High Peaks of the Adirondacks. He'd completed one-third of the peaks. There were forty-six, so he figured he'd finish up in two more winters. He'd never climbed any in the summer, and he wasn't going to, at least not until he'd climbed them all in winter first.

I had heard that Guy was recently separated after nearly twenty years of marriage and was living with another climber, Dave Ingalls, up near Columbia University. I knew Dave was talented on rock but famous for "epics" — like getting caught by darkness halfway up a route so that others had to come looking for him with flashlights. He was a student, and as far as Guy could tell, he and his other roommates were the principal suppliers of marijuana to the rest of Columbia. "Little bags all over the coffee table," Guy said. "They'd be sorting them when I went to bed and still at it when I left for work in my three-piece suit. Bill was living with me too. My oldest son." I had seen Bill hopping around on crutches at the cliffs the previous fall. Then nineteen, Bill was the epicenter of a whirl of young climbers, especially girls, and recovering from a run-in with a train he encountered in a freight yard in Winnipeg. So far the doctors had saved his leg. By spring Bill had gone back out west and Guy had found an apartment over a print shop in the Hudson River town of Marlboro, a short thirty-five minutes from the Gunks and a long two-and-a-half-hour commute from the eleventh floor of the General Electric building where he worked. It felt right, he said. He'd bought dishes and sheets and towels. "So now I live there with Ralph."

"Is Ralph your son?" I asked.

"My dog."

I laughed. He was standing in front of me with four or five climbing ropes draped over his shoulders. He wasn't very tall. But he was compact, with muscled arms, a broad chest, and a narrow waist.

"Then Jim moved in," he said.

"Is Jim your cat?" I asked.

"He's my youngest son. Bill, Johnny in the middle, and Jim." Guy laughed. I saw that he had blue-gray eyes, darkish red hair, and strong teeth. He bore an uncanny resemblance to the Kennedy brothers.

"The Planks, my landlords, are out of Dickens," he went on. "It's a tiny print shop with a huge black press. Type in heaps. Flywheels, belts flapping." He waved his arms. "When Mr. Plank throws a lever, that press makes a noise not heard since the nineteenth century."

That might have been the igniting moment, I told Guy afterward. Though I probably fell in love with him as soon as my eyes met his, like falling under a spell. This enchantment could only grow stronger when I found out he'd read every book written on the expeditionary history of Mount Everest and in fact had them on his bookshelves.

"I read *Annapurna* when I was twelve," I said, but didn't add that it had taken me most of the book to puzzle out what a crevasse was. "And when I read Sir John Hunt's Everest book I wanted to be the first woman to climb Everest." This was actually true; I wasn't exaggerating.

Guy had started climbing in 1963, and was rarely seen at the cliffs without his young sons, Bill, John, and Jim, who was known by everyone as Scooter. Since their dog Ralph, a golden-collie cross, was a fixture at the cliffs as well, when I first heard about Guy I thought he had four sons: Bill, John, Scooter, and Ralph.

That spring of 1970 rock climbing changed my life, and so did Guy Waterman. I was twenty-nine when I met him. I had not yet met a man with whom I wanted to spend much more than a weekend, let alone a life. From that first conversation I responded to Guy on a level I had never known existed. It was his sense of fun and the range of his mind. It was the way he made a game of climbing as many routes as possible, coiling his rope as he trotted down the trail along the top of the cliffs after a climb, whistling between his teeth, casting a glance back with that flashy grin to make sure I was on his heels. That green-and-blue tam in his McNeil family tartan was his trademark. During the week it gave way to the three-piece suit, but come Friday nights it held sway on his head again and he was a pixie, a leprechaun. He was also a joke teller, a storyteller, the more convoluted the better. And I was a good audience. We always talked about things I found interesting. Immediately, it all went deeper than that, and I held Guy in some unspoken place beyond my ability to articulate.

On our first commute into New York City after a weekend of climbing, he pulled out Macaulay's *History of England*. "How do you like it?" I asked. I was impressed and not quite willing to admit that I had never thought of reading this great British historian.

"He's a bit dry," Guy smiled. "No comparison with Gibbon." I owned a paperback of Gibbon's *History of the Decline and Fall of the Roman Empire*, bought with the intent of reading all three volumes, but I had never gotten more than a few chapters into it. To make a good showing, I mentioned enjoying Herodotus.

A few days later on the train Guy pulled out Ogden Nash. "Listen to this," he said with a puckish grin. "'When I consider how my life is spent / I hardly ever repent.' And here's one for your dentist appointment this afternoon: 'Dentists' anterooms / Give me tanterooms.'"

I already knew that Guy could recite the first seven books of Milton's twelve-book epic. During his lunch break, he told me, he strode from the General Electric building at Fifty-Second Street and Lexington Avenue, up the length of Central Park and back again, working on memorizing from the pages torn out of a cheap paperback.

I had read *Paradise Lost* in college but got next to nothing out of it. My world was the *Canterbury Tales* and *Twelfth Night*. For me, Milton was as ponderous as an overcooked slab of beef.

"Do you subscribe to the *Milton Quarterly*?" I asked him.

"What's that?"

"I bet you don't know about the Milton Society either," I kidded him.

"Tell me."

"Well, this year their dinner is at the Princeton Club. Want to go?"

A few weeks later we walked into a crowded room, everyone brandishing glasses, the conversation at a noisy convivial pitch. Guy looked around. "'Fit audience find, though few,'" he quoted.

"And where do you teach?" asked a pleasant-looking tweedy man who stuck out his hand to Guy.

"I don't," Guy replied with a grin.

"Then what brings you here?" the man asked.

"Well," Guy said, "I just love Milton."

"Gosh! He's here just because he loves Milton," the academic said in amazement, gesturing to Guy.

Conversation stopped. People smiled at Guy, and someone said in a cheery voice, "The president should make an announcement."

If I had not met Guy, I doubt I would have married anyone. He fully revealed himself in the very first conversation we had about books, though I saw nothing then. We were sitting on a stream bank talking about *Moby-Dick*. "Ahab knows what he is doing, and he knows he'll drag the others down with him," Guy said. "He knows Starbuck can save him, but he can't accept it." He turned toward me. "Ahab cannot act, will not act, otherwise."

He spoke in a quiet voice, and when I looked into his eyes I saw that they were bleak. But I did not understand what he was telling me about himself. His arm was around my shoulders, and already I was blinded by the desire to spend my life with him. I saw nothing of what his words foretold.

I remember also a conversation on a morning train ride into Manhattan. We'd been together more than a year and in fact were planning our future life as homesteaders. I was distressed. I was in tears. It was something about "us" that I can't remember now. But I remember the feeling of trying to get Guy to talk about something it was hard for him to talk about. His face was open; he was trying, but having trouble reaching the words. The whole conversation was a swim against the current, though before we arrived at Grand Central I'd ended up at something that felt like a comfortable spot. As we were walking off the train Guy slipped me a note he'd written on a three-by-five card. It read, "I wish I could give you a large-ish hug."

Years later, after painful conversations that Guy ended by saying, "Talking doesn't help," I recalled this conversation on the train. It was perhaps the only time I felt Guy's wholehearted willingness to dig down down down and not to cut off what he found there.

Not long after we began climbing together we were in Guy's tan Volkswagen bug, driving up to the Gunks, and he was talking about his plans for the Fourth of July weekend: he was going to the White Mountains with Ralph to spend three nights out in the Pemigewasset Wilderness. That name alone was full of wild mystery to me. I couldn't always follow the byzantine pathways of Guy's former political life in Washington, DC, but this present life of hiking and climbing was very real for me. I wanted to explore this territory. I also wanted to make mountains my world.

"What will you climb?" I asked.

The first day, he said, he'd pack up Mount Willey, that graceful peak at the top of Crawford Notch, and camp on the other side in secluded Zealand Notch. On the second day he'd "bag" three four-thousand-foot peaks — Zealand Mountain and North and South Twin — and camp at Guyot shelter. The third day he'd scamper out at dawn to West Bond, an isolated summit hanging over the Pemi Wilderness. Then he'd make the long pack over Bond and Bondcliff, down the steep path to the Wilderness Trail, and turn toward Carrigain.

"Carrigain's remote, right in the heart of the Wilderness. I'll spend the night in the summit fire tower the way I did with Bill, John, and Ralph that last night when we climbed all New Hampshire's four-thousand footers in two weeks."

I had never experienced anything like what Guy was talking about. My cast had come off a month before, and I'd begun climbing again. My lower leg still swelled if I overdid it, but if Guy asked me to come I was going to say yes. Being with Guy on this "remote" Carrigain — I could have climbed it on crutches!

"More remote than Carter Dome?" I asked.

"It's surrounded by mountains, not a road in sight," he said.

Carter Dome and Wildcat were the only big White Mountain peaks I'd climbed. I'd been up some smaller mountains, however, and had made sure Guy knew about all of them. Mount Haystack was in southern Vermont, near where my family spent the summer when I was a child. Then, when we changed allegiance to southern New Hampshire, Mount Monadnock became a daily presence for me. It occupied the horizon out my third-floor bedroom window, and every morning when I opened my eyes I beamed in on its solid shape, its rocky top glinting in the sun or darkened with cloud shadows.

I had tried to describe for Guy how I'd been affected by Carter Notch, that rugged spot with its jewel-like pond I plunged into for a sharp, cold swim. I tried to describe my utter elation as I'd sat on those huge boulders, called the Ramparts, at night, surrounded by rocky peaks. One of the boys who worked in the hut that summer pointed out the lights of the small city of Berlin, far down in the valley. It was odd to think about those people in their stuffy houses, all shut up for the night, while I sat on this enormous rock pile, formed eons ago, that filled the notch separating steep-sided Carter Dome from Wildcat.

I knew the Ramparts carried memories for Guy. It was here that Dave Seidman, a hut boy who a few years later died on a climbing expedition to Dhaulagiri in the Himalayas, first tied a rope on Johnny.

Guy knew about a trip I'd made in 1967, on a Greek freighter that called on ports within the circle of the Mediterranean and up into the Black Sea. I ended those four months with a ten-day trip through the Bavarian Alps. I had thought of it as a backpacking trip, but now I knew it wasn't since I carried neither tent nor sleeping bag and stayed at mountain lodges that served meals. I coped with bloody blisters because I was wearing new boots, something an experienced hiker would never have done.

After I returned, New York City, where I was living, had changed for me, or I had changed. I wanted to be outside in the woods on weekends. Someone told me about the Appalachian Mountain Club, and I began going on their hikes in the Hudson Highlands, in Harriman Park, and on Bear Mountain, precious wooded land for urban hikers. I was amazed to find you could go hiking in seasons other than summer and went out on a November Saturday of sleet and wet snow and soggy trails that soaked my boots. When we huddled under a shelter for lunch, I crunched a frozen peanut butter sandwich and couldn't unscrew the iced-up cap on my water bottle. Back at the cars, everyone changed out of their wet clothes except for me, who hadn't known to bring extras. Later, in my warm, dry apartment, with every stitch I'd worn draped over the radiator, I couldn't wait to get out there the following weekend.

As Guy outlined his itinerary of trails and peaks, he glanced at me from behind the Volkswagen's steering wheel. Finally he stopped talking. And I stopped showing enthusiasm for his plan. What happened next was up to him. I wanted to see whether he wanted to take me along — unproven, hardly tested, a novice with a not-yet-healed Achilles tendon.

I knew from Guy's stories that bagging these peaks was important to him. I saw from the way he climbed at the Gunks that he wasn't going to take someone along who would jeopardize his trip. I watched his face in profile. It looked like he was concentrating on the road ahead, but from the way his mouth was turned down slightly at the corners, his habit when he was thinking, I knew he was weighing this over. When he turned to me and asked, "Would you like to come?" I heard in his voice that he was taking a chance, but I also heard that he was hoping I'd say yes.

The first day didn't seem hard, but then we'd climbed Willey without our heavy packs. After supper Guy asked Ralph, who always slept inside the tent beside Guy, to sleep outside. Ralph was a big shaggy dog, and at that point a muddy one. I think Guy felt I should be introduced to Ralph's sleeping preferences in stages.

But Ralph had other ideas. As darkness came on and Guy and I settled into our sleeping bags, all three of us heard the heavy tread of a large animal, very close. Suddenly Ralph melted right through the mosquito netting, even, it seemed, before Guy had a chance to unzip it. Ralph's golden fur stood up along his back, and he was trembling. Guy looked at me with eyes as pleading as Ralph's, and I knew Ralph wasn't about to be banished again. Guy encouraged him to sleep in the back of the tent, but it was not long before Ralph had crept up between our sleeping bags, his long body fully on our pads. He had positioned himself where he wanted to be without either of us detecting any movement. So Ralph slept between our sleeping bags, and this became his accustomed place, beginning with that night spent in wild Zealand Notch.

What was it that had scared Ralph? A moose? A bear? A fabled cougar? We looked for tracks in the morning but could discover nothing. We decided Ralph had been frightened by a Heffalump, the very creature that had so terrified Pooh and Piglet and, we were certain, had never been spotted in the lonely vastness of Zealand Notch.

The next day Guy introduced me to his style of hiking. He had written out on three-by-five cards the mileages to trail junctions and summits and how long it would take to reach each point. He allowed time for rest stops — eating and drinking — and to take in views, but as he had shown me on the map, we had a lot of ground to cover, so it was important to stick to the schedule. I would be comfortably settled on a summit, Guy naming for me the distant peaks, when he would pop up and shoulder his pack and it was time to move along. Keeping an eye so closely on the time, I mentioned as he replaced his cards in his shirt pocket, didn't seem to belong in the mountains. It depended on what you wanted to accomplish, Guy pointed out, how much ground, how many summits. "When Bill and John and I hiked the four-thousand footers in two weeks, it surprised us that we kept passing people. We never felt we were pushing."

I knew that Guy could hike much faster than I, and that he was holding back, hiking at my pace. I thought over what he had said and found I liked moving along too. Like rock climbing, it just plain felt good. And it was thrilling to at last get to the summit, throw off my pack, and relish the accomplishment and the views. Peak baggers are often criticized, Guy said, for not taking in the sights along the way, but he didn't think he took in any less for moving at a good pace. He thought the most important thing was to enjoy the mountains however you liked to hike.

The third day we hit the Desolation Trail up Carrigain; just as Guy had warned, it was one of the most relentlessly steep trails in the White Mountains. By now I was curious to see how steep steep was. "Bill and John and I flew up this trail," Guy said, "but it was our last four-thousand footer, and we'd been hiking for two weeks."

By this time my Achilles tendon was swollen, and my feet were sore from the unaccustomed pounding on the rocky trails. My pack seemed heavier than ever, and steep, I discovered, was steep. So Guy suggested we try something that had worked with his sons when they were starting out. We'd walk for fifteen minutes and then take a break for five, to eat and drink something. We'd take the Desolation Trail in sections and in this way reach the top. I'd go first and set the pace. He told me the story of how one summer Bill and John had stepped aside and made a sweeping motion for their dad to go first!

As I lumbered up the Desolation Trail, Guy told me more stories of his hikes with Bill and John, as well as with Jim when he was old enough to join in. The summer after their successful two-week trip climbing all of New Hampshire's four-thousand footers, they'd concocted an adventure in the Presidentials that took them up great headwall trails such as Great Gulf and King Ravine and down all the ridge trails, including Six Husbands and Caps Ridge. After several days, high on the jagged boulders of Mount Adams, they saw that Ralph's feet were bleeding. Guy half-carried ninety-pound Ralph down the Buttress Trail. They backed off the Presidentials for Ralph's sake and finished the trip with hikes on easier footing in the Baldface Range, the Carters, and the Wild River.

Guy recounted another story about a November hike just with Ralph, in which they covered seventy miles and six summits in three days. Coming out toward evening on the last day, Ralph was so tired that he finally lay down and refused to get up. Guy thought he'd have to spend an extra night beside Ralph in the woods. But he kept Ralph moving by walking ahead of him at a slow pace. "Every time I slowed down, Ralph would too, so the distance between us stayed the same, as if a rubber band was stretched between us," Guy said.

In this way I gained the summit of Carrigain and heaved off my pack. We scampered up the fire tower, and Guy began pointing out the high ranges of the White Mountains — the Franconias, the Presidentials — naming the peaks, including the ones we'd walked over in the past few days, stretching back into the blue distance. Now I was beginning to distinguish the individual mountains, too, each one looking a little different as the angle I saw it from changed. Then we fell silent, and I breathed in the remote feeling of Carrigain, this peak so in-the-wild.

That last day, slogging out the Nancy Pond Trail, I suddenly found myself in Ralph's position. Aching feet. Sore Achilles tendon. And like Ralph, I knew I was going to keep going. I discovered then that no matter how I felt, I could always walk that last mile.

CHAPTER *four*

The greatest continue to develop until their deaths and leave behind unful-filled expectations.

— Furruccio Busoni, letter written near the end of his life to Philipp Jarnach (1923)

One day in that spring of 1970, we were walking down Lexington Avenue. Guy was telling me about Lyndon Johnson — his astonishing command as major-ity leader in contrast to Guy's first impression of the man. "Dave Kammerman stopped Johnson as he burst out of the chamber. Dave said, 'Senator, I'd like to introduce you to our newest staff member,' and when Johnson shook my hand he reminded me of a used-car salesman preoccupied with another sale, but sensing that he could take my money later, was friendly but hurried."

I laughed. Guy's stories always made me laugh. It was a sunny day in New York, or maybe it was cloudy. I don't remember. It wouldn't have mattered if it had been pouring. We were walking down Lexington, and I had my arm in Guy's.

Guy was a Republican. I voted Democrat, as did everyone I knew except my parents. But this made no difference. He launched into another story, drawing a David and Goliath scene of this young Senate aide (himself) standing up to the Senate minority policy staff director, a crafty, small-minded tyrant named Art Burgess, who wielded great power and meant to keep it. Guy felt that he was right over the issue (I can't recall what it was), and the staff director was wrong, so he went to Styles Bridges, the ranking Republican leader in the Senate, and offered his resignation. "I had the notion Senator Bridges would fire Burgess rather than lose me," Guy said.

We crossed an intersection, Guy grabbing my hand as we ran against the light. "What happened?" I kept expecting this story to turn funny.

"Burgess simply hounded Bridges into firing me." Guy sprang onto the side-walk in front of me, waving his arms. His eyes were electric.

"I would have stood up to that staff director," I said. "If you thought you were right, you did the right thing."

"After that Gerald Ford hired me to work on a big project," Guy continued, as I tucked my hand back into the crook of his arm. "And then came the 1960 campaign."

I knew Guy had been on Nixon's speechwriting staff for that presidential election. It was the second thing I heard about Guy Waterman after I came to the Gunks. The first was that he was always seen at the cliffs with his sons. The third was that he'd committed to memory the first seven books of *Paradise Lost*.

"Everyone knew Art Burgess was a madman abusing authority, but I'm sure they were asking themselves: 'What is Waterman trying to prove?'" He sent me a toothy grin, all bravado, like Bobby Kennedy. But I also picked up puzzlement in his gray eyes that said: If I was right, what went wrong?

"I had this idea," Guy went on, "that I was so good that the rules that applied to everyone else didn't apply to me. The upshot was, I was out of a job on Capitol Hill."

Guy, the fifth and last child of his family, was born on May 1, 1932. He spent his early years on "the Farm," as the Waterman family called their ten acres of fields and woodland in North Haven, Connecticut. From this country spot, Guy's father, Alan T. Waterman, made the eight-mile commute into New Haven — considered a long distance in those days — where he taught physics at Yale. Mary Mallon Waterman, Guy's mother, was raised in Cincinnati, the eldest in a family of eight, and had come east to college, as had her five brothers. Alan and Mary bought the old farm in the late twenties. Every spring Alan, with his oldest sons, Alan Jr. and Neil, plowed up the ground for the vegetable garden with the help of Dolly the workhorse. With Dolly, they had leveled land for a tennis court. One of Guy's earliest memories was of the hurricane of 1938, which uprooted the apple orchard. His father and brothers hitched up Dolly and pulled the trees upright again. There was a grape arbor, a barn where the cats lived, and a henhouse. There were always dogs at the farm, but the dog of legend was Donny — more formally Donald the Hunter, a collie-shepherd cross. Intelligent, loyal, brave, and true, Donny instilled in Guy a lifelong bond with the canine world. On Sundays, there was always a picnic down by the steep-sided brook. Invitations were open, and friends, as well as Alan Waterman's graduate students, came to partake in this Sunday ritual that they could count on even in rain or snow or sweltering summer heat. Father and sons had constructed an outdoor cooking place, much like what they used on their canoe trips in Maine, with large pots balanced on heavy cross sticks hanging over an open fire. Here Alan Waterman presided as woodsman and chef; his specialty was raised biscuits browned in "bakers" before the fire.

The legendary "canoe trips," as they were known in the family, took place during the long summer vacations of the 1930s, when Alan Waterman took his two older sons through the northern lakes of Maine and down the Allagash River. Along with the scientist Karl Compton, then president of MIT, and his sons, they were gone for six weeks, on their own in the deep woods, where to spot another party was rare. Their companion, Bill Arthur Eastman, was a Maine guide who became a close family friend. Guy remembered watching his father and Bill Arthur sitting side by side on a log in the evening, exchanging an occasional quiet word and tending the fire, first one adding a stick, then the other. Guy's father would become a licensed Maine guide himself, one of only two out-of-staters at that time.

Guy, as the youngest by six and a half years, missed out on those early canoe trips, which ended with World War II. He experienced only a few much-shortened postwar versions, much as happened with his own son Jim, who was too young to join in on the excitement of the early White Mountain romps with his father and older brothers.

Guy thought of himself as coming from a large and close family, but he grew up much like an only child, playing by himself down by the brook, creating whole worlds among the hemlock roots. The four years of World War II were an exception. During this time, university families in America agreed to house children from British university families, and Christopher and Ted Braunholtz, twins Guy's age whose father taught at Oxford, came to live with the Watermans.

The war brought other changes. When Guy was ten, the idyll at the farm ended. Alan Waterman, swept up in the scientific part of the war effort, moved the family to Cambridge, Massachusetts, where he worked at MIT in close association with his canoeing partner Karl Compton. During those years Guy went to the Shady Hill School. Right after the war, in 1946, the family moved again, to Washington, DC. There Guy's father continued his scientific career, which culminated with his appointment by President Truman as first chief of the National Science Foundation. Guy felt that his own commitment to public service sprang from his father's example. From his mother, who had an acerbic wit and was a Phi Beta Kappa graduate of Vassar, he gained a lifelong love of books.

At the age of fourteen, Guy was sent to the Taft School in Connecticut, a residential preparatory school where he spent two miserable years. At Taft he remained aloof, entering into no athletic activities — always a defining part of prep school life — or extracurricular offerings.

It wasn't until late in our marriage that Guy began to talk about just how much he hated Taft and how lonely he was there. His parents selected the school because his mother's brothers had attended it. In the Mallon family Taft was regarded as a stepping-stone to Yale. Guy didn't graduate from Taft, and he didn't go to Yale. He did well in his studies, but he isolated himself from his fellow students on the grounds that the whole place reeked of upper-class snobbishness. "The steady stream of anti-Semitic jokes," Guy wrote in his recollections, "was excruciatingly painful to me. I don't look at this as an admirable display of social liberalism, but as some kind of identification with other outcasts, which I felt myself to be."

"Did any teachers reach out to you?" I asked.

"There was one who attempted, but I was probably pretty unreachable. I was reading *13 against the Odds*, biographical sketches of African Americans I admired like Paul Robeson, Joe Louis, and Jackie Robinson, and feeling enormous guilt that I had no black friends."

I thought of Holden Caulfield — another self-styled outcast — and his branding of everyone he came across as "phony." A few years later, when we read *The Catcher in the Rye* aloud, Guy took an instant dislike to Holden. I expected Guy to identify with this alienated youth, or at least to feel some sympathy for his predicament, which, as we read the book together, struck me as not unlike Guy's. Instead, Guy said, "He irritates me. He's a whiny, spoiled, self-absorbed young man who feels sorry for himself." At the time I couldn't bear to think that probably described Guy when he was at Taft.

What relieved the gloom of his junior year — his last at Taft — was falling under the tutelage of fellow student and jazz pianist Bob LaGuardia.

The Waterman family was musical, and Guy retained happy memories of his brothers and sisters gathered about the piano in song, with Hawee — as everyone called Guy's father — at the keyboard. Alan Waterman could play just about any instrument he picked up. He kept a set of bagpipes in his office at the National Science Foundation and was known to play them there, pacing up and down the corridors. Guy had taken one reluctant year of piano lessons, and eight of violin. He spent four summers bowing away at Greenwood, a music camp in the Berkshires of western Massachusetts. Though he never progressed much beyond the back bench, this was a happy, carefree time.

Within a week of arriving on Taft's campus that fall, Bob LaGuardia, who had decided to become a clarinetist and needed a piano player to accompany him, whisked Guy off to the inner recesses of the practice rooms beneath the school auditorium and began to drill him in basic New Orleans piano style. "LaGuardia," Guy wrote, "heaped disdain on anyone as modern as Duke Ellington, had me listen to Jelly Roll Morton records by the hour, and browbeat me into abandoning all previous ideas on how to play popular music, insisting on a pure form of New Orleans piano. I developed into a simon-pure, basic Jelly Roll–style piano player."

If this was Guy's way of protesting against what he so disliked at Taft and rebelling as well against his parents who sent him there, his flight underground to the practice rooms — refuge and haven for an unsure young man who wanted to establish himself as different — carries a kind of innocence. There was no drug experimentation here, no rule breaking for the sake of violating the rules. Rather, here was honest intellectual effort with an older student in the role of mentor. The music Guy mastered was different — wildly different — from what he'd heard at home. This music sustained him all his life. With it he communicated his feelings of longing and loss, regret and despair, as well as happiness and joy — everything that was so hard for him to put into words. He told me once that his father never came to hear him in any of the nightclubs where he later played.

Guy spent the summer of 1948 at a "work camp" sponsored by the American Friends Service Committee and held at a church-run orphanage in York, South Carolina. "I believe that my parents saw that I was motivated to 'do good' and thought this opportunity might satisfy that craving to be socially useful."

Here Guy worked with the orphans, making cinder blocks and constructing a small outbuilding for the farm that was attached to the orphanage. "I loved those weeks," Guy wrote. "We were housed with the orphans and got to know them well, which I particularly welcomed as here were real-life poor people who I could finally call my friends." Then he took it all a step further in a deliberate decision to change his own image. This was his first reinvention, but by no means his last. "With my new smoking and drinking and necking, I became a flaming radical and moderately defiant of what little authority was exerted over me."

The defining moments of that summer were the much-anticipated football matches held during the last three Sundays of the camp, "campers" versus "orphans," tackle football played without equipment. In the first game the orphans trounced the campers. In the second the campers won back the crown, scoring four touchdowns to three; that game set the stage for the final winner-take-all contest. Guy, the smallest but one of the fastest, played center and found himself looking across the line at the orphans' star back — a brawny, fast, and very tough sixteen-year-old, and a big scorer on his high school team. Guy did well, hurling himself into the crushing tackles to the cheers of his teammates; his performance was contributing to his new image. In the final game, a rip-snorting seesaw battle, with four touchdowns apiece, the star back slipped through the campers' frantic efforts to bring him down and won the game. After the cheering and congratulations, Guy recalled "going into one of the outbuildings all by myself and lying down on the floor and crying uncontrollably, not for grief at losing but for joy at the great effort expended, and the comradeship we had all felt."

But I think he was sobbing for something more. The summer was over, and a high point had been reached that could never be regained in the same way ever again. Guy intuited what this loss meant, and the sadness of it was unbearable to him. In some sense this was his tragedy. The final party where he was voted "friendliest," and the final image of himself playing catch in his good clothes with two of the orphans who had become his friends before boarding the bus back up north to Washington, must only have deepened his sense of loss.

That fall Guy went to Sidwell Friends School in Washington, DC, where his parents felt he would be better off socially if he repeated his junior year. Though still privileged and admitting no black students, at least Sidwell was nonresidential and coeducational. Guy consolidated his image change and found himself swept up by a fast crowd of seniors — the social elite — his entrée being his magnetic piano playing and his penchant for getting drunk at any opportunity. He began going around with one of the popular senior girls. Not long before Emily's graduation, the couple had gone to a movie, then hung around downtown until it was so late that she was afraid to go home and confront her father, who had a violent temper. The upshot was that they ran off together, heading for York, South Carolina, the scene of those idyllic times for Guy at the orphanage the previous summer.

They were two young kids hitchhiking, and eventually they were stopped and questioned by the police in Charlotte. Guy asked the cops to call his parents rather than Emily's, because she was terrified of her father's reaction. So Guy's father and his older brother Neil drove down from Washington, a full day's drive, to pick them up and bring them back in time for the first big family wedding, the marriage of Guy's sister Anne, for which everyone had already assembled from across the country. The wedding proceeded smoothly, but afterward, in Romeo and Juliet fashion, the families managed to keep the two young people separate for the rest of the summer. That fall Emily was shipped off to college at Cornell without seeing Guy.

Guy had one more year at Sidwell Friends. "I basked in the notoriety of the rumors over just what Emily and I had done the previous May," Guy wrote. "I was arrogant to teachers and adults and openly defiant about getting drunk at weekend parties despite parental warnings."

That fall Guy had made the football team, but he played in only one game. He quit the team, despite the entreaties of his coach and his parents to stay with it, and took a "real" job, his first, as a soda jerk at People's Drugstore on the corner of Forty-Ninth and Albemarle Streets, for sixty-five cents an hour. "I loved football and the prestige of being on the team," Guy wrote. "But I carried a sense of guilt about being of the upper middle class. I craved being an ordinary working stiff." This action too could be seen as rebelling against the adult world, but the pendulum had swung in a different direction.

Emily left Cornell after only one semester and returned to Washington. And the couple could not be kept apart.

By this time, at his parents' urging, Guy had begun weekly sessions with a psychoanalyst. This did not go well. Guy wrote, "I was defiant and the doctor took the posture of being completely unsympathetic and caustically critical of my conduct."

One Sunday evening, Guy's parents told him they were all going for a meeting with the psychoanalyst, where they would meet with Emily and her parents, as well. "At this session the doc announced that I was a deeply disturbed young man," Guy wrote, "and he recommended prolonged psychoanalysis. In fact I was not to return home that night. I was hauled off to the psycho ward in George Washington Hospital, and incarcerated there on a floor where the stairway doors and elevators were locked. I was kept for several days of tests — including one session where they administered some kind of truth serum and questioned me about my musical friends, who had marijuana. It felt like jail to me. I was very unhappy."

After that, Guy's parents deemed that he would be better off far away from the Washington, DC, scene and sent him to finish out his senior year of high school in West Carrolton, Ohio, where he lived with his sister Bobbie and her husband Joe. In a sense, Guy found there what he wanted. This was a working-class town, with African Americans in the classroom. Even so, Guy fell back into the kind of isolation he'd experienced at Taft, making no friends and spending long hours playing his sister's piano. He also discovered that the education in West Carrolton, where only two in his class of forty were headed for college, was far below the standard he was used to in the "privileged" schools he'd attended. "We read no Shakespeare," Guy told me, "and when I mentioned to my English teacher I was reading *The Mayor of Casterbridge*, I was stunned to find out she had never heard of Thomas Hardy."

Here, also, he had to travel into Dayton several times a week for sessions with the psychoanalyst. In this case, Guy said, both doctor and patient sat in silence.

Meanwhile, continuing in the mode of Romeo and Juliet, Guy and Emily had found a way to communicate through the intermediary of Emily's sister and concocted a plot to meet in the Charlotte, North Carolina, airport during the interval between the end of classes and Guy's graduation ceremonies.

This time they pulled it off, journeying from Charlotte across the border to York, South Carolina, where the age of marriage without parental consent was eighteen. The ceremony was performed in the back room of the county clerk's office on May 20, 1950. Guy was the legal age by three weeks. The newlyweds sent a telegram to Emily's sister quoting the final words of the civil ceremony: "Whom God and the laws of South Carolina have joined together, let no man put asunder." Though the families welcomed the young couple back into the fold, as Guy said of himself at the time, they were "defiant to the end."

By 1951, he and Emily were living in Washington, DC. Guy had embarked on a career as a jazz musician and was both a full-time student at George Washington University and a family man. Their first son, Bill, was born in 1951, and Johnny followed just seventeen months later.

At George Washington, Guy, as in the past, took no part in college life. But he was possessed by a desire to learn and studied relentlessly between classes, at first in his car, until it got too cold; then he found out where the study halls were located. His excellent grades reached the notice of the president, who wrote him saying, in effect, we don't know who you are but want to congratulate you on your outstanding work. Guy made Phi Beta Kappa in his junior year, graduating number one in his class with a major in economics in two and a half years.

Meanwhile, at night he changed into his tux and red bowtie — the outfit he wore as a piano player with a Revival band called the Riverboat Trio, led by trumpeter-vocalist Scotty Lawrence. From 1951 through the first half of 1953, matching his college years, Guy played in the cocktail lounge of the Charles Hotel in the 1300 block of R Street, N.W., and as the off-night band on Tuesdays at a huge nightclub under the K Street Freeway known as Jazzland and sometimes as the Bayou. Guy relished the fact that these spots were in the black sections of segregated Washington, DC, as his presence there pointed out just how far he'd traveled from those miserable years at Taft. Following ex-alcoholic Scotty's abstemious lead, Guy drank coffee, strong and black, during the breaks.

Shortly after he began playing in Washington, DC, Guy met Roy Carew, who, as a typewriter salesman in New Orleans around the turn of the century, had become an early fan of jazz and was friends with Jelly Roll Morton. Mr. Carew had begun collecting ragtime sheet music as it came out, especially Scott Joplin. His dining room cupboard was stuffed with it, Guy said. He began to visit Mr. Carew almost every month, borrowed two rags, slowly mastered them (he was a poor sight reader), then brought them back to play for Mr. Carew, when he'd borrow two more. Gradually Guy learned almost all of Joplin's forty or so rags and began playing them in Washington, DC nightclubs at a time when no one else was.

In 1953, he wrote two articles about ragtime that were published by a minor jazz journal called the *Record Changer*. "I saw this," Guy wrote, "as an effort to demonstrate that ragtime fully deserved respect as a music independent of jazz." These articles were anthologized twenty years later as the interest in ragtime and Scott Joplin grew.

Guy gloried in the image of himself as a jazz piano player and in the nightly ritual of moving up to the bandstand, where he stood a moment to light a cigarette and survey the crowd. Seated at the piano bench, he played a couple of chords and gave Scotty his A, then waited until Scotty gave the signal to launch into "I Can't Give You Anything but Love, Baby," the song they invariably opened the evening with. Guy wrote, "On my better nights, I could stand the audience on its ear with a powerful rollicking barrelhouse style, or tormented gutbucket blues."

By mid-1953 it was over. "I recall a feeling," Guy wrote, "of deliberately bringing the hitherto productive relationship with Scotty to an end." The breakup of the trio Guy attributed to "that self-destructive streak in me which, throughout my life, has tended to surface and destroy whatever good things come my way. After that, I began to drink again."

When I met Guy I knew very little about jazz and had barely heard the word *ragtime*. I was brought up in a household where classical music, almost exclusively opera, my father's great love, commanded the airwaves. That's what my ears were adjusted to. I can remember, when I was about thirteen, being in the car with my father when he switched on the radio for the news but instead got Teresa Brewer's hit-of-the-moment "This Old House." For a few seconds her high-powered, hard-driving nasal sound filled the car. My father said, "Do you like that?"

"No," I said. From the look on his face I knew my father didn't like it either. Yet I also knew this was what kids my age were listening to.

I instantly took to Guy's piano. To my ears Joplin sounded classical. Guy opened up a new musical world for me. At our apartment in Marlboro, after the train ride out from the city, he'd put on a stack of records: Fats Waller, Bessie Smith, his Jelly Roll Morton recordings from the Library of Congress series; maybe some Pete Seeger — Guy had known the Seeger family in Washington, DC, and jammed with Pete's brother Mike.

Often during a weekend of climbing, friends would come to our place for dinner, or we'd find ourselves at someone's house with a piano, and Guy would play, with a grin on his face, his tam at that jaunty angle, his climber's forearms hammering out the tenths. When he played for our friends like that I was shot through with an unstoppable happiness watching how everyone responded to his music: glowing faces, tapping toes, swaying bodies. I loved being with Guy, this amazing man who could make people laugh, who everyone wanted to be with just as much as I did.

Guy had big hands. He had muscled, stocky fingers and thick palms. His knuckles bore nicks and scrapes from climbing. He had a way of splaying his fingers on the keyboard that allowed him to cover bunches of notes. This flat-and-spread hand position was the antithesis of how I'd been trained to curve my fingers above the keyboard. If this had been anyone but Guy, I would have been musical snob enough to have trouble overlooking what I considered improper training.

The way he grabbed for the notes, then offered them in fistfuls, typified how he communicated best. He poured into his music all he couldn't say in words. It was oblique, and often I wanted words. But after he had lost his sons and there were no more words, when he played "Over the Rainbow" — a song he connected to Johnny — I would find my eyes wet. I knew he had found release, and I had too. The strains of the day would dissolve as Guy's message reached me through his music.

By the time Guy was twenty-nine he had already burned through two careers. His adolescent decisions, aimed at the dramatic, the rebellious, the grand gesture, rang as a cry for attention from both the adult world he was at war with and from his peers, who he sought to be a part of yet held himself aloof from. A self-destructive streak lay behind his exit from the Washington, DC scene, as well as from his truncated career in jazz. I saw none of this. Instead, I was drawn to the heedless boy who didn't want to grow up and put on a coat and tie. I too wanted that enchanted life on a faraway island. There was as much Peter Pan in me as there was in Guy. In Guy I had found the other half of my own response to childhood, my own wish to throw off serious adult responsibilities for adventures and just plain fun. But I also saw in this Peter Pan a bedrock integrity, an innate honesty, a commitment to standing up for values he believed in.

Guy told me about his drinking problems the first evening we had supper together in New York, when I had a glass of wine and he drank ginger ale. After he left Washington, DC, and took a corporate job in New York, he had drunk himself into a stupor nearly every night. The General Electric job was flat. Gone was the excitement of giving all he had for issues that mattered, working until 2:00 a.m. over a speech a senator needed at eight the next morning. Still, he rode that commuter train for the next twelve years. He was in demand as a speechwriter among the senior officers at General Electric because he was good, but he knew he was just coasting, carried along on the reputation for rapid, accurate work he had earned in Washington, DC.

"How did you break out of the drinking?" I asked him.

"It was climbing. I wanted to be fit. I wanted to take my boys to the mountains."

All my parents' friends at the Lawrenceville School drank, and the stories about teaching classes with hangovers always got laughs. I'd grown up helping myself to the cherries at the bottom of their cocktail glasses, also considered funny. But I was thinking about my own family. My father was usually drunk by dinnertime.

Guy had stopped drinking. That was all I needed to know. On some intuitive level — there was nothing rational about it — I knew he would stay sober.

It felt to me then that what each of us believed deep down, even what drove us, was similar. Partly it was. But back then I couldn't see that what drove Guy was often very different. All the same, from the beginning I felt in tune with Guy. I trusted him. I felt at home. I couldn't imagine not feeling this way toward him. Though I cannot say about Guy what Catherine Earnshaw says about her soulmate Heathcliff in *Wuthering Heights*, "I am Heathcliff," there was some of this. But basically I wasn't thinking. I just knew that what had started as enjoying the same books and sharing a love of climbing had plunged to a deep spot that had more to do with how Guy could make me laugh. I saw that he longed to do the right thing, an impulse also strong in me. With Guy I could keep on growing. I could have articulated none of this. All I knew was that what I had been searching for I had found in Guy.

From our first conversation a bridge spanned between us even though he had told me: "I disappoint the ones I love most. I let people down."

I didn't understand, and I didn't ask him to explain. But I was convinced he would never disappoint me or ever let me down.

Years later Guy posted this quotation on the calendar we kept at Barra. It's from T. H. White's *The Once and Future King*, and I give it here the way Guy copied it out.

> Merlin:
> Well, anyway, suppose they did not let you stand against all the evil in the world?
> Wart: I could ask.
> Merlin: You could ask.

That intangible quality behind the "I could ask" Guy never lost. His desire to do right stirred in me something impossible to explain, because how can we explain love?

❀ ❁ ❀

CHAPTER *five*

The weight of this sad time we must obey;

Speak what we feel, not what we ought to say.

The oldest hath borne most: we that are young

Shall never see so much, nor live so long.

— William Shakespeare, *King Lear*

During the school week when I was growing up, the family dinner table was the battleground. My parents occupied either end, and my younger brother and I the flanks, pinned in the crossfire. When their arguments flared into open warfare, I found myself ducking as they hurled words back and forth across the table. The food turned to paste in my mouth, and I held on to my knife and fork in an effort to keep myself from shaking. Even though my parents seldom argued, the possibility left me feeling that it happened every night. Because every night the atmosphere was dense as my mother held herself tense and alert, monitoring my father's studied effort to act as if there were nothing wrong, nothing wrong at all.

Before dinner there was the cocktail hour. "Bourbon, dear?" My father asked this question at six o'clock, and every evening at six my mother said, "Lovely. I'll be right there." She was in the kitchen fixing dinner.

My father carried their drinks into the living room, setting his on the end table beside his armchair. He sat down to wait for her and removed a Chesterfield from the silver cigarette case with an engraved inscription that read

> To Thomas H. Johnson
> with respect and affection
> from his colleagues

And when he'd finished, he would stub his cigarette out in a silver ashtray, also engraved

To Dad on his Birthday
with love
Laura and Tommy

My father wore a tweed jacket and silk tie and sat with his right leg crossed over his left. When my mother arrived she occupied the sofa, one arm resting on the back, a leg folded under her. Her drink was there waiting beside her ashtray.

I was doing my homework upstairs, with an ear cocked to what was going on downstairs. My brother was playing in his room down the hall, and I knew he wasn't paying any attention. If they fell into an easy back-and-forth flow, with a lilt of a laugh from my mother, I settled into my math and lowered my antennae. But if my mother offered conversation in a tight voice and there was an interminable pause before my father gave forth with a monosyllabic reply, my pencil froze. I couldn't distinguish their words, but I only needed to catch my mother's tone, jammed with all the words she wasn't saying, to dread dinner. I heard her get up and stride into the kitchen with a footfall that rattled my pencils in their mug, and when she announced that dinner was ready, I was filled with fear, because in her voice I heard that she was close to giving up on the whole situation.

I looked at my watch. It was six thirty. We ate every night at six thirty. I started downstairs. My brother bounded out of his room, slid around me, and landed in the dining room. "I win," he hooted.

I didn't pay much attention. I wasn't interested in racing.

"Slow down, Tommy," my father said in his warning voice. He stood behind my mother's chair, leaning on it. My mother walked back and forth from the kitchen, putting food on the table. Finally she emerged with her apron off. My brother and I had already sat down. My mother walked toward her chair, and my father pulled it out. "Kiss the cook," he said and leaned toward her. And she returned his kiss. Then he walked to his end and sat down. My mother laid her hands on the table palms up, as if she wanted to hold hands. She put on a bright smile, looking first at my brother, then at me, and finally gazing straight ahead at my father. I was flooded with hope: maybe tonight everything would be all right.

Then my father pushed back his chair and stood up. He hung over the meat with the carving knife in his hand and started sawing. The roast slid around, emitting a strong smell of the gravy. His knuckles clipped his glass, and the water slopped out in big drops. I reached to move his glass to a safer position. "Thank you, Laura," my mother said. She sat very straight in her chair.

"What?" My father lifted his head and flung a look across the candlesticks. His eyes were pale, innocent and blue, his cheeks puffy, and the carving knife wobbled in his grip. She didn't say anything further but put her fingers to her throat, and I heard her inhale. It seemed she was holding her breath. There was a tiny smudge of lipstick at the corner of her mouth.

He went back to the meat and levered a ragged slab onto the top plate from the stack of four in front of him. Gravy slopped onto the table, catching the edge of his mat, but he wasn't aware of the brown stain that was spreading into the threads of the lace. My mother drew herself a notch tighter.

He handed me the plate, and I passed it to my mother, who received it and splatted out the mashed potatoes with a silver serving spoon. I braced myself in case she hurled, "You're drunk." She'd only said this once. He'd flung back, "You're drunk," which resulted in an argument. Normally she held herself in check, her eyes on him not giving an inch, and the silence that flowed toward my father like a current was packed with anger and all her unspoken words.

Finally, we were all served and sat before our heaping plates. "Sit straight, Tommy," my mother said. Across from me my brother sat sideways in his chair, as if ready to bolt from the room. He squirmed a quarter-turn toward center. I sat in my chair like an insect pinned to the mounting board, studying first my father's face, then returning to my mother's. She picked up her fork. I did, too, even though my appetite had vanished. Everyone was silent. My father sat round-shouldered, staring at his food. He fumbled with his fork, which rattled against his plate. My mother sat so straight that her back arched like a bow six inches from the chair. She turned to me and said in her party-bright voice, "What did you do in school today, Laura?"

My father, Thomas H. Johnson, was a brilliant man, a scholar and a gifted teacher. I was told he had the kind of clarity of mind that could illuminate textual analysis with the concentrated focus of a magnifying glass. He was known for his infinite capacity for taking pains, and colleagues who sought his advice found their academic papers subjected to a razor-edge scrutiny that lifted up their work at the same time as it left them feeling like schoolboys. His contribution to American letters as Emily Dickinson's editor was, some have said, the most important piece of scholarship in the twentieth century. Among the things I learned from him was discipline. He rose at 4:00 a.m. every day of his adult life and wrote at his desk until my mother called the family for breakfast at 7:15.

Though I cannot recall my father expressing his emotions in words, he was an emotional man. He loved opera and played his recordings of the great voices of his youth at full volume — Caruso, Melba, Rosa Ponselle, Galli-Curci, John McCormack — in the evening after I was in bed. He made no allowances for a young child trying to fall asleep.

On Sunday afternoons my father often listened to his records with Mr. Marsh, a heavy-set bachelor who wore musty-smelling three-piece suits and taught music at the Lawrenceville School, where my father also taught and around which our lives revolved.

"Mr. Marsh is coming this afternoon," my mother would announce with a smiling voice at breakfast, and I knew I'd be included in this adult occasion at which my father served sherry, treating the event as a command performance for the whole family. He did not feel it necessary to explain the opera's story, or even sketch for us what we were hearing, but nonetheless I knew my father wanted me to be there as I took my place beside my mother on the couch, my brother under her arm on the other side.

My father's record player was a Victrola the size of a chest of drawers, with a metal arm to wind it up. The whole household spoke of "Dad's records" in hushed tones: they were breakable disks, one song per side, with plenty of background crackle.

On those Sunday afternoons my father was in charge of operations and ritual. He began with the "Jewel Song" from Faust. As the great Geraldine Farrar gained momentum, his face drew together, his eyes lost focus, and the music took him over. As the singer's voice ceased he sat immobile for several long seconds, his head bowed. The record on the phonograph whirred louder. "God damn!" my father ejaculated in a voice that sounded like a sob and hit the arm of his chair with his fist. This propelled him to his feet, and lifting the needle off the record, he turned to Mr. Marsh and began a discussion about the voice they had just heard.

I listened, but mostly I watched my father. His reaction was so strong. It wasn't that unnamed terror I felt at the dinner table, but he was scary, and my mother's grip tightened across my shoulders when he pounded his chair. Mr. Marsh sat large and unmoving as a walrus, however, as if my father's reaction to the music was the most natural thing in the world.

"The human voice is the greatest instrument," my father said to Mr. Marsh. I didn't understand this, though he said it often. But I saw how the human voice affected him. And this was his greatest gift on those Sunday afternoons, the one he gave without knowing he was giving it: letting me see what moved him.

Ambiguity was my father's favorite word. Others were *paradox, innuendo, conundrum,* and *profound.* The word others used to describe him was *opaque.* "Tom, that was a thoroughly opaque remark" became an oft-told story, because the headmaster who called my father on one of his philosophical profundities did what no one else would have dared to do. After my brother and I were grown, we concluded that it wasn't what Dad said that caused friends to regard him with awe, but his delivery. First came a preamble of throat clearing that could silence a room, then an elongated pause that drew all eyes to him. Meanwhile, his eyes became steely or watery, depending on the tenor of the oracular statement he was about to impart.

There were stories about my father in the classroom, his brilliance in leading his students to the brink of understanding, then encouraging them to make the leap. I remember a discussion of free will at a midday Sunday dinner, the meal for which I was most grateful, because my father was at his brightest and best, since it took place when he was still sober. He asked me to consider what I would do when I took the train back to school — I was home on vacation and was to leave the next day — and arrived at my station. Would I get off the train? Or would I stay on and keep going? I tried to imagine myself remaining in my seat while everyone else got off, the train pulling away to parts unknown, me still on it. Classes starting at eight the next morning and my place vacant. In this way he led me to see that I wasn't as "free" as I thought.

It was a well-known secret, at least in the English Department, which he chaired, that Thomas H. Johnson was an alcoholic. But in those days everyone at the Lawrenceville School drank. It was the way these adults socialized. Alcoholic or not, words like *great man* and *genius* attached themselves to him in trails of glory.

What no one beyond the family saw was that "the great man" was slurry to the point of incoherence four nights out of seven. The clarity he was revered for was muddied, as though a heavy stone had dropped in the wellspring of his mind. But which four nights would it be? There was no predictable pattern to his drunkenness, so I dwelled in a perpetual state of watchfulness, gauging by a repeated footfall, by the click of a closet door, by the splash of liquid into a glass, what he was going to be like by dinner.

I never gave up hoping that my father would stop drinking. But I hoped with the powerlessness of a child. I clung to wishful thinking and the off chance of a miracle.

In 1952 we spent the year in Copenhagen, where my father had been invited to set up a program in American studies at the university. When he returned to his teaching at Lawrenceville the next fall, he began his work on Emily Dickinson. It was that fall also, when I was in seventh grade and my brother Tommy was in fourth, that my father's normally opaque pronouncements at the dinner table crossed the line into a kind of gibberish. So, as I later came to see, at the moment my father was at the height of his powers, poised to make his most important contribution to American letters, he had also begun the unchecked downhill slide. Perhaps there was good reason that *paradox* was one of his favorite words.

"What did you say, Dad?" I found myself asking nearly every night at dinner. I was missing something important. If I asked him to repeat enough times, perhaps I could make come clear what I couldn't understand.

After supper I asked my mother, "What's the matter with Dad?"

"He's tired," she said.

That made sense. He got up so early. Often at dinner his pale eyes were more watery than ever, and he went to bed before my mother and I had finished the dishes. I just needed to be patient when his talk made no sense and he moved his knife through his meat as though it were a piece of leather, then let it sit on his plate. His face was growing jowly. My mother kept the conversation going, and I did my best to help her out.

One night after dinner was finally over and my brother had escaped back upstairs, I heard my mother in the kitchen call him back to help with the dishes. I was in the dining room watching my father as he headed for the door. His shoulders were stooped. His legs seemed about to buckle as he pushed a hand along the wall, then reached for the door jamb. He was only fifty-two, but he seemed old, and it made me sad.

In the kitchen dishes clattered in the sink. "What's wrong with Dad?" I said. This time I had to find out.

"Don't you know?"

"No," I said in a small voice. There was something I should know, but I didn't.

"He's drunk." She didn't shout, but her words exploded out of the kitchen.

I stood alone in the empty dining room. Now she was telling me the truth. I felt guilt for not knowing this thing that the rage in my mother's voice told me she had known for a long time. I walked into the kitchen.

She tossed me a dish towel. We worked in silence, and I was full of questions I didn't know how to ask.

When my father's study door was open I could walk in, even if he was at his desk. The room smelled of his tobacco, his books, and the mustiness of a man who dwelled with books. Sometimes he showed me what he was working on. Or he might say, "Here's a poem you might like to memorize, Laura." In this way I learned by heart "How happy is the little stone" and "I like to see it lap the miles" — Dickinson's verses that children like. He had tacked Emily's (as the family called her) poems to the pine paneling. These "photostats" showed her wispy handwriting in chalk white on a jet background, and he moved them around as he discovered new ways of dating her poems. We met over books, my father and

I, but I knew from what went on at our dinner table that he couldn't be counted on for emotional or even practical support.

That meant I had to count on myself.

But I could also count on my mother. When I was in high school I believe she wrestled with leaving him. Then something changed, because I no longer felt the threat that our family might come apart. It seemed she had made a commitment to herself — to her family — to stick this out. She must have paid a high price.

Perhaps the turning point came the year my brother was in seventh grade and entered the Lawrenceville School. I was, by then, a sophomore at Princeton High School. My mother wanted to work at a real job, for pay. My father didn't want her to work. He was "adamant" about this, he said. Her going to work would "belittle" him. It implied he couldn't support the family on his teacher's income.

"You're a tyrant." I caught my mother's sentence as I sat upstairs in my bedroom over my hated math.

"If you're bored, go back to indexing for that Princeton professor."

"I'm not going to do that, Tom," my mother said. She wanted to be out of the house. She wanted a career. She stuck to this, and she won.

She studied for her broker's license and then sold real estate in Princeton for many years, though it often must have seemed a Pyrrhic victory. My father "stipulated" that she be home to fix his lunch and that she not take clients out on weekends. I see my mother — an intelligent and surprisingly resilient woman — as the unsung hero of our family.

When I was growing up our house was alive with talk and friends, many of whom were contributing to American literary scholarship. When a colleague arrived with his briefcase he'd be greeted by my mother, who, with a wave toward the study, would say, "He's in there with Emily."

When they came with their wives, everyone glided into the living room on a spin of laughter and my father fixed the drinks. Their cigarettes overflowed the ashtrays. I sat on the stairs taking in this adult talk about their work that left me feeling there was nothing so exciting in the world. If the gathering included Perry Miller, a white-haired, florid-faced, whale-sized man and a prodigious consumer of my father's drinks, the talk hinged on Cotton Mather, Jonathan Edwards, and other Puritan "divines" my father and Perry had written books about. I sat listening with my chin in my hands to their well-turned sentences intended to dazzle, their knee slapping, the gusto of their laughter as they unleashed those Puritans, three centuries dead, right into the room.

I took in as well the sad failures. Dick Martin was, for a time, my father's closest friend and colleague at Lawrenceville. When Dick burst into our house without knocking, I'd run downstairs to hug his legs and we'd waltz around the hall, me standing on his shoes. Then he'd disappear into my father's study. The story, years later, was that Dick was "always going to" get down to a big work on Melville. As Dick sank deeper into alcohol my father lightened his teaching load, but nothing worked, and by Christmas another Lawrenceville family, the Pecks, had taken in Dick's wife Ruthie and the three young children. Word spread that Dick was holed up at home with a shotgun. That jagged, boisterous Christmas Day at the Pecks, we children ran around upstairs, jumping on the beds, while the adults circulated with martinis downstairs. Whenever I came down to see if dinner was ready, there was Ruthie with a box of tissues in a corner of the couch, hovered over by the wives. Dick hung on for another two years, only to slide out with a whimper at his own kitchen table. Poor Dick Martin, my father's friend and mine, had certainly never lived up to his promise.

Had my father? If one were to judge by his published works, the ledger was dense with checks in the credit column. After *The Puritans* came *The Literary History of the United States*, which had involved a team of scholars; my father was responsible for volume 3, the bibliography. On the heels of his success with Emily Dickinson, he was asked by Oxford University Press to write *The Oxford Companion to American History*. This came out in 1966, the year he retired from teaching. He made it to the end of both of these efforts with forbearance on the part of the Lawrenceville School, which let him reach retirement age before cleaning out his classroom, and an assist from Oxford, which called in a "consultant" to help him wind up this monumental work for which he would have needed no assistance a decade before. He lived for nearly another twenty years, going out of the house less and less. In his reclusive habits he was increasingly compared with the Amherst poet who he had spent so many years studying and in whom he had found not just a kindred spirit but a version of himself. When I came home on infrequent visits I saw with a stab that he appeared always a little smaller, more florid about the nose, more jowly, and more sunk in his customary chair. But he was still wearing his jacket and tie, still sitting with his right leg crossed over his left, and still filling the silver ashtray, given to him by my brother and me so long ago, with his unfiltered Chesterfields. I took in as well that the tabletop and the Oriental rug at his feet were a little more scarred with cigarette burns. I sat across from him on the couch, unable to concentrate on my own reading as I watched how he held his well-thumbed copy of *The Oxford Companion to American History* open on his lap. Was he reading or dozing? I couldn't tell. The winter sun slanting through the picture window behind him cast too weak a light.

When I was in college I risked everything to "save" my father, though I was far from understanding what I was doing at the time.

I selected Hollins College in part because of a program called Hollins Abroad, one of the earliest European study opportunities, offered in 1958, when I entered as a freshman. The Hollins program was based in Paris. Students lived with French families and studied at the Sorbonne. The year spanned from the sophomore second semester through the first semester of junior year, with the summer spent touring Europe, including countries behind the Iron Curtain. This was called the Summer Tour.

I wanted this experience more than anything. My parents agreed but told me they couldn't afford any costs beyond my college tuition. I won a scholarship and began reading André Maurois's *History of France*. In an attempt to balance the scales, my mother gave me Art Buchwald's lighthearted *Paris for Christmas*.

Dr. Degginer, the program's director, and a dedicated Francophile, reeled off all the ways we could turn ourselves into Parisians during our year. Sitting in cafés reading the newspaper. Eating patisseries on the grass in the Tuileries. Buying a long baguette and walking home with it under one's arm. Getting up in the dark and taking the Métro to Les Halles to haggle with the fishwives. I took notes. Daddy Deg, as we called him, explained French bathrooms: the john had a pull chain; the bidet looked like a john to uninformed American eyes but wasn't; the tub was in a little room separate from the john. Newspaper was used instead of toilet paper. There was alarmed discussion about the newspaper. And not long after that one of the girls told us her father had calculated how many rolls she would need for the year at three squares a shot. Water down the experience like that? Not me!

That winter in Paris was dark and rainy. Or so it seemed. I was supposed to be having a French Experience, and to me that meant meeting scads of French people, talking French, and going to museums and cafés after classes with French friends. But I wasn't making any French friends. So I walked around Paris by myself, from the Latin Quarter on the Left Bank, crossing the Seine to the Place de la Concorde on the Right Bank, stopping in a patisserie for a *tart aux fraises* as I marched from la Tour Eiffel up to the Arc de Triomphe. On the Métro I pulled out *Strait Is the Gate* by André Gide. That winter I worked my way through a depressing dose of Gide as well as Camus and Sartre. Finally, it was April, and we had three weeks off for Easter. I made plans with one of the Hollins girls to travel in England and Scotland. I was really looking forward to speaking English and touring with someone besides myself. Bill Marsden, an English student of my father's who had spent his senior year at Lawrenceville, had invited me to visit. It was there I met two French boys who lived in Paris.

After I returned one of them called and asked me to a movie. It was fully spring now, and my Parisian life suddenly looked a lot brighter.

The movie the French boy took me to wasn't shown in a movie theater but in a large house surrounded by gardens. This was not what I expected, but it was a lovely place, and afterward the French boy asked me what I thought, as did a Danish girl and a few adults I met that evening as we drank coffee and ate cakes and they told me about their organization, called Moral Re-Armament (MRA).

I didn't know what to think. The movie was about their founder, an American named Frank Buchman, who had come up with an "ideology" that appealed to all religions: Catholics, Jews, Protestants, Hindus, Muslims, Buddhists, and Confucianists. The world was in danger morally, Buchman said. For instance, there was far too much drinking, especially among college students (no doubt about that!). Buchman was committed to making a "hate-free, fear-free, greed-free world" and fighting communism. That seemed like a good thing. We were still recovering from the Cold War, and no one I knew wanted to be labeled a Commie.

But mostly I was glad to be meeting people my age who weren't Americans.

Classes were almost over, and the Summer Tour was about to begin. I had planned to spend the two weeks before then with friends my family had made in Copenhagen in 1952, but these Moral Re-Armament people wanted me to come to their European headquarters in Switzerland instead.

That night I talked this over with my roommate. "It's a wonderful chance to see the Swiss Alps," I told Abby.

"But what about this group? What do they do?" Abby asked. She could be annoyingly practical.

"They fight communism," I said.

"What will your parents think?" Abby was sitting on her bed facing me from her side of the room, her feet flat on the floor.

"Oh, I'll write them," I said.

My new friends were there to meet me when I got off the train. We drove out of the valley up into the mountains, which looked just like I knew they would from reading Heidi when I was ten. The air was excitingly clear, and the sun bore down as though nothing could stop it. We arrived at a sprawling red-roofed structure surrounded by gardens in the glory of June. Several hundred people were staying there.

Before that first day was out I had made friends with another American girl, Joanne, the daughter of a well-known labor leader, who told me she had come to Switzerland while her father had gone to MRA's headquarters in America on an island in Lake Michigan.

"Is your mother there too?" I asked.

Her mother wasn't interested. "It's very hard on my father. But we're working on her. How about your family?" she asked. "Are they members?"

I had to say no. "I'm not really a member myself," I added.

"Well, I hope you'll decide to join us," she said, hugely beaming. I liked her. She reminded me of a girl I'd played field hockey with in eighth grade who could turn fringe players like me into part of the team.

After breakfast we gathered in the main assembly room for prayers and announcements led by Peter Howard, Frank Buchman's right-hand man, since Dr. Buchman was ill. Mr. Howard was tall, a whippet-thin Englishman. He had round eyes, dark and deep, that gave his face a cavernous, burning look. I was introduced to him but had no idea what to say. Everyone said he was very caught up in his work, which I didn't doubt since my views of him were always from a distance as he melted out of sight down a hallway or through a closed door.

That first afternoon in the room I shared with the Danish girl, my friends told me about Moral Re-Armament's important principles of sharing and guidance whereby it was made known whether a person was right for the group or not. They asked me to examine my life through four windows: Was it absolutely honest? Pure? Unselfish? Loving? I had to write down my shortcomings in each category. Then, as a group, we would discuss my "confession." This was the sharing part, and they also urged me to mail it to my parents.

In the absolute honesty column I confessed to having ruined a good silk scarf of my mother's. I had tried to force it through a funnel when I was watching my mother's teenage helper iron sheets. The only way out of this was to cut apart the funnel, which ruined the funnel and, worse, put holes in my mother's scarf. I had felt so bad about this that I folded the scarf very neatly and buried it in the back of her bureau drawer. Even though my mother had found the scarf and long ago forgave me, I thought this was the sort of dishonesty MRA would like to know about.

How had I acted selfishly? I'd been pretty consistent about grabbing the larger piece of cake, leaving my little brother with the smaller.

Was I absolutely pure? They meant sex here. Men and women. I felt enormously relieved that I hadn't slept with any boys yet. But what level of detail would I have to go into? And girls? they asked. Think hard, they said. Finally I came up with my friend Taffy, whom I'd known since I was three and she was almost five. We climbed trees and went to all the ball games on the Lawrenceville campus, running up and down the bleachers, buying cokes and Mars Bars.

"Did she touch you?" one of my confessors asked.

"What do you mean?" I asked.

"In private places," she said with a stern look that made me feel that she thought I was keeping something hidden. "Feelings don't always have to turn into actions," she added.

In the confession I sent my parents, I ended up stating that I had "lesbian feelings," as they phrased it, for my childhood friend.

We moved on to absolute love, and I had to confess that I didn't always feel loving toward my father, and then the whole family secret of my father's drinking came out. I was embarrassed, ashamed to admit this. It was like telling them my father was a hardened criminal guilty of a white-collar crime like embezzling that could lead to an extended stay behind bars. But on another level I felt a strange sense of relief at being able to say anything at all about the biggest, saddest, scariest, most hurtful, harmful, and awful thing in my life. The thing I had never told anyone.

"Aha!" My friends assured me, "If your father embraces the tenets of Moral Re-Armament, he will be free of his alcoholism." Why, they said, the founders of Alcoholics Anonymous had used MRA's principles to form their famous twelve-step program!

Then we all sat around and applied the second important principle of guidance, which meant asking God for guidance in my particular case. Evidently word came down that I was worth their time and effort, if I was interested. By that time I was very interested. So I was congratulated and made welcome and experienced joy at being a part of this group that was making the world a better place. And besides, I'd found a way to help my family, since if my father embraced MRA he would ipso facto have to stop drinking. All this occurred within forty-eight hours of my arrival in Switzerland.

The next thing was to inform Professor McQuiggan, the faculty adviser who had come to Paris with us, that I wasn't going on the Summer Tour. I'd had him in psychology. He belonged to the Skinnerian School, which frowned on words like *soul*. He told us we didn't have "minds," we had "brains." Everything we did was in response to "stimuli" of some sort. We were like rats, Professor McQuiggan said, as we went through life trying to press the correct lever, the one that delivered the food pellets, not the electric shock. I didn't get on with Professor McQuiggan, but I wasn't too concerned about phoning him. By now I saw that he was a Communist; in fact, all my teachers at Hollins were Communists, or at least had Communist leanings. I knew my parents weren't Communists — at least not the card-carrying kind — but for certain their academic friends were.

My parents called me — that is, my mother did. They had read my "confession" and didn't think what I was doing was such a hot idea. They wanted me to go on the Summer Tour. But I resisted. It was easy to say no when I knew I was doing the absolutely right thing.

By the third phone call with Professor McQuiggan he said, "Is someone pointing a gun at your head?"

"Of course not!"

"Have you talked to your parents?"

"Yes."

"What did they say?"

"They want me to go on the Summer Tour."

"Are you coming?"

"No."

"Then," Professor McQuiggan announced, "you will be expelled."

"Expelled?"

"From college," Professor McQuiggan explained.

College felt very far away. I didn't see how I could be expelled because I hadn't done anything wrong like flunk out or get caught with booze in my room.

When my mother called again (transatlantic phone calls in 1960 were expensive and were made only when the situation had reached a state of emergency), she said she'd bought a ticket for Geneva and I was to meet her plane. "Good!" I said. Things were going to work out after all. I had been there a month. Now my mother was coming, and she would see how MRA could help Dad.

As soon as my mother got settled — she'd been given a lovely room with a view of the mountains — she announced, "I've come over here to take you home." This didn't really surprise me. I could tell that after she'd got a grasp of what MRA stood for, she had heard enough. She joined me for meals, but she wasn't socializing. She smoked in her room, another vice MRA frowned on, and poured herself a cocktail now and then from the bottle of bourbon she'd brought in her suitcase.

"But what about Dad?" I asked. I had told her about MRA's stance on alcohol.

"Your father," she said, "would never be interested."

I knew it wouldn't be easy to win Dad over, but I kept hearing their voices rising over cocktails in the living room. My father pounding his chair, delivering his ultimatum — "I am who I am" — when my mother, very occasionally, confronted him about his drinking. I saw my young self, alone in my room, bearing down harder on my math problems, which made absolutely no sense.

On the Fourth of July we had a celebratory dinner with the Americans and British in a private dining room where the Stars and Stripes shared the centerpiece with the Union Jack. My mother was at a far end, and every time I looked her way she was in animated conversation with the gentleman on her right. I was glad she was having a good time. Perhaps she would change her mind about Moral Re-Armament. At the end of the meal I heard her say, "May I have an ashtray?" A waiter scurried around, and a little dish was brought, since there were no actual ashtrays. A silence fell over the long table as my mother pulled out a Chesterfield. Most people began to concentrate on dessert. The man she had been talking to lit her cigarette with her lighter. She sat there, filling the pure air of MRA's dining room with a steady flow of foul smoke. I had lost most of my sense of humor over the last few months, so I was surprised to find that as I stared at my mother I found this funny.

Back in her room my mother said, "That man I was sitting next to asked me what I was doing here."

"What did you say?" I asked.

"I said, 'I've come to collect my daughter.'" She paused. "I really made him laugh."

All this time she'd been urging me to talk to Louis Rubin, my college professor and faculty adviser, who was teaching summer school at the University of Marseilles. After a week of this I just didn't see how I could keep on saying no. Besides, I was devoted to Mr. Rubin, who knew my parents; my mother had contacted him before she left the States.

We would rent a car, my mother said, and drive through the Alps, across northern Italy, and into France down to the Riviera. I had to admit that sounded pretty appealing. "But," I told her, "I'm leaving most of my clothes here."

That first night we stayed up late talking over a seafood dinner in a restaurant Mr. Rubin knew about. He smoked his pipe and wanted to hear all about Moral Re-Armament — how I got involved, what they stood for, where I saw my life going from here. Mr. Rubin and my mother had cocktails and wine with dinner, but I didn't touch a drop.

When my mother and I were preparing for bed back in our hotel room, my stomach began to cramp, and I just made it to the bathroom in time to lose all that langouste — my main course — in the toilet.

The next morning, when I mentioned this to Mr. Rubin, he said, "How did you feel after that, Laura?"

"Oh, much better!"

"I think this change of air is doing you good."

My mother laughed.

The second day I continued trying to explain to Mr. Rubin about fighting communism and all that.

"Ideologies can be very seductive," he said. "But they don't have much to do with living one's life in the real world."

"But they're trying to change the world!"

"That's what I mean," Mr. Rubin said. "Groups like that see things only one way, their way. Their beliefs — it's a nicer word than *propaganda* — don't allow for much straying from the party line."

"But what they say includes all religions," I said. Why couldn't I make Mr. Rubin see this?

"Do you want to live your life in service to one idea?" Mr. Rubin asked. "In a cloister? At nineteen?"

"It's for a higher cause," I said.

"When people turn themselves over to one overriding idea they are called fanatics," Mr. Rubin said.

I didn't see how I was a fanatic, though I could see how this word applied to that hollow-eyed Peter Howard.

The next day Mr. Rubin proposed that we drive out along the ocean to Monte Carlo, where Somerset Maugham had lived. It was supposed to be very scenic. Mr. Rubin drove our rented car. My mother sat in the passenger's seat in front, and I sat in back, though I was nearly on the floor, on my knees, so I could see down toward the ocean, which was alive in the sunlight, and up into the hills toward the tile-roofed houses clustered just as I had seen them in my art history book.

"Have you read *Rain*, Laura?" Mr. Rubin asked.

"Maugham's *Rain*?" my mother asked.

"No, I haven't," I said.

"It's about a missionary. He's a pretty intolerant guy. Then he meets Sadie Thompson. I think you'd find it interesting in the light of your MRA experience." Mr. Rubin smiled to himself. "Sadie Thompson is a prostitute. I'll lend you my copy."

Somewhere on the road back to Nice I agreed to go home with my mother. I didn't understand what had happened to me — either why I'd been drawn to Moral Re-Armament or why I was now returning home. But between Mr. Rubin and my mother, I'd been unbrainwashed enough to see that my life didn't belong to a cult. At any rate, that evening at dinner I joined them in a glass of wine. Mr. Rubin advised us to drive straight to the airport in Geneva, but I said I wanted to pick up my clothes and say good-bye. "In that case," Mr. Rubin announced, "I'm coming. I want to make sure you get on that plane." He winked at my mother, but he looked very solemn too, his teeth clenched around his pipe stem.

On the drive back we stopped at a bistro for lunch, and my mother allowed as how she was dying for a martini. She hadn't had a decent one since she'd left the States.

Mr. Rubin spoke to the bartender, who had no notion of what a martini was. So Mr. Rubin pointed to the gin, the dry vermouth, the ice, and mixed up a pitcher himself, pouring it out into three glasses: one for my mother, one for himself, and a small one for the bartender, who took one sip and, elevating his brows and narrowing his eyes in the inimitable French manner, handed it back to Mr. Rubin without comment.

When we got back in the car I mentioned that MRA's no-alcohol policy had been a big reason why I got interested.

"Why was that?" Mr. Rubin asked.

"Because of my father," I said. I couldn't say anything more.

Mr. Rubin glanced at my mother. He was behind the wheel, as usual.

"Well, Tom drinks too much at times," my mother mumbled.

"I wish I knew his brand," Mr. Rubin said.

When we pulled up in front of the grand entrance back at MRA's headquarters, Mr. Rubin said he'd wait at the car, adding, "I don't even want to use their bathroom."

My mother sailed up to the front desk. I was right behind her. I didn't want to stay, but I felt a little bad about just walking out when they'd all been so nice.

"My daughter will be returning home with me," my mother announced in an even tone to the gentleman behind the desk.

"I'm sorry to hear that." He looked at me.

"I guess I'd like to pick up my clothes," I said.

"I must owe you something for my week here," my mother added.

"Not at all, madam. You were our guest."

My roommate, the Danish girl, wasn't in the room. I quickly packed and on the way down the hall ran into the American girl, Joanne, who had been so friendly on that first day. It seemed a long time ago now. "I'm going home," I said by way of explaining my suitcase. She looked at me, then at my mother, and I felt like I was letting the old team down.

Back outside Mr. Rubin was leaning against the driver's door, grinning, his pipe clamped between his teeth. On the way to the airport he told me he'd see what he could do about getting me readmitted to Hollins.

❀ ❀ ❀

It all came to naught with my poor, dear alcoholic father. He was my underlying "cause," but a hopeless cause, since he wasn't asking for anyone's help. I was unable to articulate, even to myself, how much my father's drinking hurt me, so the thought of actually telling him never crossed my mind. I had felt so helpless before the terror of the dinner table that I had put at risk my college education and my future. But the path I had chosen couldn't work and made no sense. I chose it because I could.

This story had far-reaching consequences for my life with Guy: after the watershed year of his son John's death in 1981, I began to live in fear in my life with him without knowing it. What I have now come to recognize as Guy's depression generated a tension between us that I was never able to resolve. Yet since I so longed for resolution, I strove like a mighty Trojan at great cost and in the only way I knew how — always to be in a state of peace and harmony with my husband.

CHAPTER

six

Be favorable to bold beginnings.

— Virgil, *Georgics*

Barra began on an ice-climbing trip to Mount Washington's Huntington Ravine in February 1971.

I wasn't along. Guy had driven up from New York with our friend Brad Snyder and a young climber named Dave Troe. On the drive up and back, on the walk into the Ravine, and at the Harvard Cabin, where they spent the night, the three friends talked about what they wanted to do next. All of them felt unhappy with their present lives.

Dave, who had just graduated from high school, wanted to build fine furniture but wasn't sure he could make a living. Besides, his parents weren't too thrilled with this out-of-the-mainstream plan.

Brad taught German at Mount Holyoke College but knew that it was no longer right for him. He was attracted to land conservation but didn't see his next step.

Guy's job writing speeches for the top executives at General Electric had not turned out as he had hoped. He had taken the job with the understanding that he would be writing statements of conservative economic policy for a company known for being willing to speak out on economic issues. But in December 1960, the very week of Guy's arrival at corporate headquarters in New York, news broke of the largest antitrust scandal in US history, a massive conspiracy of price fixing by the electrical equipment manufacturers. General Electric was at the center of the scandal. Company morale plummeted as employees went from perceiving themselves as part of the top company in America to feeling like they worked for the top crooks in the business world. After the dust settled Guy was assigned to the new president, Gerald Phillippe. Though Guy admired Phillippe, the antitrust trouble had silenced the company's political voice. Guy found the work tedious and lacking in the sense of urgency and mission he'd thrived on in Washington. He stuck with the job because he had college tuitions on his mind. His family had increased to three with the birth of Jim in 1955.

By the time I met him, Guy was thirty-eight and determined not to spend the rest of his working life at General Electric.

On that trip to Huntington Ravine, Brad and Dave told Guy about a book they'd just read called *Living the Good Life* by Helen and Scott Nearing. The subtitle ran: *How to Live Sanely and Simply in a Troubled World*. That seemed to sum up their predicament.

The Nearings' book, published in 1954 about their twenty-year experiment of homesteading in Vermont, was reissued in 1970 at the height of the back-to-the-land movement. It has remained vigorously in print, and the Nearings themselves have become the patron saints of the homesteading movement.

Helen and Scott Nearing, disillusioned with city life, had a story to tell to anyone who wanted to make the "good life" in the country a reality. "At the outset," they wrote, "we thought of the venture as a personal search for a simple satisfying life on the land, to be devoted to mutual aid and harmlessness, with an ample margin of leisure in which to do personally constructive and creative work."

Guy saw in the Nearings' story a way out. Scott was a trained economist. He had taught in various universities during the 1920s, but his politics, a kind of deviant Marxism, had eventually rendered him unemployable. Like Scott, Guy too was an economist who had found himself out of a job in Washington. Though Guy was a registered Republican, these two men were not as separated politically as it might appear. Both were idealists, both were committed to sustainable living and resource conservation, and both had a vision for their lives.

What had always stopped Guy from buying a farm, he told me, was that farmers have no time for anything but taking care of their animals. Guy wanted time for the mountains. Reading the Nearings' book had shown him that he could be relatively self-sufficient by raising his own food and supplying his own fuel from his woodlot. The Nearings had supplemented their income by selling maple syrup. Guy was a writer. Writing might be the way he could continue to earn money.

When Guy had left Washington to become a New York commuter, he had moved his young family to Stamford, Connecticut. During those years his drinking worsened. Discovering hiking, and especially rock climbing, had restored some meaning to his life. It had helped him give up alcohol and offered a way to spend more time with his sons by taking them hiking. By the late 1960s, Guy had come to grips with his failing marriage. He had stuck with it, he said, because he didn't want to walk out on his sons. But now the two oldest were on their own: Bill was starting college, and Johnny was climbing full-time. Guy thought that the divorce would be hardest on Jim, who was in high school. But reasoning that the home atmosphere was probably no better for Jim if Guy stayed, he finally moved out — briefly into the city, then to Marlboro, New York. This gave him a two-and-a-half-hour commute into Manhattan.

In the winter of 1971, I joined him for nearly every trip to the Adirondacks, speeding through Friday night up the New York State Thruway to the Northway and on up the smaller roads to the High Peaks. There we set up our tent on ice-covered Chapel Pond and spent the weekend snowshoeing mountains and ice climbing. We zoomed back to Guy's apartment on Sunday night, beat but happy, except that we had to be up at 4:45 a.m., and on that commuter train the next morning. Our life wouldn't have appeared either simple or sane to the Nearings. To Guy, who was unhappy in his job, it felt downright schizophrenic.

He bought the Nearings' book. When he showed it to me I said, "I looked at this in the bookstore." I had put it back on the shelf.

I knew my life in New York was headed for a change, but I wasn't as desperate for a way out as Guy was. Adopting the Nearings' kind of life was a very radical step, different from anything I'd thought of. But since I'd discovered climbing and met Guy, I was having a hard time staying interested in my editorial job with Atheneum. I wanted something else, though I didn't know what. Whatever it was, I knew I didn't want it to be in an office from 9:00 a.m. to 5:00 p.m. I wanted to be outside. I mulled over getting a degree in outdoor education, but that would mean going back to school, which I didn't think I could concentrate on either. I remember becoming aware of mail carriers and dog walkers. I liked the idea of walking around all day. Despite knowing my life was headed for some kind of upheaval, I never would have come to homesteading on my own.

As I had listened to Guy describe the commitment he'd felt to his work in Washington, I knew I had never experienced anything like that — I wanted to. Though I couldn't imagine myself doing anything besides working with books — it's what I'd come to New York for — it had never given me that saving-the-world feeling Guy talked about.

Guy was looking for a life's work. What he was thinking about — homesteading — needed two people if it was to be successful. Sure, I could pour myself into this. But back in the planning stage, I knew nothing about homesteading and it took a far, far second place to spending every day with Guy. When we talked about how we could make it work, I pictured the two of us living in a tent while we constructed our house.

"And if the house isn't finished by winter," I said, "we'll just keep on living in the tent."

"I don't think so, Laura," Guy said. "Tent living is fine for winter climbing weekends, but the house has to be built before the snow flies."

That part didn't concern me at all. I could think of nothing nicer than to spend the winter with Guy in a tent. At any rate, our discussions about homesteading didn't progress beyond the talking stage. That couldn't happen until Guy decided he wanted to spend the rest of his life with me.

In May 1971, we went on a climbing trip to the Alaska Range. Our small party failed miserably on the then-unclimbed North Face of Mount Hunter, yet Guy and I had gotten along in an effortless, carefree way before which difficulties dissolved. When we returned home I felt like I was on the other side of something. We'd been together for a year. I was ready to marry Guy. We had a teary conversation standing in the kitchen of the Marlboro apartment.

"Laura, I just got out of being in a bad marriage for nineteen years."

"I know. You said you weren't going to marry the first woman you went out with. Who happens to be me."

"I still feel that way. I'm happy the way we are."

"But I can't go on and on and on the way we are now." Something within me was making it impossible to stay with Guy if he didn't care enough about me to make it a permanent arrangement.

"If you don't want to marry me," I said, "I have to move back to New York."

On Sunday, June 6, Guy drove me back into Manhattan. It was a hot day, and we had the windows rolled down. Truck exhaust made it hard to breathe in the car. Guy drove across the George Washington Bridge in a tangle of traffic. I gazed down at the Hudson. There was a tugboat moving a long way below, looking so peaceful in its soundless island of calm.

"If I married anyone," Guy said, "I would marry you."

This didn't help. The tugboat grew smaller. I had forced the issue, and Guy was taking me back to New York. I knew he wasn't going to change his mind. I wasn't either, though it was awful to move back into my old life that didn't fit me anymore.

I stumbled into Camp and Trail Outfitters, where I was working at the time, on Monday morning. At the end of the day Harry Hunt, who ran the store, said, "What's the matter, Laura? Did someone die?"

I went home to Lawrenceville that first weekend. Ordinarily I would have been climbing, but I wasn't ready to face the Gunks scene. Guy would be there. But we wouldn't be together. I didn't talk much with my mother about what happened. I could hardly talk at all. Sometime on Sunday, before I went back to New York, my mother said, "You really love him, don't you?"

That next weekend I went to the Gunks. Guy would be there, but I wasn't about to give up climbing just because I had a broken heart. Sooner or later I'd have to confront seeing Guy, so it might as well be sooner. Herb Cahn, a climbing friend who lived in the city, drove me up.

"Guy and I get along great," I babbled as the car streaked up the New York Thruway. "There's no reason other than his just plain not wanting to get married."

"Do you want him back, Laura?" Herb asked.

"You bet."

"When you see him, act as though you do."

What was Herb talking about? How could I act otherwise?

Herb had said what he did, Guy told me later, because by Tuesday Guy was having second thoughts. He called Herb and two or three other friends of ours and asked if he could talk. He was beginning to think he'd just made a horrible mistake! He was suddenly in a panic that some other guy was going to snap me up. I didn't feel it necessary to tell him, right then, that that was absolutely impossible. Herb had offered to bring me up to the cliffs that weekend. Guy told Herb that if I showed any hint of being friendly, even just the glint of a smile, he'd ask me to come back — and he'd ask me to marry him.

That evening the climbers gathered at the Bavarian Restaurant, a German place a few miles from the cliffs. When I walked in Guy was already there, sitting at a table and talking with his usual animation. I couldn't tell if he noticed me or not. Just before dessert he came over to where I was sitting at a different table and said, "Laura, would you come outside with me?"

It was a cloudy night and very dark. We stood between the cars in the parking lot, just outside the thick wooden door of the Bavarian. When we walked back in together everyone looked up with concerned faces. Then broke into wide grins.

Sunday, June 6, the day Guy drove me back to New York, was forever known by us as Black Sunday.

That summer of 1971, we began making plans to become homesteaders. I knew I had already acquired certain strengths through climbing that would be useful to me, including self-reliance, discipline, and the ability to master something difficult. Climbing had also taught me perseverance and given me inner strength. And it had certainly contributed to my good health and kept me in good shape. But climbing is regarded, even by climbers, as a useless activity of no social value. Perhaps the same could be argued of homesteading. Why spend all that time chopping wood when you could heat your house by turning a dial on the wall? Why invest so much time growing your own food — fighting drought and deluge, punishing wind, heartbreaking late frosts, and menacing insects — when you can buy your food already packaged? Think of all the time you could save and thereby put to the good of society! The answer for me was, at first, the same answer as to why I climbed. It was fun. It was self-competitive in a way that I learned from. It was deeply satisfying, that is, to my soul.

I think Guy saw homesteading as his last chance to reinvent himself. In it he found what he had lost when he left Washington, something large that he could believe in and throw himself into, something that would ceaselessly challenge him mentally, creatively, and physically. All his life no one was as determined as Guy to be his own man.

I wanted to be with Guy. It didn't make a great deal of difference how, as long as it felt useful and fun and took place mostly outdoors. Homesteading seemed like a good idea, but I didn't really have a clue as to what this new life would give me.

There was something else about homesteading — and about climbing too — that went deeper, even deeper than my longing to be with Guy. All my life I had resisted the idea of becoming what I called in my head a "real adult." The stereotype I had was a briefcase-toting, three-piece-suit type from the suburbs who boarded the 7:08 a.m. train five days a week for a lifetime. Since I had grown up in the fifties, this was the form my fear of entrapment took: for me a "real adult" was someone in a trap. A real adult was stifled, suffocated in a life that felt like a prison sentence. Yet on the outside it was the accepted thing. It was the kind of life you were expected to have, but ever since I was a kid something deep inside had resisted it. I had no idea what I wanted for my life, but I knew there was a certain type of adult I didn't want to grow up to be. The truth was that I didn't want to grow up to be an adult. I wanted to stay a kid. For me life was all about what happened on Saturdays. Climbing captured that. Guy and I often joked that climbers are children at heart. You don't find real adults, we said, in the climbing world. We felt superior talking this way, as though just by knowing how to have fun we were in on a secret real adults didn't know.

Guy, of course, was taking that commuter train, and I was taking it with him. We had a two-and-a-half-hour commute each way to New York City. But we had only a half-hour drive to our favorite climbing cliff, and this seemed to make all the difference. This shift in balance changed the nature of the game. When Guy suggested that we turn ourselves into homesteaders — rely on our garden for most of our food and on our woodlot for cooking and heating — I thought of it as a high-stakes game that sounded like fun. Not only that, but it seemed to have everything to do with how, deep down, I wanted to live my life, because it sounded like play. Hard work, yes, but play too, because it was the sort of thing kids did on Saturdays. I could hold on to Peter Pan. Yet, unlike Peter, who remains stuck in Never Never Land, I wanted to do something useful with my life. This seemed to me the only good reason to grow up and become a "real adult" that I could think of.

So from the beginning homesteading appealed to me, but I could have never guessed the soul-deep contentment of getting to know my own trees to the point that every day we worked in our woods was a visit with old friends. It appealed to me to grow my own food, even to get to know my own soil, but I could not have foreseen the gut-calming sense of place, this feeling of belonging to something much larger than myself, and much more enduring, that it would give me. When we moved to the land I was not particularly concerned about lightening my impact on the earth; I hadn't really thought about it. But this idea grew — and took on compelling meaning — as we began to live lightly. What Guy suggested felt right on some intuitive level, and I embraced in full measure the onerous idea of "responsibility" — which I had spent my young life trying to avoid — now that I had found something, a way of living, I could give my whole heart to.

We began to talk about where we wanted to homestead. We considered seriously mountainous West Virginia and Alaska, but discarded the notion of West Virginia because the winter climbing season wouldn't last long enough. From our climbing trip in May, we found out that Alaska wasn't for us. Those mountains demanded an expedition. We wanted mountains we could make short, frequent trips to. We knew our homesteading life wouldn't allow us to be away for much more than a week at a time. Also, the Alaskan forests of unrelieved spruce, fir, and stunted birch weren't woods that spoke to us.

We needed the northern hardwoods: maple, ash, oak, beech, and tall, graceful birches — trees that leafed out in summer, then raised bare arms against the sky in winter. We needed a rural countryside of alternating pastures and woods revealing a farmstead cupped in the folds of the land. We needed small villages where the houses clustered around a green or along a riverbank. We were looking for a landscape where humans could fit in.

In short, we learned we were already there.

In the summer of 1971, we began to look for land in northern New England and around the High Peaks in the Adirondacks, areas that were familiar to us from climbing. We ruled out acreage around the Shawangunks as being too built-up and too expensive.

We talked about the qualities we wanted our land to have, and Guy made a list. We knew we couldn't find everything we wanted in one spot, but making the list helped us think out what we were looking for.

Forty acres (more or less), mostly wooded, but three to five acres
of open land with a good house site
Woods: mixed hardwoods for firewood, but sufficient softwood
of spruce, fir, hemlock, and pine for building purposes
Stone walls
Old apple trees
Sugar bush with perhaps an old sap house
Rose hips
Wild blackberries and raspberries
A stream or old well
A cellar hole or old building we could use for lumber
Views, preferably of mountains

That summer we tramped over more than fifty properties. Most were easy to eliminate: the woods were too scrubby, there was too much open land and not enough forest, it was on a busy main road, and water was inadequate. But by looking at what wasn't right, we were finding out what was.

Sometime in July we called Bryce Thomas, a real estate agent in Newbury, Vermont. He drove us around and showed us a couple of parcels that didn't work. It was getting on in the afternoon, and we'd seen enough land for the day. Besides, we weren't too drawn to Mr. Thomas. He was a little too intent on selling.

"I have one more piece I want to show you," Mr. Thomas said.

We reluctantly agreed.

He drove us into a small village, made a left-hand turn across a bridge on a dirt road, and kept going.

"This land out here, two hundred acres, belongs to a man named Anderson," Mr. Thomas said. "He's divided it into parcels over ten acres. Most of them have been sold."

We continued on along a rutted road that looked like it would need a lot of work and through a nice piece of open land that he said was recently sold to a family named Wells from Long Island. Then we bounced up a track that had never seen traffic — tree sprouts and high grass were dinging the car's undercarriage. We emerged in a clearing of about three acres with three branchy white pines growing in it. Mr. Thomas skirted his large, American-made four-door under some red oaks of enormous girth and pulled up at the top of a thin-soiled knoll with a good view out over the Waits River Valley.

"I'll sit here," the real estate man said. "The land runs down this hillside, across a little stream, and up into the woods there." He pointed toward a hardwood forest in which stood a few clumps of darker evergreens.

We scrambled down what we later came to call Pavilion Hill. I was wearing shorts, and the thorny brambles scratched my legs.

"Blackberries," Guy said to me, and smiled.

We walked into the woods, under the regal hemlocks that formed the edge separating clearing from forest. The sunlight slanted down, falling on the trunks of three or four toppled elms that had lain there long enough to become hosts to several varieties of mosses. We examined the ancient trunks, touching the soft moss with our hands. We looked up into the canopy of sugar maple, red oak, and ash, mature trees stretching upward for seventy feet. Guy and I were suckers for large trees.

The stream, which lay a few steps farther into the woods, was meager, but we thought it might do.

We came out of the woods and into the clearing. Guy knelt down and scratched in the dirt. "What do you think?" he asked, letting the topsoil sift through his hands.

I knelt down too. I had no idea what made up good garden soil. But this was loose and fine. I was sure it could provide a start for a garden.

"It looks good," I said.

"The house could go here," Guy pointed up the slope, directly above the flattish spot where we were standing. A rock ledge rose steeply up behind and merged into a forested hillside of a few hundred feet. That would give protection from the north. The house would tuck in below the brow of the hill and face due south.

We stood a moment in the clearing and looked around at this land that was all sloped and wooded. It formed a high valley. "I like this," Guy said. "It feels like its own contained world."

We walked up to where the house could perch, about fifty paces above the garden, and then along the old wood track under the rock ledge to where Bryce Thomas sat in his car.

"This would be the place to put your house," the real estate man said, indicating the hilltop where he was parked.

Guy and I exchanged a glance. We climbed back into Mr. Thomas's car, and he started the engine.

This land was worth a second look. We would come back.

We bought the land on August 23, 1971. Guy suggested naming it Barra, after an island in Scotland's Hebrides, the ancestral home of his mother's family. Guy was a great namer, and his naming of our land was the beginning of what he named at Barra, which grew to include the rock ledges to the north behind the house (Arads), the bare hill we looked out on to the west (Pavilion), and the wooded slope to the south (Colby Hill) that led up to the Highlands, where stood our largest-girthed maples, named for the 8,000-meter peaks in the Himalayas. By naming Barra, Guy began to create a world — his world But it was mine too, since I embraced this plan.

That Christmas, which we celebrated at my parents' house in Lawrenceville, Guy's gift to me was a navy-blue three-holed notebook. The title on the spine read "The Book of Barra."

On the first page Guy had typed the following:

> The Basic Plan:
>
> — To go to live on a 38.8-acre section of land in Vermont, and to create a relatively self-sufficient homestead there.
> Under the heading "General Objectives" Guy outlined:
> To live simply
> cheaply
> unhurriedly
> basically (i.e., concerned with basics like food and shelter and fuel)
> And to maintain our interest in climbing and hiking, in reading and music, and possibly in writing or other interests which we may decide to develop.

This was followed by a page called "What This Life Will Entail":

> Raising our own vegetables, fruit, berries, and sugar; storing food for nonseasonal consumption; buying other food needs (generally in bulk).
> Building our own shelters, expanding them slowly over a 20-year period, using purchased lumber and other materials as necessary (especially at first), but placing heavy reliance on our own logs and stone.
> For fuel (cooking and heating), using wood from our land.
> Minimizing other financial expenditures, by building our lives around interests and activities which do not require sizable financial outlays.
> For cash needs, relying mainly on substantial money savings (1973–1991) and then on Social Security (1992 on). The modest additional amounts needed will be scrounged from one or more of several possible sources, including: (a) developing some regular cash-producing crop or activity; (b) undertaking small income-producing jobs; (c) writing; or (d) holding major scheduled expenses below estimates.
> Keeping up our interests in reading, music, possibly writing, relaxing hobbies.
> Maintaining a strong interest in hiking and climbing, and keeping up our contacts with climbing friends and organizations.

Next came a quote from the Nearings' book, as well as these words from Thoreau's *Walden*.

> I went to the woods because I wished to live deliberately, to front only the essential facts of life, and see if I could not learn what it had to teach, and not, when I came to die, discover that I had not lived. I did not wish to live what was not life, living is so dear; nor did I wish to practise resignation, unless it was quite necessary. I wanted to live deep and suck out all the marrow of life, to live so sturdily and Spartan-like as to put to rout all that was not life, to cut a broad swath and shave close, to drive life into a corner, and reduce it to its lowest terms, and, if it proved to be mean, why then to get the whole and genuine meanness of it, and publish its meanness to the world; or if it were sublime, to know it by experience, and be able to give a true account of it in my next excursion.

We had talked over and over about what Guy had written down in "The Book of Barra." But by committing the vision to paper, Guy was articulating the kind of world he wanted to live in. He was giving our experiment shape and immediacy, even legitimacy.

We would be successful, I knew, if Guy's skills as a planner had anything to do with it. I was aware that by stepping out of the nine-to-five structure we needed to impose an order of our own on our lives. I already knew how organized Guy was. We never ran out of household items, because Guy had a backup for every item. That is, when the paper towel roll was empty, Guy made a note on his shopping list that he kept on a three-by-five card to purchase more paper towels, in this way restocking the backup. The list he kept of routes he wanted to climb at the Gunks was not unusual — many climbers do this. But Guy climbed about twice as many routes as most climbers because he got up in the dark, drove to the cliffs in the dark, ran up the talus rocks, and was at the base of the climb when it was barely light enough to see the holds. We were dubbed "the Dawn Patrol" by our friend Bill Thomas, who frequently joined us. When I began climbing with Guy I joined this game too. I didn't like getting up in the dark, but after I was on the rock, held in the sun's rays just striking an east-facing climb and turning the air spring soft, when I could hear the birds in full morning cry and knew all the other climbers were snoring in their sleeping bags for another two hours, I could imagine no better place in the world.

Guy was a driver, a pusher. He was extremely demanding of himself. If I wanted to climb with Guy, I had to fall in with the program. There was something in me — the Saturday kid? Peter Pan? — that responded to the challenge, to the adventure, to just plain being with Guy. But what if I had said no? Guy was looking for someone to climb with — to share a life with — and he was setting the pace. I fell into his vision without even thinking about it because it fit me also. If it hadn't, nothing would have happened between him and me. I saw none of this at the time.

Though Guy was casual in nothing and the words "laid back" least described him, I didn't feel run over by his drive or his planning. I had lived a well-organized life before I met him. The difference between us was that Guy needed to make lists, to keep track, to write everything down. What kept his planning from feeling overbearing was that in our climbing, and especially in Barra's early days, Guy turned this organization that was so essential to the smooth running of his own life into a kind of play.

"The Book of Barra" was a starting point. After Guy had put the vision for our future on paper, we put the navy-blue notebook away. We had no need to look at it again. We began to live it.

For the rest of 1971 and all of 1972, we prepared ourselves for this great new direction.

We set a date, June 9, 1973, for the actual move to our land. This was twenty-two months away, but knowing we had a definite day to aim toward made the commute easier. When the train was overheated and delayed and we looked around at the sweaty tired faces of our fellow commuters and saw only resignation, we told ourselves that we were going to be stepping out of this world. It wasn't going to last much longer.

In the spring of 1972 we planted a garden in Marlboro. The only gardening experience I had had was as a reluctant child-weeder for my mother in her flower beds. I could recall an asparagus bed and some tomato plants my father had in Lawrenceville, and I could dredge up a picture of my parents canning quince jelly from our quince trees, my father laying open the hard fruit with a hatchet.

Guy had been raised on the home garden at "the Farm." As an adult, he'd put in a few gardens in the various places he'd lived.

"We'll plant radishes," Guy said. "They pop right up — gives you a real feeling of accomplishment."

We began to subscribe to *Organic Gardening and Farming* magazine (as it was then called), and *Mother Earth News*, a magazine that grew out of the back-to-the-land movement of the sixties. Though Guy was still wearing his three-piece suit, and I hose and heels, we'd stepped into the counterculture. Our life at Barra began in the context of the late 1960s and early 1970s, though unlike the hippies of that time, we were looking for permanence. We were staking out what we wanted to do with the rest of our lives.

On Memorial Day weekend of 1972, we began preparing the ground for a garden at Barra. We drove up from Marlboro with Guy's oldest son, Bill, and of course Ralph.

It was unseasonably hot. Guy and Bill worked bare-chested, their shirts tossed over a large rock we'd selected as a corner marker of the garden; Guy named it the Barra Stone. We cut out strips of sod with our spades, piling them off to one side. Then we loosened the ground with our long-tined garden forks. Bill removed his sod strips twice as fast as I did, the sweat pasting his blond hair to his forehead. Ralph lay in the shade under the white pines at the edge of the woods, lifting his head now and then, and watched us work.

We cooked over a fireplace we constructed. Guy and Bill had run up the steep hillside behind where we planned to build our house to roll down larger and larger rocks, whooping with laughter.

I liked to be around Guy and his sons. Since Bill had been in college out west, this was my first experience of the two of them together. It was a world not known in my family. "Dad never plays catch with me," my brother had said. Watching Guy and Bill made me wish my father could have gone out in the backyard and tossed a ball with my brother. It wasn't about how well you threw the ball.

In 1968 Bill had met with an accident in a freight yard in Winnipeg. He was sitting with his leg over a rail, half-dozing, in what he felt was an out-of-the-way spot, waiting to hop a freight later that night. A string of boxcars was "bumped" way up the line, and a wheel ran over Bill's leg. The doctors had managed to save it, but the leg continued to be so painful that Bill had recently had it amputated. Now he had a prosthesis. From the way Bill was throwing himself into work and play on this Memorial Day weekend, it seemed like he had made the right decision to take this radical step.

On the drive back we had all the windows open. It was very hot, and Bill had taken off his leg and given it to me up front. This gave him a little more room in the backseat with panting, hairy Ralph, who had a tendency to lie at full length, taking up much more than his half of the seat. We stopped at a service station some place in Connecticut, and the attendant came over to pump gas. Bill wanted to get out of the car, so he asked me to hand him his leg. The guy pumping gas happened to look up as a leg wheeled through the air into the backseat. The three of us watched the attendant's eyes bug out, but we didn't dare exchange looks, holding our explosion of laughter until after we got back on the highway.

This is my best memory of Bill. It was the only time he saw Barra.

Building an actual dwelling sounded like a tall order to two people who hadn't even built a doghouse, so Guy suggested we start on something small as practice. In August 1972 we came up to Barra for our vacation. Since we were to be married at the end of the month, we dubbed these two weeks our "moonhoney." We wanted to make sure we were capable of erecting a roof that would withstand a Vermont winter. So we built a three-sided shelter, or lean-to, where we could store our belongings the next summer as we worked on our house. We would sleep in our tent. I was really looking forward to that. In fact, I couldn't imagine anything more idyllic. We would be living outside — camping out — for the entire summer while we built our house!

During those two weeks in August we dug up another section of garden, pulling up blackberries and hacking out small saplings. Our clearing had been grazed until not long before we bought the land, so we needed to take down only a few of the taller white pine that would have shaded the garden. We continued working into the fall, on weekend trips, until we had a thirty-by-forty-foot plot. Then we sowed our first cover crop of winter rye.

Our initial plan was to build a stone house, as the Nearings had done. But we knew this couldn't be done in a summer. First we had to gather the stone. So we decided to erect a tiny cabin from purchased lumber with no foundation, one room we could live in for at most three years while we worked on our stone house. Later we'd turn this one-room structure into a toolshed or guest cottage.

We ran into our first major problem right there.

On that two-week trip in August, when we checked the zoning requirements for our town, we found out that dwellings needed to have full foundations and a square footage of 500 feet.

So we changed our plans and decided to build the house out of planed boards, purchasing the lumber. We could get away with a minimal foundation that went down four feet, and we'd add a stone wing later. The square footage was 512.

As it turned out, we had no stone walls on the entire 38.8 acres. After we began to amass stone, Guy roamed our land, crowbar in hand, unearthing rocks wherever he came across them. To collect them he instituted his "two stones a day" program: he carried two stones a day during the snow-free months of April through November up to the west side of our cabin, where we planned to locate this stone wing. I carried stones too, but not every day. Guests seemed intrigued by this slow but steady way of accumulating stone and often helped carry a stone or two. To do something useful with these rocks until we got around to building with them, we constructed a wall at the entrance to our orchard. Guy broke down all our laborious jobs this way.

We never did build the stone wing, but we used those stones in terracing our garden, making borders around our flower beds, and laying the foundation of the guest cottage we built years later and called Twin Firs Camp.

That winter in Marlboro we continued living as a family of four, counting Ralph. When Guy's high school–aged son Jim moved in, Guy gave him the only bedroom. Guy slept in the alcove sitting room on a camping pad that he rolled out every night. Since most of this area was taken up by his Steinway grand, the only room for him — and me when I joined the household — was wedged half under it. Ralph curled up at our feet and, if truth be told, made himself comfortable on Jim's bed by day, when left all alone in the apartment.

Guy had decorated the walls with climbing pictures, taken from calendars and magazines, showing fabled ranges around the world, from the Canadian Rockies to South America, from the Alps to all the 8,000-meter peaks. He had a poster from the first US ascent of Everest in 1963, with a quote from Goethe under a climber headed up the West Ridge: "Whatever you can do or dream you can do, begin it. Boldness has genius, power, and magic in it." I had bought that same poster in the fall of 1969 when I had begun climbing. Now we had two.

Guy and I got home around 7:30, and Guy, Jim, and I fixed supper together. I was impressed with how grown-up Jim seemed. He had a maturity I had been very far from feeling when I was his age. The divorce couldn't have been easy. And here I was, moved in and an integral part of his father's life, taking away time Guy might have been spending with Jim, though I didn't see that then. We didn't talk about the past. We talked about climbing: climbs we'd done that past weekend and the climbs we planned to do on the weekend coming up. We talked about our friends — all of whom were climbers — and about our climbing gear, which hung on a pegboard rack Guy had made just for this purpose. Jim, one of the best young climbers at the cliffs, climbed with a group of teenagers who called themselves the Degenerates. Oh, they had long hair and smoked pot, but they were also strong environmentalists and fiercely protective of the Shawangunks. The sound of someone pounding in a piton high on the cliffs could rally a swarm of Degenerates who would first yell up that pounding pitons widened cracks; if the pounding persisted, they'd climb up to straighten the poor guy out.

In the evenings in Marlboro we encouraged each other to crank out one more fingertip pull-up on the three-quarter-inch board over the door frame. I never managed more than five, while Jim and Guy could go on endlessly. We worked on our forearms by squeezing a tennis ball, tossing it back and forth among the three of us, being careful not to knock off the elephants (glass, china, wood, ivory) that lived on the shelves and every other flat space. Guy had collected 367 of them during his Republican political days.

Mostly I remember a perpetual feeling of carefree relief during the three years we spent in our tiny apartment in Marlboro, though I couldn't have articulated it. This was, for sure, a different world from life in my own family, who were so hard for me to be with but for whom I often felt an aching love. I was proud of my father and his contributions to the world of scholarship. I relished our conversations when he was sober Dr. Jekyll. But when he turned into that monster Mr. Hyde, I found myself counting the minutes till I could escape from the house. Being with Guy in this happy family life with Jim and Ralph felt like perpetual vacation. I had gotten lucky! I had skipped out! And I wasn't about to give any of it up, though I felt twinges of guilt over my inability to help my own family, who on the outside looked perfectly normal but on the inside were torn apart by the awful, tension-packed thing we couldn't talk about. I felt helpless when I thought about my parents, alone with each other in that sad house filled with the suffocating fog of alcohol and cigarette smoke.

Between weekend climbing trips to the Adirondacks that winter, we constructed a few useful items for our new life. These were mostly made by Guy, since he could grab the occasional weekday off to do General Electric work at home.

One was a bin for dry food, something in which we could keep grains, cereals, and flour safe from the nibbling appetites of our rodent friends. As soon as we moved up we'd be living outdoors and would need an animal-proof place for food. We already knew about the porcupine family that lived in the ledges behind our house. Ralph had paid them a social call, much to his (and our!) regret.

Guy drew the plans for this food bin to the specific dimensions of the entryway of our cabin — its final destination — 5½ feet long by 2 feet 10 inches high by 11½ inches deep. There were three openings in the front large enough for fifty-pound sacks of flour. The top opened in three sections for storing smaller bags. We covered the framework with two layers of different-sized wire mesh that allowed for plenty of air circulation. We painted it white with green trim and attached brass hooks for keeping the doors shut. Guy called it "the Has-Bins." It was the first — and perhaps the most successful — item we ever built.

Guy also designed an outhouse seat. We painted the top traditional white, but with sides of green, red, and blue. He planned it to fit exactly into the building itself, which we would build later. Our experience with backwoods outhouses that employed the type of plastic seat-lid arrangement found in modern indoor johns had taught us that in winter these are penetratingly cold. Our seat was made of wood, with the sides of the opening carefully rounded and smoothed. We had already dug a hole in an appropriate spot, up on the hill a short walk from where our house would be located, and far far far from our water source.

That first summer we used just the seat over the hole, taking with us an umbrella for when the trip up the hill had to be made during a rainstorm.

We bought Rex Roberts's book *Your Engineered House* and a few other books on stud construction. Guy worked on house plans at his desk at General Electric, and we went over them every evening on the train ride back up the Hudson. He was writing speeches for three of the top executives at the time, and each one, conscious that Guy worked for two others, was careful not to overload him with work. As a consequence, Guy had time to draw not only the floor plan but the detailed placements of each board, from the basement headers and stringers up to the rafters. Then he made a list of exactly how many boards we'd need and what sizes, priced it out, and tinkered with it until he got it to fit into the $7,000 we'd budgeted for the cabin. All this design work, which most at General Electric would have regarded as subversive, was accomplished on GE's time.

Guy fit his piano — a full grand — into our 512-square-foot living space, locating a window to throw light on the keyboard and music rack. The question most often asked of us over the years was how did you get the piano into the cabin? The visitor asking that question would have just walked nearly a mile to reach us. But getting the piano to Barra was easier than moving it out of our second-floor apartment in Marlboro. Guy had brought it up the front flight of stairs, but it wouldn't come out that way. It refused to make a crucial turn around the door and down the stairway. We ended up calling on a number of our climber friends and taking the piano out the back and down a set of rickety outside stairs. For this move we put the piano on belay and lowered it as we would an injured climber — a 600-pound climber — down a cliff face. Once the piano was on the ground, Guy took off the pedals and detached the legs. We tipped the piano on its side and onto a dolly we'd especially made for this purpose. Now the piano was only a foot or so wide and somewhat lighter. We loaded it onto the truck of a friend who drove it to Vermont. Since we had not yet closed our road, we could drive the piano to the door, ease it off the truck, wheel it on the dolly across the floor, reconnect the legs and the pedals, and tip it upright into its new home under the west window.

We knew that by adopting this "good life" we'd be drastically reducing our income. Guy in particular was being well paid by GE, and we started pouring money into the savings account. We stopped eating out and going to movies. We started taking sandwiches to work, and if either of us was invited out, we pocketed our homemade lunches until the next day.

During the course of that winter of 1972, we turned ourselves into vegetarians. Jim seemed willing to go along with this too. Though he wouldn't be making the move to the land with us, he was very much involved and planned to give us a hand when we reached the building stage. We became vegetarians for economic and practical reasons. We weren't going to have refrigeration, since we weren't going to bring in electricity or try to make power by other means. It was an essential part of our bare-bones financial plan that we would have no debt and no bills to pay.

Both Guy and I had been brought up in families for whom meat was the centerpiece of the meal and the roast on Sunday was obligatory. Neither of us had philosophical or moral objections to eating meat. Those came later, after we'd been vegetarians for several years. We liked meat and knew that changing our diet would be hard. We started slowly. First we cut out bacon at breakfast. Since we ate meat every night, Guy suggested we whittle it down to six nights a week, then five nights, and so on. For our first cold turkey (so to speak) vegetarian meal we selected vegetables we absolutely adored, purchasing them fresh from the farm stand: peas, asparagus, potatoes, and a big salad from our garden in Marlboro. This meal looked appetizing, but would we feel full? We expected to be hungry if we didn't eat meat. To our surprise, we felt perfectly satisfied. This was working! Eggs were the hardest. Guy and I loved eggs. But we didn't need them, so we weren't going to buy them. The only way we could make Barra work financially was by cutting out all unnecessary expenses.

At Barra we lived on a budget of $200 a month, which over the years, because of inflation, increased to $250. This meant that for our nearly thirty years at Barra we lived on $2,400 a year, which shaded up to $3,000. When Guy went on Social Security at sixty-two and began drawing a check of $500 a month, well, we could eat all the ice cream we wanted!

We didn't have to make the belt so tight. We debated sticking it out in the city one more year and saving more money. It would have made a difference. But Guy said that if we put it off another year, things might come up that would cause further delays. He was desperate to get out. I enjoyed my job at Backpacker, but when Bill Kemsley, the publisher, hired me, I had told him about our plan to homestead and said I could give him one year. My mental clock was set for that. I, too, was ready to leave New York.

Guy made up a budget. We needed to figure out how much of our savings we could draw down on a yearly basis for expenditures like food, gas, hardware, garden items, postage, some clothing. The big expenses were property taxes and car insurance. These were our only bills. We never paid a federal income tax, since our income put us below the poverty level. We paid a Vermont state tax of around $70 a year. We limited the car insurance to us hitting the other guy — liability only. We dropped health insurance, relying on healthy living and good luck.

It was a calculated risk that worked. We incurred a few medical costs through minor injuries, but we never came within a fraction of paying out what annual insurance premiums would have cost us.

Guy called our financial plan the "Twenty-Year Plan," because in twenty years he would be eligible for Social Security. In 1972 this seemed impossibly far off. In the meantime, Guy could cash in his GE pension in seven years, though he took a big cut by not waiting until retirement age. We had initially bought two contiguous pieces of land with the intent of selling one. Despite these income sources, we knew we'd have to find some way to earn more money.

Guy was concerned about financing the college educations of his sons and had long been building up the college account. In 1973, when we moved to Barra, Bill had left Western Washington State and showed no signs of going anywhere else. Johnny was traveling and climbing, though he talked about college, possibly the University of Alaska. Jim had just graduated from high school and had no immediate college plans, but might later. Guy felt that he could handle his sons' college tuitions — just barely. He knew he'd be better off if he worked one more year.

Despite all of this, we kept to the June 9 date.

At the beginning of planning for Barra and before our marriage, we'd had a conversation about children, whether we wanted them. It was a brief discussion. Guy said he had had one family and felt no interest in starting another. I felt no empirical urge to become a mother. What we were planning together seemed fulfilling in the way I imagined motherhood could be to other women. So we were in agreement. It was a decision I did not regret.

Early that spring of 1973, we began our Barra garden in our apartment in Marlboro. We built a tall, narrow structure and set it on casters so we could roll it in front of a sunny window. On its five tiers of shelves we set our flats of tomatoes, beans, broccoli, cabbage, Brussels sprouts, peppers, leeks, and companion flowers such as marigolds, nasturtiums, and zinnias. We started the seeds in cut-off gallon milk cartons. Guy called this structure "the Sun Shelves."

Guy suggested we name our seedlings. So we chose names from the Marlboro, New York, telephone directory for 160 tiny plants. If we lost one, we marked the spot with a toothpick cross and x-ed out the plant's name on our garden chart. In this way we bid farewell to Irving Blemard, Walt Metzer, and Albert Lee, who perished, I'm embarrassed to say, because of overzealous watering.

The Sun Shelves structure had a major design flaw: it was tippy. Yes, it was very tippy. One day when Guy had been doing GE work at home he met me at the train station with a long, sad face. In the process of wheeling the Sun Shelves to a sunnier spot he lost control, and the plants on the upper shelves came crashing to the floor, spraying dirt and tiny new leaves everywhere. A mess! A terrible tragedy! It took him about two hours to put things to rights again. Though we sustained great losses, Brian Bushweller, Father Gregory, and many others lived to thrive in our first garden.

By the time June 9, 1973, rolled around, we were as set as we were ever going to be. Dave Datsun was loaded with all our seedlings and most of our belongings; there was barely enough space left for Ralph, who was now ten and would only be with us another three years, to curl up in the backseat. Jim and our friend Brad Snyder saw us off. As we pulled out of the drive Brad said, "Hey, wait a minute! Don't you want to think this over?"

CHAPTER *seven*

If you don't go beyond, you get nowhere — nowhere.

— Nick Clinch, quoted in Robert Roper, *Fatal Mountaineer*

Trips to the mountains blended easily, as we had hoped, into our life at Barra. Our homesteading work kept us in good shape for climbing. Our active involvement in the mountain world kept us from becoming isolated.

Though we lived halfway between the White Mountains in New Hampshire and the Green Mountains in Vermont, we traveled mainly to the White Mountains. Here we found the perfect mix of trails and rock climbs in summer and ice routes and mountaineering in winter. Bushwhacking, or off-trail hikes, we enjoyed at all times of year.

We stuck close to our garden during planting, from late April until the end of June, when the threat of late frosts was past. That is not to say we couldn't take a day to go climbing. But longer trips were out, and we learned this the hard way. On June 14, 1978, we planned an overnight down in the Boston area so I could do some research on Miriam Underhill, America's foremost woman mountaineer during the 1920s and 1930s. That night, in the suburb where we were staying, temperatures dropped into the forties. This made us nervous, and indeed, we returned home to find that the "blond assassin" had paid a call. Our frost-sensitive plants — five rows of beans, thirty hills of squash, the cucumbers, six rows of corn, and all the tomato and pepper plants we'd grown from seed — had wilted, blackened leaves.

We strategized that the plants shouldn't have to fight to maintain their hopelessly dead leaves, so like surgeons who clip off frostbitten toes to save the leg, we amputated. Our garden was a pretty sad sight for several days, but the life force kicked in, and we ended up losing very few plants.

After the Fourth of July, when the frosts were behind us and we had the garden well mulched, we always planned a longer trip of three or four nights, timed for that window of time after we'd canned the peas but before canning the broccoli. During the rest of the summer we could go on trips whenever we liked.

We made a weeklong hike in mid-September, *after* the killing frost and the first stage of our harvest. We covered portions of Vermont's Long Trail this way; the leaf-strewn paths in the hardwoods spread themselves under our feet like Oriental carpets. We visited less frequented country in the White Mountains like the Baldfaces, the backside of the Carters, and the Wild River region that Guy and his sons had explored over a decade earlier. In late October and into November we fitted in trips around our wood collecting and other tasks that prepared us for winter, often with our friend Lou Cornell. The three of us camped in our roomy two-person tent and sipped tea while Lou read aloud from Murray's *Mountaineering in Scotland.*

During the 1970s, for the seven years Guy was on the board of the Mohonk Preserve, the land trust that safeguarded the Shawangunks, we made trips there four times a year for meetings — and of course to climb. We spent, in total, a good month out of the year there, and our life fell into a very pleasant routine — the kind you're not even aware of when you're in it, time passes so lightly. But when you look back after it's gone, you remember you were happy.

After we'd cleaned up from sugaring in mid-April, we headed for the Gunks. We didn't need to be back at Barra until it was time to plant the peas. We stayed with our friend Brad Snyder during the week and camped at the base of the cliffs so as to be closer to the climbs on weekends.

The Smiley family, who owned the land and created a preserve of over five thousand acres, understood the importance in people's lives of forming ties to land. Our conversations, often on walks through the woods with the two brothers, Dan and Keith Smiley, instilled in us a sense of stewardship for land as well as a strong desire to reach our fellow hikers and climbers with the message. In the early 1970s, land managers across the country were seeing the damage caused by an increasing army of hikers: trail erosion, polluted streams, compacted campsites. It seemed that if we were *all* made aware of the damage we caused, we would strive to do the right thing out of a regard for the land itself. The themes of the books we would later write, *Backwoods Ethics* and *Wilderness Ethics*, grew out of our connection to the beautiful land at the Shawangunks and our talks with Dan and Keith Smiley.

Winter! That was our time to climb. The garden was put to bed, the wood collected. In late fall Guy drew up a list of all the places we'd talked about exploring: the trailless ridges, the cirques, the slides and gullies, the headwalls, the frozen streambeds that often made great routes up mountains. Though we fit in three trips a month of three to five days out, as well as a few day trips, we always had more trip ideas than we could crowd into the short winter months of January, February, and early March, when we were back to sugaring again.

Guy also set aside five or so days for what he called his "solos." These trips gave him a physical challenge, but I came to see that he needed the encounter with wildness most of all. He returned from these solitary tramps easier in his mind. These pilgrimages, his tussles with the wild and uncontrolled in nature, somehow appeased for a time the turmoil within. I saw also that whatever drove him out to be alone in the winter woods with a week's food in his pack was not in me.

I said goodbye to him many times and watched him walk down our snowy path. I could not be sure he would return, not because he had thoughts then of not coming back, but because his trips took him to isolated places. His was a quest for the unbeaten path. If he had fallen in a steep place, broken an ankle above the tree line, or become hypothermic in a driving snowstorm, he would have had a hard time rescuing himself. But he always came back, and at the hour he said he would, because he never wanted me to worry.

Each day I followed his progress in my mind. He wrote down his itinerary on a three-by-five card that I kept next to me at the table where I worked and ate and read. During the days he was gone I settled into my own routine, though I kept to our same schedule of meals and water fetching and weather readings. The cabin felt silent. I felt silent, as if half-alive. I was not so much lonely as aware of the absence of the vitality that was Guy. But I made the most of this time by myself. As the years passed and Guy's dark moods deepened, this time alone came as relief. I could not admit it then; I was not even aware I had let up on the vigilance.

On the day he was due back I went out and sawed wood in the late afternoon, often looking up from my work and down the path, even though I knew it was too early to expect him. As the light began to fade I went inside to lay the fire, keeping an ear cocked for the sound of his snowshoes crunching back toward the house. As soon as I detected this I dropped what I was slicing for supper and rushed out to the porch without my coat. He was back. It was too dark to see anything more than his shape, bulky with his pack on, but as I hugged him I smelled the woods in his clothing and felt his face fresh against mine. Holding his rough fingers in my hand, I drew him into the warmth of the cabin.

"Tell me how it went, Guy." But already I knew. I could tell if his trip had gone well, or ill, by the way he took off his pack. I could tell by how he plopped down on the ash-log seat by the door whether he was weary because of a hard trip successfully concluded or whether he was dissatisfied with himself, second-guessing his decisions, feeling that he had failed to meet the challenges.

If it had gone well, he launched into the story as he unlaced his gaiters, grinning up at me and saying, "Some kind of large cat paced around my camp. I saw his fresh tracks every morning." The mellow glow of the kerosene lamp fell upon his hands. And I was filled with joy because he was sitting so solid on the ash-log seat and the cabin was alive again.

Guy needed big goals, big projects. His most ambitious was a plan to climb all forty-eight White Mountain summits over four thousand feet in winter from all four points of the compass. This meant that he would climb each peak four times. He had gotten a good start on this project from previous years of climbing, and continuing to pursue this goal sustained him for around four years as he fit these trips into all the other hikes we took in winter. I joined him on some, as did our friends, but he did many solo. It was his practice to write up his day of climbing, while sitting in his tent at night, as a letter addressed to me. It served as a record of his trip, but for me his notes carried an immediacy that told far more about what really happened on the adventure than he ever could have conveyed to me later. Here is an excerpt from a weeklong trip in 1987.

> Sat. Jan. 10 (Camp of the Unknown Ladies)
> Dearest Laura,
>
> . . . Today I got casual and overconfident. Before I knew it I became very confused. An all-day snowstorm began about 9:00 a.m., so I had no views at all to help guide me. Soon I felt genuinely lost, but knew that if I kept going uphill and south I would have to cross the Appalachian Trail. Then I ran into the famed Twin Range Scrub, and battled it for about 2½ hours. *Dense!* Not even any tracks of Rashleigh the mad hare, and it is well known that he is a hair mad. All this time the snow never ceased, and I got completely drenched. Then, crossing Guyot there was a terrific wind, so I became ice encrusted as well. You recall what wind on Guyot can be like!
>
> What worried me was having 5½ miles to go after that, even had I not gone over to West Bond, which made it 8. I came very close to passing up West Bond for fear of being too tired later, but really wanted that peak. I noted my time at each landmark, and realized I'd be OK as long as I didn't strain a muscle or something. I thought a lot about our first hike, when you were so tired on that very trail. I tried to figure whether you were more tired that day (17 years ago this summer) or me today. I realized that I probably never appreciated how tired you had been. . . .
>
> Sun. Jan. 11 (Zealand Hut)
>
> The snow which began yesterday continued all night, so I awoke to find a foot or so of new snow. I broke camp, and when

I started up the slope it did not take long to see that I would be totally exhausted trying to pull the Bemis Tiger up that one mile and 700'. So I elected to ferry loads. First I went up with my day pack, encountering very tough trail-breaking and terrible spruce-traps and getting very wet — it was *still* snowing. Then when I finally reached the trail (between Hale and the Hut), I was so wet and cold I put on my wool nets, left my pack, and started down. This gave me a bit of a pause, with *no* life sup-port system — no 1st aid kit, no parachute cord (if a snowshoe broke), not even my wool shirt and sweater. But I got back down fine and put on the other pack and towed the Bemis Tiger empty. The Tiger was great, bouncing along behind, rushing up on my heels at the slightest downhill and responding enthusiastically every time I cried C'mon Tiger. So about 2 p.m. I finally had everything up to the trail, but I was so cold and ice-encrusted I gave up on Hale, and slowly sledded into the Hut. As I got closer, I was sad to realize that my time alone was coming to an end, and went slower making little side-trips to the cliffs and caves of Cioffredi Peak, even though I was so wet and cold. I expected to see a sizable Sunday-night crowd at the Hut, but to my great surprise, I turn out to be the *only* guest, and the caretaker is the floater, Bobby Dery. So now I am drying everything out on the ceiling racks, and sitting at a table to write. I had a warm meal for the first time since last Wednesday. . . .

I sure like being out by myself in the middle of the moun-tains. I appreciate your tolerating my doing so. This time I was 80 hours without seeing anyone. But, boy, you do get wet. So I am not sorry to be at the Hut tonight. O boy! Tomorrow I see *you.*

Love,

Guy and

Ludwig [the Hut cat] (who has been trying to sit on this let-ter pad as I write)

and

Rashleigh (the Mad Hare) who is a hair mad:

and

CLEM (guardian angel of the mountain men).

When Guy completed the four-points-of-the-compass project — on Mount Moosilauke with me and our friend Dan Allen on March 8, 1987 — he felt both elated by the accomplishment and bereft of the goal. He thrashed around for a few years, trying to recapture what he had so recently enjoyed. During Christmas week of 1989, he went over to the White Mountains to explore the remote and steeply wooded flanks of Carrigain, one of his favorite peaks.

Dec. 22, 1989
Dearest Ms. L —

Our first message from Fort Pileatus — so named because on our arrival, a pileated woodpecker flew off. We are about 6 miles in from Rte. 302, at about 2,000', with splendid views of Carrigain, the Captain, and the sprawling massif of Hancock, the White Mountains' most underrated mountain. Sheep and Mr. Rat are comfortably seated by my side, and dinner is started. We are having no trouble with black flies or mosquitoes. As we came in for the last time at 4:30 p.m. it was -1°. The air has that deep cold feel of Jack London's prose or Robert Service's poetry. Sheep and Mr. Rat are being very brave, and I have told them that I am very proud of them, and that Ms. L will be very very proud of them. The sterno is humming away, plus 3 candles — 4 candles now (just added a tall one for seeing into the pot better).

Dec. 24, 1989

On the whole, I am quite discouraged tonight. I had difficulties with these snowshoe bindings on the descent again — just after I thought they had done quite well on the ascent and in the thickets on the ridge. I fixed them, but I don't know how much downhill they can take.

But it is all part of a general deterioration in our winter gear, which money cannot fix, because we have no money. These snowshoes, my old and not very warm sleeping bag, Johnny's wind pants, old REI gaiters, etc. Well, really it's not so much the equipment as the deteriorating man inside. I just seem to move very slowly these days. Partly it is less strength due to age. Maybe some general waning of the fire inside. Perhaps the completion of *Forest and Crag* [a book that took ten years to write and came out that fall] coming on the heels of completing the 4,000ers-from-all-4-compass-points has magnified my sense of having no more goals. I *do* have goals, but only the ones involving Barra seem definite. Well, it is too cold to continue writing tonight, I just finished dinner and stepped outside, and the temp is -6°. I still do have some gut left, tho, just to be sticking out my full 4 nights in this cold. The sleeping bag is not worth much, but I am using all the resources I have — keeping clothes dry, using candles just right, getting hot drinks. Wonder how the last night will be. Wonder how cold tonight will be.

On Christmas Eve, three of your beloved animals send their warmest love to you you —

S, Mr. Rat, and G

[Sheep and Mr. Rat were small animals that could easily tuck into a corner of a pack. They made many trips to the winter mountains, alternating with Ben the Bengal Tiger or Lion or Rocky the Raccoon or Hazel the Rabbit or Killy the Snow Leopard, whom Guy had come across in a wild part of the White

Mountains called the Kilkenny. These animals, among others, inhabited our bedroom and maintained a close watch over us by day and by night. Killy and Ben accompanied Guy on his last trip up to the Franconia Ridge.]

Then, as if to belie his concerns about his strength, Guy climbed a major ice route called the Black Dike with our good friend Mike Young on the second day of the new year. My journal entry read, "Mike and Guy were back by 4:00 — with big *smiles* on their faces. Guy just loved it! He said he'd thought about me a lot when he was up there — that climb, which we'd done thirteen years ago — is so vivid still for us."

Mike Young gave Guy a pair of boots he couldn't use anymore, and our friend Sue Deming made him a pair of wind pants just like his beloved old orange pair that had belonged to his son Johnny, who had been given them after climbing McKinley by his teammate Tom Frost, who was getting rid of them. That was in 1969. Johnny passed them on to Guy in the early 1970s. I had patched those wind pants, so often snagged by his crampons or on White Mountain scrub, until there was very little of the original orange left.

Replacing worn-out gear turned out to be easier than finding another big project. Nothing seemed to work. Guy talked about exploring in the Kilkenny Range, a nearly trailless area in northern New Hampshire. He talked about tackling some wild country in Maine. He seemed to be looking for wilder mountains with greater opportunities for solitude. I wasn't so sure I liked the Maine idea. I didn't know those mountains. Because I could visualize where he'd been when he came back from his White Mountain trips and told me about everything — the ridges he'd climbed, where he'd camped, every summit he'd been on — I felt connected to what he had experienced and it felt safer somehow. I didn't want him to make the long winter drive to Maine, over unfamiliar roads, so far from home. But if Guy had found such a project, if he had found the spark to light again the fire within, I would have been happy to watch him pack his pack, readying himself for the next adventure.

Though I often stayed at Barra, I also used the opportunity of Guy's solos to climb with some of my women friends. We women climbers wanted to see what we could do in the winter mountains on our own, without boyfriends and husbands, who somehow ended up making the crucial decisions if they were along.

In the winter of 1980, Natalie Davis, Debbie O'Neil Duncanson, and I made a successful winter crossing of the Presidential Range, the first ever for women. The next year, 1981, ten of us traveled to Katahdin in northern Maine. Again it was a first winter ascent for women, but after that I decided I preferred smaller groups. Perhaps my most successful trips were with my friend Sue Deming. We used the same tactics to climb mountains that Guy and I found so satisfying. On the first day we hauled sleds into the area we wanted to explore and set up a base camp. During the next few days we climbed the open slides with crampons or bushwhacked up thick slopes to the summits.

These trips with Sue gave me confidence in my own mountain judgment that I could never have found if I had only gone on trips with Guy. As did the years we spent instructing at the Winter Mountaineering School. For fourteen winters — from 1973 to 1987 — Guy and I taught at this program run by the Appalachian Mountain Club, which was held between Christmas and New Year's.

The ice climb that meant the most to Guy and me was the Black Dike, the route that the world-renowned climber Yvon Chouinard described as "a black, filthy, horrendous icicle 600 feet high." It occupied the shadowy void separating the Whitney-Gilman aréte from the rest of Cannon Cliff in Franconia Notch. The sun never shone on this north-facing strip of ice-and-snow-plastered rock, a "frozen maelstrom of malignancy," as Guy called it. It just sat there in the gloom, the ultimate dare for any ice climber.

On our first attempt in March 1975, we didn't even reach the bottom of the ice. We arrived at dawn to find Franconia Notch enjoying its own private blizzard, but we walked up the snow-covered talus slope anyway because, who knew, it might suddenly clear. It took us fifteen minutes to strap on our crampons — normally a four-minute job — because of the swirling snow.

We'd seen, with some surprise, another car in the parking lot. Now we heard scuffling and calling from a party directly above us, in the act of rappelling down the Whitney-Gilman route. This turned out to be Andy Tuthill, a young climber of our acquaintance, the only guy we'd expect to see out on a day like this. Andy, crampons scraping on the rock, landed beside us with a thump and said "Hi." Then he began coiling up his rope.

If it wasn't a day for Andy, it certainly wasn't a day for us either, but I began uncoiling our rope anyway, getting ready to belay Guy up the snow ramp that led to the first pitch of the Black Dike, when suddenly, appearing from behind us out of the mist, up strode Big John Bragg — the only other climber we weren't surprised to see up here.

We suggested that John precede us up the Dike, since he was a party of one (and a *much* better climber) and would move faster. Meanwhile, Guy was cramponing up the snow ramp when we heard an unmistakable *woomf* and the snow sheared off, taking Guy with it. He whizzed past John, who leaned out to grab Guy by the scruff of his neck but stopped himself, considering what might happen to him if he grabbed hold of a fast-moving object. The mini-avalanche petered out; Guy stood up, and we exchanged looks that said, Enough of this nonsense.

"Why don't you come over to my cabin and have a hot drink," Andy said.

Indeed!

As we headed back down the talus slope, we kept looking back up into the swirl. Our last view was of Big John Bragg hanging on his ice tools, head bent, parka hood up, as the spindrift passed over him.

"He's off to Patagonia day after tomorrow," Andy said. That explained it.

We were back a few days later. The weather was with us, and this was lucky because we were terribly slow. On the second pitch I stood, my back to the ice, belaying Guy for two and a half hours as he tried a way that turned into a cul-de-sac; he had to down-climb and try another. During that long belay, as I wiggled my toes in my boots to ward off the cold, I tracked the sun as it moved along the cliff face on the opposite wall. Occasionally huge icicles would drop and crash down to the talus slope.

I climbed the last steep pitch in fading light, and it was hard. We were using long axes then, and my arms were tired; I thought I was going to spend the rest of my life flailing away on that last bit of steep ice. I was mad at myself that my wrists had turned to jelly. When I finally popped over the top onto firm ground, Guy reached for me in an enveloping hug. Suddenly he was sobbing, his wet face against mine. Perhaps at that moment he sensed, in the way we can know the unforeseeable, that the climbing wasn't going to get any better. Like that ultimate football match between the orphans and campers so long ago, Guy had given this great climb all his energy, concentration, and desire. There had been less than a handful of previous ascents, none by a woman. Perhaps Guy had seen that together we had reached a summit, and that the long path ahead lay only downhill.

In 1980 we began taking care of the Franconia Ridge Trail — 1.8 miles, all above tree line — under the Appalachian Mountain Club's Adopt-a-Trail Program. That work grew to mean to us as much as our work at Barra: the Franconia Ridge became an extension of our own backyard. Our routine was to pack up to Green-leaf Hut, located a mile below the summit of Lafayette, and spend two or three nights there. As trail workers, we were granted free lodging in exchange for work.

Forest managers were concerned about the beating the fragile alpine vege-tation was taking from the heavy foot traffic. The sheer exposed beauty of the Franconia Ridge Trail attracted the crowds. Hikers who lived in Boston could make the eight-mile loop as a day trip: ascending the Old Bridle Path to Lafayette, crossing over the summit of Lincoln to Little Haystack, and descending the Falling Waters Trail. In the late 1980s, we counted as many as 300 hikers up there on sunny weekends.

We saw the challenge as twofold: protecting the plants and educating hikers into wanting to safeguard these plants. It was really threefold: achieving both of these goals without compromising everyone's experience. It was important, we thought, that hikers not lose that precious sense of freedom, that sense of wildness, that being in the mountains gives. It might seem hard to find on crowded days, but the wildness was there on this narrow windswept ridge, this sky traverse through alpine glory. It was embedded in the rocks, held fast in the impenetrable scrub at the tree line, and heard in the heart-stoppingly clear note of the white-throated sparrow.

It was our profound privilege to think deeply on these things for nearly two decades. The terrain in which we worked, and the hikers we met up there, gave back to us far more than we could ever give.

Friends got interested, and several of them adopted adjacent trails. By the mid-1980s we were helping each other on our trail sections and had dubbed ourselves the West End Trail Tenders. The Franconias are located at the western edge of the White Mountains, and the acronym described the conditions we often found ourselves working in: WETT! We formed a sturdy, dedicated force that appointed no officers, held no meetings, charged no dues, drafted no bylaws, hired no staff, and built no clubhouse. We had one "rule": when we were working on your trail section, you were the boss.

The WETTS got together for two long spring and fall weekends, but Guy and I didn't let three weeks go by without getting up on the Franconia Ridge. Over the years these trips took their toll on my knees, and it all came to an end on May 26, 1991, when I was descending the Falling Waters Trail on a muggy day. I'd just gotten off a steep section and was feeling the relief in my knees, when my left knee gave way. I stumbled, but saved myself from falling with the aid of my hiking poles. I was about a mile from the trailhead and limped on down. It had been a big weekend. Everyone's knees were hurting. Since I didn't want this to be anything worse than the way I normally felt after a big descent, I didn't say much. But I knew it was worse: as it turned out, I'd torn the cartilage in my left knee — and that was my good one.

I was fifty-one. I had always struggled with what Guy and I referred to as "Laura's bad knee." Many climbers suffer from knee problems. Mine began when I was seventeen. My first knee surgery was in the mid-1960s. I felt a strong identification with Mickey Mantle and his problem knees. But he kept going, and I kept going by lifting weights, wearing knee braces, chewing anti-inflammatories, and using trekking poles, which turned me into a four-footed creature, as my doctor put it.

As my knees worsened, when Guy suggested a bushwhack, I could feel myself twinge, and I pictured the downed trees stacked like jackstraws, their criss-crossed trunks making up the terrain of the summer bushwhack. I could see in the way Guy held himself, watching my face, that he wanted me to say yes. We didn't do that much summer bushwhacking, and in winter this underbrush was covered in snow. I didn't want to confront the fact that I couldn't do anything I wanted in our home mountains. I didn't want to say no, so I kept on saying yes and again felt a twinge (which I ignored) for the "discomfort." I knew my knees would feel pain. Just as I could not see into the pain of Guy's soul and he wasn't talking about it, much the same thing was going on with my knees. Guy knew they gave me trouble, but he could not know how much, because I wasn't talking — not to him, not even to myself.

I continued to cling on. In January 1991, we packed up to Tuckerman Ravine with a group of ice-climbing friends with plans to climb in both ravines, Tuck's and Huntington. I could tell I made the others nervous as I stumbled over ground where, if I fell, I would land on the rocks below. It was an awful feeling, knowing this terrain was too much for me now.

Later that same winter I went with friends to climb some ice that was an easy walk from the road. That should work. No big descents. But this experience was, if anything, worse. I found myself flailing at the ice, unable to make my crampons grip. I knew this wasn't just an off day. I was awkward and ineffectual and weak. I felt my hold on the mountains loosen.

It made me think of Hans Kraus, who put up many first ascents at the Shawa-ngunks back in the 1940s and 1950s. By the time I met him, Hans was gray and a little bent, but I never thought he would stop climbing. One day Guy and I passed Hans as he was starting up a climb, a route he'd put in years ago. We took in the rope coming down from above that attached Hans to his climbing partner up on the cliff. Hans wasn't leading and Hans always led. Then we took in Hans's form. He was clawing at the rock. He was unable to move upward. We knew about his arthritic hands. As a teenager climbing in the Dolomites, Hans had caught his partner in a long fall, and the rope, running through his bare hands, had burned them to the bone. We hurried past. This was too painful to witness.

I promised myself this would never happen to me.

But it did. On the ice that was an easy walk in from the road. I sold my ice tools later that winter.

In early November 1992, I had surgery, but my knee didn't recover well. My last crossing of the Franconia Ridge was July 24 to 25, 1993. We met a group of friends at Greenleaf Hut, two of whom dated back to Guy's Shady Hill School days. Everyone had come to see the alpine plants, and it was a glorious mountain day. The descent was laborious — very unpleasant — for me. If others hadn't been along, I would have been in tears. Not just because of the pain, but because I knew I had no right to be in the mountains anymore. Because of my weakness, I put my companions at risk. Finally, we reached the trailhead. As we gathered for a group picture, I took in some young hikers nearby. They lolled on the grass, their boots unlaced, their damp gear spread out, exuding that sweaty, dirty look of having been out for several days. I heard the joy in their laughter with a stab as our little band threw arms about each other's shoulders for a snapshot. I was filled with longing for something I knew was already in the past.

As my knees began winding down, Guy had begun contouring our paths at Barra. He put in a zigzag path to the outhouse, eliminating the steep uphill. He established what we called "the Winter Route" for our walks out to the village. This eliminated the steep parts of our road.

Now I had time to plant more flower beds at Barra.

Guy and I had time to volunteer at the library.

I encouraged Guy to go to the mountains. He went, but not as often, and he began saying to friends who invited him on trips, "I'd rather have Laura without mountains than mountains without Laura." I took this as a joke, a kind and thoughtful joke, but a lighthearted remark nonetheless. I have come to see it was not a joke. It was lighthearted perhaps — Guy was often that — but being in the mountains together had meant everything.

Surprises sometimes happen.

That summer of 2000, after Guy had died, my friend Lou Cornell asked me to join the Labor Day crowd for climbing at his place near Franconia Notch.

I said yes. Right then I was saying yes to everything.

But I was putting myself in a tough position. I found it hard to be around climbers when I couldn't climb too. That's why I'd stopped going to Lou's Labor Day events.

I wrote Lou that I planned to arrive late Friday afternoon, stay for dinner, and spend the night. This would give me a chance to catch up with old friends, and I'd head for home when everyone left to go climbing.

Then my old climbing buddy Bill Thomas wrote to say he'd pick me up. He was going to show his slides, many from the old days at the Gunks, some of them of Guy. He had so many slides that showing them would take two nights.

Two nights!

I wrote to Bill, saying I absolutely had to be back home on Sunday morning. I had a commitment to meet friends in Bradford at 3:45 for our monthly play at the community theater.

I resigned myself to being stuck in Franconia for a whole long day while everyone went climbing. Except that I kept thinking about climbing myself. What about those slab routes on Whitehorse Ledge? I was pretty confident that my knees would be fine on that easy-friction, low-angled rock that involved no big step-ups.

Lou called, and I heard myself saying: "I'm going to bring my climbing shoes." And he said: "If you can get up, Laura, they can get you down."

That Friday evening Linda Collins said she wanted to climb Beginners' Route with me the next day. I was so excited I could hardly sleep.

Saturday morning was overcast and misting. The plan was for Linda and me to leave her husband, John Dunn, and their three-year-old Laura — my namesake — to spend the day at Santa's Village. In the parking lot there was some dithering around as we debated retreating to North Conway for a second breakfast while the weather made up its mind. Finally, Linda and I decided we'd go check out the slabs. We told John we'd very likely be back.

Beginners' Route wasn't exactly dry, but it was dry enough. Linda led. As soon as I started up the rock, every sinew, tendon, joint, blood vessel, and brain cell clicked in, and I was taken over by the pocked and dented granite under my fingers as I padded up those beauteous slabs that swelled like motionless waves. The rock was gray, like the sea on a cloudy day. Linda said, as I stepped onto the belay ledge high up the cliff, "Are you thinking of Guy?"

"Oh, yes! He'd be so happy!"

I made plans to climb the next day with John.

Sunday was, if anything, more threatening; the cloud level rested halfway down the cliff face and never lifted. As I climbed upward, I slowed my mind to focus on the roughness, the dull sparkle, the secrets hidden in the granite. I felt possessed of an enlarged vision that pulled the past — all my climbs, so many with Guy — up into the light of this present. It was as if I were held in the firm embrace of a dear friend not seen in years, one with whom I felt an abiding connection that could never be broken, even if I never saw my friend's face again.

When John and I reached the top a raven flew in, croaking, and touched down on the slabs about twenty feet away.

"Do you think that's Guy?" John said with a quiet smile.

Neither of us believed that large black bird was Guy, but we saw in the raven's flight, and heard in his raucous call, the delight that Guy had taken in the romp up the rock.

Bill drove me back home on Monday morning. As we motored slowly through the town of Bradford I pointed to a building and said, "That's where we go for the thea —" I gasped, clapping my hand to my mouth. Bill threw me an alarmed glance.

"I forgot! I totally forgot! I was meeting Sally and Tek here yesterday at 3:45!"

Bill started to laugh. "You were drugged, Laura," he said. "Drugged on rock!"

CHAPTER *eight*

Well, I can only teach you two things — to dig, and to love your home.
These are the true ends of philosophy.

— T. H. White, *The Once and Future King*

Guests often asked if I found it hard to cook on a woodstove and live without running water. My answer was, not at all. We're all just creatures of habit, I'd explain; it was just a matter of getting used to a different habit. Of course it all went much deeper. Living the way we chose to live was much more than setting up different routines for cooking and doing the dishes afterward. But that was the part that was harder to explain to visitors. I didn't understand it that well myself.

"I've found someone who will play in the woods with me," Guy often told guests. He believed if you could turn your grown-up work into the kind of play you played as a child, you could make a satisfying life. He'd gesture toward the root system of a hemlock, intertwined and needle-filled, and tell guests how he'd created whole worlds while playing around such roots on his family's farm in Connecticut.

Our first summer, when we were building our house, we cooked outside over an open fire. That September, when we moved inside and I began preparing meals on a woodstove, I realized how much I liked handling wood, picking up a piece and thinking red oak, as I stoked the fire, knowing that chunk of hardwood was going to burn slowly and maintain an even temperature in my oven. I liked the process of damping down the fire, finding that fine line between a clean blaze and a smoking stove.

As a child reader of Laura Ingalls Wilder, I had longed to go west in a covered wagon and be a pioneer. That was the play I had played, and now I was coming close to living it. Using an outhouse and making do without running water and electricity never felt like hardship. To me, hardship would have been living in the suburbs within commuting distance of some large East Coast city. That life, the dream of many in my generation, was one I wanted no part of. I knew this before I was thirteen. But what did I want? I'd loved growing up on the Lawrenceville School campus, so I thought I'd marry a schoolteacher like my father. But before I was out of high school I knew that life would be as deadening as that red brick house on the spacious lawn. I told myself I needed more room, though I didn't exactly understand what I meant by that. But it had something to do with what my mother said after she had grown old: "You know, Laura, I never played by the rules." So the kind of life Guy proposed was one I embraced without thought before I'd even tried it on, even if it meant living without running water, flush johns, or a telephone. Those things seemed unimportant compared with finding work that felt like play and freedom to live by my own rules. With Guy, I could light out for the territory.

"It's good to take care of a piece of land for a while," Guy often said. Each spring, when we unlatched the garden gate and plunged our sturdy garden forks into the soil, we greeted a new beginning. We had the knowledge gained from the season before inside us, and from the season before that. The same held for the work we did in our woods. We learned from our trees. The connection strengthened the more we spent time with them.

John Williams, our friend from the village, told us a story of a dairy farmer who, when asked why he was so successful, drawled, "Well, I guess I was always there."

We couldn't claim that. We weren't always at Barra. But in a way we were. Deep down we never left our land.

When we first moved up we heard a lot of stories about ambitious back-to-the-landers who worked out systems for pumping water right into their kitchens, generating power, and otherwise trying to duplicate the conveniences they had left behind. Then we'd hear they had moved back to the city.

"How come?" we'd ask.

"The water system kept breaking down," we'd be told.

Too many systems. Reliance on systems that kept needing repair. That was often what drove people off the land.

We had no "systems." Guy knew that attempting to install plumbing or rig up some kind of solar power would cause him immense frustration. "If it breaks down, and I can't fix it, it makes me dependent on someone else to fix it." It was important to Guy to have nothing at Barra he couldn't fix. And Barra thrived because Guy had worked out a way of life that suited him. He had come to the end of the road in the "real" world. He had made the leap and found his own. But first, he had found me.

In our last months together Guy said, "Our life isn't a model for anyone. People have been telling us for years we should write about it, but really, what we made work for us wouldn't work for anyone else." This was disappointing to Guy.

At the time I didn't really agree with him. But I was too inside my own life to say that while no one would want to make a blueprint of our lives, what we had done — deliberately creating a life that means something — was important. That's what visitors saw: that it was possible to follow the beat of that distant drummer of the heart. But that was only half the message. The other half was the practice of how we lived — lightly and sustainably. Neither of us saw, when we moved to the land in the early 1970s, that by the end of the century resource consumption would be an even more pressing issue, and even further from resolution. At Barra we were living at the far far end of the consumer curve. Visitors saw this, and they knew you didn't have to homestead as stringently as we did to achieve it.

But still, we saw something, even if it was only how right the life was for each of us. In the spring, when we forked under the garden — a two-hundred-by-seventy-foot piece of ground — or in the fall, as we faced each other on either end of the crosscut saw, Guy would catch my eye with a grin and quote Kipling.

> There are nine and sixty ways of constructing tribal lays,
> And — every — single — one — of — them — is — right.

We struggled to find the balance between undertaking too much and allowing ourselves enough leisure time. By leisure time we meant giving ourselves time to enjoy our work at Barra in an unhurried manner, as well as time for writing, climbing, playing music, and being with friends.

We understood the importance of not overscheduling. Guy was in charge of drawing up the schedule, which he did on a three-week basis. He wrote it out on a three-by-five index card that I would find at my place at breakfast. I looked it over for spots that felt too crowded, and we talked about how to shift things around. Sometimes we settled for the jam-up if it was spring and the work was pressing. Or if we both longed, for instance, to fit in a particular climb with a friend. When we were satisfied with the shape of the next three weeks, Guy posted the schedule on the bulletin board by the door.

On my own I would not have planned the way Guy did. But living an organized life, the habit of routine, agreed with me. I often found myself referring to the schedule so that I could look ahead. If I were down for laundry, say, I knew that my work would be over before midmorning and I'd have time to tinker with the short story I was working on or weed a patch of garden. Weeding for me was never "work." Far from being onerous and dreaded, weeding produced in me, when I stood back and gazed upon the weed-free patch, a sense of satisfaction that is at the heart of all useful work, all work that has meaning.

It was Guy's ability to plan that kept Barra running in a highly productive and efficient way. After the watershed year of Johnny's death in 1981, it seemed that Guy needed the planning to help him keep control of his own life. This screw continued to tighten, but so gradually I wasn't aware of it. Guy's planning always made sense to me. It wasn't until our last year that I began to see that he was driven by the three-by-five cards he carried in his shirt pocket. And had been for a long time.

Aside from the daily schedule, Guy kept a list of separate jobs he wanted to accomplish during the day. This, for him, was where the real difficulty lay. It became a problem for me because it was so difficult — impossible really — for him to resolve.

He needed to keep the pressure on. When he got it right, when he turned up the heat and kept the pot at a steady rolling boil, all went well. But if he adjusted the controls upward — that is, if he added more to his list of afternoon jobs — the pot frothed over. Then he'd begin darting about from task to task, hovering only to pull out his three-by-five cards. I'd hope he was checking jobs off, but from the strained, squinty look he threw me I knew he was miserable, and it made me feel miserable as well. My saying "Go easy on yourself, Guy," made no difference. I coped with his distress by continuing with my weeding. Being diligent about my own work was the only way I knew to help Guy or to help myself. But I often had a thought I couldn't keep from crowding in — that next to the urgency of Guy's work, my own work wasn't important. All I could do was witness his desperation from someplace off on the sidelines and stick to my task. But the way he rushed around made me feel crowded out. I knew this made no sense. My work was often the same as Guy's. I never mentioned these thoughts; in fact, I kept them so well submerged that I didn't acknowledge them as thoughts at all.

Still, Guy continued to joke about "unspecified recreation" — his term for when one or the other of us wasn't engaged in a specific job, like planting or canning or bread making or wood collecting, and we could do "whatever we wanted." I picked what I liked doing anyway, often weeding my flower beds or the strawberries or the asparagus patch, while Guy headed off for the woods with axe and saw.

When our friends learned that we felt pressure too, they seemed surprised. Perhaps they wanted to see Barra as an idyll, a haven, a place exempt from life's stresses and strains. And it was true that we'd stepped off the traditional treadmill.

The pressures at Barra were different, and I felt them in a different way from Guy. Because he was such a careful scheduler, I knew everything would get done — the garden would be planted, the wood collected — just as it always had. The pressure I felt came from the pressure Guy put on himself, which increased as his own storm clouds thickened.

Perhaps what people saw at Barra was a certain freedom. Admitting to feeling pressured or rushed or overwhelmed didn't seem to go with freedom. The freedom was certainly real. We had chosen a way of life, and we were free to make our own structure within its bounds — boundaries set by the seasons.

In early spring the schedule looked like this.

April	Th	27	plant (peas, strawberries)
	Fri	28	wood
	Sat	29	bread
	Sun	30	(hosting birthdays weekend)
May	Mon	1	laundry (clothes)
	Tu	2	write
	Wed	3	plant (onions, greens)
	Th	4	bread
	Fri	5	laundry (sheets & towels)
	Sat	6	garden (tend asparagus, rhubarb, build compost pile)
	Sun	7	write
	Mon	8	hike/climb
	Tu	9	plant (brassicae: cauliflower, broccoli, Brussels sprouts, cabbage)
	Wed	10	bread
	Th	11	garden (manure and mulch raspberries, blueberries, fruit trees)
	Fri	12	wood
	Sat	13	write
	Sun	14	wood
	Mon	15	plant (carrots, beets, rutabaga, parsnips)
	Tu	16	bread
	Wed	17	hike/trail work
	Th	18	write

We began in spring with digging under the cover crop of winter rye. Not all at once — the garden was too big for that. We worked on it about twenty minutes after lunch each day. That was the routine. It was Guy's idea to break big tasks down into manageable segments. I always welcomed the "digging up," as we called it. Forking in manure and winter rye and wood ash collected from winter fires as we prepared our soil for planting kept me in touch with how it looked. We picked out stones and set them aside for later use in building projects. We kept our eyes peeled for worms (good!). But if we spotted fat white grubs or orange wire worms or mean-faced cutworms, we put them in a jar. Guy called this the Better Barra Beetle Bottle and joked with visitors that the offending creature could gain freedom by producing two letters of recommendation. So far, he said, none had.

Other spring jobs included building the compost pile as well as mulching and manuring our rhubarb and asparagus beds, blueberries, strawberries, and raspberries. We used a manual reel lawn mower to cut the grassy paths in our garden and around the flower beds. We trimmed the borders with hand clippers.

In May I began canning, starting with the rhubarb, which I turned into jam and several kinds of condiments; I also put up just plain rhubarb stewed with maple syrup, which we ate at breakfast during the winter. I made all our jams, jellies, and condiments with our maple syrup. The canning progressed through the peas, broccoli, beans, cauliflower, corn, cabbage, cucumbers, tomatoes, and pumpkins, ending in a grand finale in October with apples.

Work, yes, but when we ate raspberries in January that I'd put in syrup the previous July, we could taste the sun in them. When I descended the ladder to our root cellar for a jar of beans for supper, my eyes ran over all the jars stored there, six deep on the shelves. There was ample food to last us for a year. I knew the personal history of every vegetable I had canned or layered in sand, like beets and carrots, or heaped in the slatted bins, like potatoes and onions.

We spent an average of twenty-three days a year collecting eight cords of firewood for the cabin and the sugar shed, using an axe, bow saws, a crosscut saw, and our invaluable peavey, a logger's tool that can lever, roll, and twitch trunks too heavy to lift. We began in May and ended just before Thanksgiving, collecting wood in multiples of four feet, carrying it to the house, sawing it into four-foot lengths, and stacking it in cord sections.

Nearly daily we worked up firewood. Guy split while I sawed, and this was a task we also worked on for twenty minutes or so each day. In the winter months, when we burned more wood and had more time to spend on it, we worked longer. The more wood I sawed, the more I loved to saw wood. It produced the same soul-deep contentment that weeding did. If I didn't saw for a few days, I missed it. "Perhaps I'm half-beaver," I said to Guy. "My front teeth will grow long if I don't keep gnawing down trees."

White ash, I'd think, or rock maple, naming to myself each four-foot log I put on the sawhorse. When I told Guy I did this, he said he did the same. We also discovered that we counted saw strokes, something we'd each done for years without the other knowing. When I began writing short fiction, I found that ideas came into my head when I was engaged in the meditative work of sawing wood or weeding.

Guy carried water to the house every morning — we consumed two to three gallons a day — and picked up the temperatures, which he read at three different locations: in the woods, at the garden, and at the house. I took care of the kerosene lamps, keeping them filled and cleaned.

I made the three-mile round trip out for the mail about three times a week, in the afternoon. The mail was our only means of communication with the outside world. It was the way we handled all our work with magazine and book editors; it was how we kept in touch with friends and family or made plans involving others. Once, when we walked into the post office with our friend Bonnie Christie and she saw the hunk of letters we pulled out of our box, she said, "Boy, you get a lot of mail!" Our postmaster at the time leaned out of his window and said, "Yep, we're a higher-class post office because of Guy and Laura." He was joking, of course.

Then, on the day we were down to plant the corn, it might rain. That meant shifting the schedule to an indoor task like writing or baking bread or laundry or canning. The weather had a big say in everything we did. If the spring was dry, for instance, we watered the garden every evening, for forty-five minutes to an hour, hand-carrying the water from our stream in watering cans. I carried so much water, so many buckets of sap to the sugar house, and so much cow manure to the garden from where we had dumped it a quarter of a mile uphill, that by the mid-1980s I had tendinitis in both elbows and had to begin using a yoke. I was very fond of that yoke. Now I see it was a symbol too — of the work Barra exacted. It made no difference that Guy never developed any serious joint problems and never used the yoke; he too was yoked to Barra. We were a yoked team.

Ongoing tasks included maintenance to our buildings and upkeep on our paths and road. We also had seasonal jobs, like cleaning our chimney and stoves twice a year and taking down the big window in our outhouse in spring and putting it back up in fall. We cleaned out and often repainted the rain barrel behind our cabin. In winter we shoveled snow off our roofs. A big job was clipping back the undergrowth that threatened to turn our three-acre clearing into forest again. For many years we also clipped back the young saplings around our sugar shed that had sprouted when we thinned the forest to give room to certain sugar maples. We wanted to move around our woods easily, especially when we were collecting sap, and so we began clipping out these saplings over an area of perhaps five or six acres. When we had a young family visiting once, we persuaded ourselves that they might find this work interesting. They stuck to it until all had dropped out but the father, who went on doggedly wielding the clippers, engaging us in conversation of such jetlike intensity that it was clear even to us that while he could stick this out, such an effort was entirely too labor-intensive, and probably useless in the end. After a few more years we gave up on this Sisyphean project, rationalizing that by now, surely, the canopy had filled in enough to slow down the sapling growth.

Guy gave me a hammock as a birthday gift one year. It was a symbol, he said, with a knowing look. We hung it between two trees behind the house. We made a point of lying in it a few times, staring at the sky way up there through the leafy green. We strung up this hammock every spring and took it down in the fall. Eventually that was all we were doing with it, so we gave it away.

We spent our afternoons "working" too. We'd do lighter tasks like weeding or the mowing and clipping. Perhaps we'd turn the compost pile or work for a few hours on Twin Firs Camp. But when I stop to think about it, what else would we have done in the afternoons? Perhaps we would have taken more walks.

Would I have worked this hard if it hadn't been for Guy? I was looking for meaningful work, and I had found it. The desire to strive is strong in me, passed on by my Yankee forebears. Alive in me also is the outdated, outmoded belief in the perfectibility of character (mine) through hard work. With Guy, and through the work at Barra, this belief, like cream, rose to the top.

At the beginning the tone of the work — the way we carried it out — was lighthearted. It was play. Though the streak that lay in Guy to turn it grim was there, it rarely showed itself. When the balance was overturned and Guy's need to keep control of his world intensified, the way in which he went about the work also changed. Guy's moods affected me, though I tried to hide this from him and from myself. But the work — solid, tangible, with soul-satisfying results — sustained me. It was refuge. It confirmed our partnership.

We welcomed many visitors to Barra. In 1973 and 1974, we hosted 110 individual guests, many overnight, some for the day. Guy kept a list of course! Many were friends and relatives. Some were acquaintances, and others were friends of acquaintances. All came to see what this strange couple was doing out in this place they had to walk to. Most came to lend a hand. Winter saw the fewest visitors, but beginning in March with sugaring and continuing through to

November, we often had people at Barra for more than half the days in each month.

We knew it wasn't easy to get there. In the first place, they had to find us. Guy had made a map that we mailed to first-time visitors. The land was hilly, however, and the path forked several times, and though he often redrew our map in response to the suggestions of visitors who took the wrong fork, we never entirely solved the wrong-turn problem that sent newcomers wandering around the woods carrying their heavy backpacking gear.

Guests couldn't pick up the phone and call to set a date or to change plans at the last minute. They had to make arrangements entirely by mail and well in advance. If something unavoidable came up, they couldn't let us know. Nonetheless, there were very few instances of visitors just not showing up.

Sugaring was a wonderful time for visitors. The diverse tasks lent themselves to many hands: collecting sap, sawing wood and stoking the fires, adding sap to the evaporator, and drawing off the syrup. A very pleasant moment came in the late afternoon after the day's sap had been collected and we were letting the fire die. I would boil up a pot of tea laced with new syrup, and as the shadows lengthened our conversation deepened, drawing us a little closer to the smoldering fire.

The rest of the year we shaped our work to the visitor. Some came to garden; others enjoyed the workout of hauling wood or the unaccustomed fun of using axe and saw. We were careful not to inflict the weeding or the mowing and clipping on anyone — the unskilled labor we did with the reel mower and hand clippers. Work on our guest cabin, Twin Firs Camp, lent itself to many hands using mallets and chisels.

Working with guests had the effect of making Guy and me work harder. The visitor always worked hard, and we didn't want to let our end down. Many of our friends returned to Barra year after year. They came to feel, I believe, a sense of community with the land. They came to partake in the immediate meaning in working for one's food and fuel.

Our friend Brad Snyder, who had introduced Guy to the Nearings' book, took an interest in our project from its conception. It was great to have Brad around when we ran into snags. In fact, we saved for Brad our toughest problems, like conceptualizing the placement of the stringer and header logs for Twin Firs Camp. This was a complex problem, because Guy and I had broken up the straight lines of this little building with a lot of angles so that we would be able to lift the logs ourselves.

We also saved for very close friends the job of moving the outhouse. We did this every four or five years and had a neat system of three adjacent holes, dug three to four feet deep. We had constructed the building so we could remove the plywood sides and lift off the roof, leaving the stud frame, which we moved on roller logs the few feet over to the next hole. We rotated the holes about every twelve years. By that time what had gone in had turned to a rich, dark soil that I could put on my flower beds.

Guests often brought food to Barra, packing in items they knew we didn't grow, like grapefruit, oranges, and bananas; cheese, fresh milk, and eggs; green peppers and eggplant in the dead of winter; and often (very often!) ice cream. Guests quickly found out that Guy and I had a profound disagreement on one point: he liked vanilla, and I went for anything chocolate.

Our guests' offerings of food, especially when they were packing in three or four grapefruits, a pineapple, several big round melons, and even a coconut, were not to be taken (ahem) lightly. When we expressed appreciation and surprise at the sheer quantity they'd carried in, they often said such things as, "Well, we didn't want to tax your supplies."

I never understood why guests said this until the winter after Guy died. I was living in the village, and one day I walked up to Barra to help Lisa Troy, the winter caretaker, prune the fruit trees. Lisa was stirring squash soup on the cookstove as I arrived. I felt reluctant to eat Lisa's soup, as well as her homemade bread. I'd brought some food myself and quickly laid it out on the table feeling, I realized, much as our guests might have felt. It was an interesting reversal. What our guests had seen was the work we put into our garden and how dependent we were on it. They saw that what we couldn't grow, like rice or peanut butter, had to be packed in. I was stunned by my lack of perception. I had been too caught up in living my life to be able to see around the edges.

Occasionally we were surprised by unexpected visitors. We were always working on some task, and I would watch Guy's eyes get that squinty look that told me he found the interruption hard. It meant he'd have to carry those jobs he had wanted to finish that afternoon over to the next day. But he'd drop his work to say hello and take the guests up on the porch, then go in the house for glasses and fresh water and some of the crackers I made when I baked bread. Guy had told me years before how important it was to him to act the welcoming host. The guests often offered to lend a hand, saying they didn't want to take us away from our work. Eventually the squinty look would ease as Guy became absorbed by the visit from these friends who had been kind enough to stop by and whom we had not seen in months.

A question we were often asked by first-time visitors as they looked around our cabin was, "You don't have a radio? How do you get news?"

"Well," Guy would answer with a mock-serious face, "we subscribe to two papers, *Baseball Weekly* and the *New York Review of Books*. If it's something important, we'll hear about it sooner or later."

"People send us clippings in the mail of news they feel we'd like to know about," I'd add in an effort to help out.

The visitor would smile politely, and the subject was usually dropped. Perhaps it seemed that a newscaster's voice coming out of a little box didn't fit with a life that encompassed hand tools, no motors, no evidence of a car. No electricity. Not even a hand pump in the kitchen. An outhouse. And there was that mile walk in. The Watermans lived closer to the pony express era than to email, but why, the visitor might have thought, didn't they subscribe to a daily paper?

I had always maintained a very loose connection with the news; I never read a paper on a daily basis, not while I was in school, not even when I lived in New York. But what about Guy? He had lived a life of intense political involvement when he worked in Washington, DC. He often told me that he liked either to involve himself to the point of immersion or, if he got out, to do so completely, though perhaps these breaks were not as clean as he imagined. For instance, after he had left Washington, he attempted —and failed — to get into Connecticut politics when he began working in New York. But after he moved to Barra, no news reached us over the AP or any other wire.

During our first summer together at Barra, 1973, Watergate was at its height. Nixon, a president Guy knew and had worked for, was going through the impeachment process, but Guy did no more than glance at the headlines in the newsstand in nearby Bradford. "They found another tape," he'd say. But he never bought the paper.

As I've come to see, Barra was Guy's creation. It was his last attempt to reinvent himself. He talked often about his Washington days, going over and over the what-ifs. He saw his time on Capitol Hill as the most exciting and intense period of his working life. But I came to see that it had contained disappointment, even heartache. Guy was plagued by the feeling that he could have done better, that he had let himself, and others, down. Bringing the news into Barra was, I believe, the last thing he wanted to do. Since I had never been much in touch with news, I never noticed, or even thought about, its absence.

Opera was much more important to me than news. When I was living in New York, I had sat in the Family Circle at the Metropolitan Opera House every two weeks, on average, for six or seven years. I rarely missed the Saturday afternoon broadcasts. But now, between my absorption in climbing and our life of homesteading, opera had just dropped out. It belonged to another world, and I didn't miss it.

It was Guy who had seen, on the very first day we walked onto our land, that the shape of the hills turned Barra into its own contained world. He dubbed the graceful white birch at the entrance to our clearing the Gabriel Birch, after the archangel who guarded the portals of Eden. For me, whenever I had been away and I walked back into Barra, it was as though I returned to a country where past memory is erased — like Ulysses in the land of the Lotus Eaters. But the image that resonated deepest for me was Barra as Huck Finn's raft. That raft is a happy place. On the raft Huck and Jim are at a safe distance from the perils of the world.

But occasionally Huck and Jim have to leave the raft. This got harder for Guy. "I'm fine at Barra," he'd say, "though you have to put up with my bad moods. It's dealing with the outside world that's hard."

As for me, beginning in the early 1980s, my trips away increased as problems related to old age caught up with my parents. After my father had died and we had moved my mother to a retirement home closer to us, I continued to visit old friends in Lawrenceville and always stopped to see my friend Annie Barry, who lived in New York.

"It's hard to leave Barra," I'd say to Guy. But I had learned that once I was on my way, I had a good time. In fact, though I didn't see it, and would never have admitted it, the break from Guy was good for me.

I made these trips in winter, the quiet season. The night before, Guy lashed my suitcase onto his packboard. My bus left White River Junction at 10:40 a.m. Guy figured we needed one hour to snowshoe out, scrape ice off the windshield, and stop by the post office, and another hour for the drive. Then he added an extra half-hour in case the car didn't start or the driving was bad or anything else unforeseen came up. That would get me to the bus station early, but I much preferred waiting there to running into a delay that had me nervous about missing the bus.

This morning as we mushed down the path in the frosty light, I swung a look back at our cabin hunkered beneath the steep hillside, smoke curling out of the chimney. Then we entered the woods, and the clearing — our Barra world — disappeared.

At the bus station I bought my round-trip ticket. Guy, standing beside me at the counter, seemed pulled into himself. He was heading out the next day to the mountains on a solo trip, and I knew he was keyed up. But that didn't explain why he seemed so down. He was just down. I picked up a schedule, and we checked the arrival time of my return. "Do you want to keep this?" I asked, even though I knew we had a bus schedule at home.

He started to tuck it into his shirt pocket along with his three-by-five cards, then put it back on the counter. "I won't need it," he said. The moment had come to say goodbye, although the bus wasn't due to depart for another twenty-five minutes. Guy sat down in one of the plastic seats, and I sat next to him. He stared at his boots, which were making puddles on the floor. The corners of his mouth were drawn down, and his big hands clenched in his lap. His knuckles glared, enlarged and red, in the fluorescent lights of the bus station.

"You can leave if you want, Guy," I said. I had placed one foot into this trip, and I knew it would be easier for me if he just headed back to Barra and finished up his packing for his trip.

"You'll be all right?" he asked.

"Yep," I gave him a silly, confident grin I knew was out of tune with his mood. Out of tune with my own.

We stood up, and I walked with him to the door of the terminal. The place reeked of exhaust. More people in heavy coats were coming in, and a line had formed at the ticket counter. We hugged each other hard.

I stood on the inside of the plate-glass door and watched him cross the snowy parking lot and get in the car. A puff of white came out of the tailpipe. He backed up, and as he pulled past me he raised a hand in farewell, but he didn't grin. I stayed by the door until the white Subaru had disappeared.

I returned to my seat and pulled out my book. I knew it wouldn't do me any good to think too much about how Guy was feeling. He would be there to meet the 8:10 p.m. bus a week from Sunday in a better mood than when he left. What could stop him would be an accident on the road or ordinary car trouble. We had a plan if he didn't show up. I was to call our friends, the Cornells. Way, way stuffed in the back of my mind was the thought that he might not come out of the mountains. But it was only when I knew he was low in his mind that my thoughts went in this direction. The faith that he would be there to meet my bus went along with trusting that he would never drink again. I was very good at trusting.

On the bus I pulled out the food I'd fixed the night before and looked around at the other passengers with their coffee in plastic cups and McDonald's French fries. I crunched a rooty, earthy-smelling carrot. The light coming in the bus's tinted window bleached it an unhealthy yellow.

In New York's Port Authority Bus Terminal, I purchased a ticket for my trip out to New Jersey. "How much?" I asked the face behind the window a second time, forcing myself to focus. I could feel the line behind me — people shifting their packages — impatient with this person from the country who was taking too long.

But first I was spending a few days with Annie Barry. As I walked down the sidewalk on my way to her apartment in the East Village, I tried to stride along like everyone else. But I knew, from their quick sidewise glances, that I appeared to be an alien in my "big mudder" boots with a pack on my back.

I was very conscious of horns honking, cars squealing, buses farting, and people, people, people moving at high speed past me. The rap of their heels on the pavement exuded efficiency and purpose. My rubber-soled boots made a soft scuffing, hardly audible even to me.

Barra felt very far away. I ran my hand along the side of a building and examined the grit that covered my fingers. It was impossible to tell where the city grit began and the Barra dirt left off, but I began to feel better. There was the market on the corner with its appetizing display of fruits and vegetables. The bookstore I used to visit looked much the same! Suddenly, I was striding along, caught up in the thrum of the noise and hustle and smell of the city, even though I was sweating into my bulky country clothes.

At the end of the week, heading home, as soon as the bus crossed into Vermont, I couldn't concentrate on my book. I knew Guy would be there. That is, I couldn't believe he wouldn't. He always made a point of getting to the station early. I myself was ready, pack on, scarf on, hat on, suitcase in my mittened hand, perched on the edge of my seat. As the bus pulled in, I caught sight of him standing solid outside — a man wearing a tam at a jaunty angle. I was the first to spring off the bus.

In the car I had him tell me everything that had happened at Barra first. We couldn't stop talking, and when finally I snowshoed past the Gabriel Birch, Guy behind me with my suitcase strapped to his packboard, I had, once again, safely returned to Huck Finn's raft. It was dark, but I knew that to my left lay the garden under the snow; straight ahead sat the cabin, secure on its slope, protected on the north by the steep hardwood hillside.

CHAPTER *nine*

What novelty is worth that sweet monotony where everything is known and loved because it is known?

— George Eliot, *The Mill on the Floss*

Even before we came to Barra, we agreed that Guy would keep the statistical record while I kept a narrative comment on our daily doings. I wasn't so sure I liked my half of the deal.

"My brother found my diary when I was sixteen and went around singing 'Laura loves Bobby,'" I said.

"Don't write it like that," Guy said. "Just say what we did every day."

"Okay," I said. "No personal stuff."

"Well, you can put in 'Guy loves Laura' if you want."

I began this journal on June 9, 1973, the day we started living on our land.

I never missed a day. This sounds ridiculously compulsive, but so is brushing one's teeth, and for me these daily journal entries turned into that kind of habit. I could be in bed, realize I hadn't written in my journal, and get up to do it.

The first entry read as follows:

> We left the Merritt's in Lenox, Mass. around 6:30 a.m. and arrived at Barra at 11:05. We stopped at McLam's to talk about our lumber order on the way, and picked up a rather large supply of mail at the post office. John and Freda Williams were working on their garden, and we chatted briefly before driving into our property. Then something happened we weren't expecting. We didn't get up our first hill the first time! A combination of a very wet spring and construction trucks going up and down our road. We tried again, staying to the far left side, and made it. We were consoled when we saw the shelter — still in one piece with contents intact — and the garden. Everything we'd planted in May had come up! And the peas looked superb. We decided just to unload the plants which were the worse for wear, having suffered on the drive up. We were afraid it was going to rain and needed to make a trip out for groceries, potting soil, and lime.

This we did. And, though the sky blackened, it did not rain. Disturbing incident on the way out — ran into three trail bikes just before the road turns into the wood. Pleaded with them not to go up our already rutted road. We are free of subways, noise, and city rudeness — but not of mechanized and destructive toys.

Spent the rest of the afternoon planting. Peppers and cabbages and leeks. The peppers improved soon after we put them in the ground. Decided to arrange the shelter for permanent living and then started dinner. We cooked on our camp stove and made a great vegetable stew. About 6:30 John and Joan Bennett and Craig Campbell arrived. John and Joan were looking for property in Vermont and Craig owns some land near Thetford. They cooked dinner and took a walk around our property. We had the feeling that our land grew on them. We all went to bed around 9:00. Guy and I almost caused a fire by setting a candle too close to a rafter in the shelter.

Another incident happened that first evening that I didn't record. Darkness was settling down into our clearing when, to our surprise, we heard footsteps, punctuated by occasional thrashings in the underbrush. Suddenly, a man clad in the brown uniform of United Parcel Service stumbled out of the woods. Breathing hard, he looked at us, down at the parcel in his hand, and back at us again. A desperate light shone in his eyes.

"Guy Waterman?" he gasped." "I hope!"

Guy's record keeping was in many ways the heart and soul of Barra. That may seem like an oversentimentalized view of statistics, but in keeping records we kept in touch with an astounding number of details having to do with all aspects of our life on the land, from the weather to the birds seen and heard each day, to the wood collected and consumed, to the garden yield, to the number of nails and screws used in Twin Firs Camp versus handmade pegs, to the sap produced daily by each of our sugar maples. Keeping records like this gave a shape, an order, to our lives.

To mark our first decade at Barra we celebrated by throwing the Ten-Year Anniversary Bash. We invited all our friends — the Shawangunks climbers who had helped us build our house that first summer as well as all our new North Country friends. Of course, we had a task lined up for so many willing workers: replacing our eight-foot garden fence erected to keep out jumpers like deer and diggers like woodchucks. Guy and I had already prepared the ten-foot posts from trees in our forest and carried in the rolls of galvanized fencing. At the time our garden was 70 feet wide by 160 feet long.

We were influenced in our record keeping by our friend Dan Smiley, a naturalist who kept all kinds of observations pertaining to the natural world, including the weather records at Lake Mohonk, New York, which at the time were heading into their ninetieth year. Dan had said, "You don't know what you're going to discover when you start." And we found that, indeed, the usefulness of the accumulated data comes as time passes and the records build. Another reason to keep records, I soon discovered, is that close observation increases perception, and memory can't be counted on.

"*Last* January I bet we'd had three twenty-belows by now," I said to Guy, who wisely didn't say anything but just reached for the clipboard on the wall where we kept our weather records.

"By today's date," he intoned, "we'd had eight straight mornings of ten degrees below, two fifteen-belows, a seventeen-below, and three nineteen-belows, but actually, no twenty-belows." He replaced the clipboard with a smug and knowing wink.

The statistics we kept on weather were useful to us in many ways. For instance, if the garden temperature read forty-eight degrees by 7:00 p.m. on a clear night in early June, we knew we'd better cover our plants to protect them from frost. If we were feeling lazy, we kept an eye on the thermometer to see how fast it was dropping. If at eight o'clock it had dropped only another degree, we might decide not to cover the plants, since clouds could develop during the night. But if the temperature had plummeted three or four degrees, the night was probably going to stay clear, and the temperature could be below freezing by morning.

We kept thermometers at three different locations — at the house, in the garden, and in the woods near the stream — and took readings at 7:00 a.m., 1:00 p.m., and 7:00 p.m. We also read the barometer at those hours. We noted wind direction once a day and kept track of rainfall and snow accumulation. We monitored our water as it flowed through the sluice at gallons per minute. We recorded the temperature in our root cellar. In general, Guy gathered the weather statistics. But if he was away for the day, or if it was just easier for me, then I got them.

On an index card Guy kept a list of birds seen and heard on a year-round daily basis, transferring it to the master list in the evening. If we heard the indigo bunting when we were working in the garden, one of us would say, "There's the indigo," and we'd both look up to try to spot this lovely bird, the male an iridescent blue. Keeping records on birds made us take time to stop what we were doing and look around. In this way the birds, as they went about their daily lives, became a part of our lives too. In fact, everything we kept track of worked this way. It was as though by keeping records we had grown antennae, like insects, and these feelers kept us a little more abreast of what was going on in the world around us.

All these records drew us into a deeper connection not only with the land but with each other, since we were both tuned to gathering the data and liked talking about it.

"What were the temperatures?" I'd ask Guy every morning. Or, "Thirty-six asparagus spears, eight radishes, and fifteen rhubarb stalks," I'd report on my return from the garden to fix supper so that Guy could make a note of the day's garden yield on a chart kept for this purpose.

The records we kept on our sugar maples moved us into the kind of working relationship with our trees that the farmer must feel for his draft horse or the hunter for his hunting dogs. Call it reverence. A bond develops over years that can end only in death.

When we went out to collect sap, we carried with us, along with our gathering pails, a three-by-five index card with each tree's name listed on it, a pencil for recording the number of quarts picked up, and a stick marked to measure quarts. In this way we got to know the dripping patterns of more than 200 sugar maples. Plantagenet, for instance, gushed sap early in the season, then suddenly tapered off. Swamp Fox, dwelling deep among the hemlocks, could be counted on to produce at the end of the season, after the temperatures had moderated and his roots had warmed up. Mad Dog, our best tree, was unstoppable early or late. In the part of the forest we called the Highlands a stand of big old gnarly sugar maples kept us busy making repeated trips up the hill. Some trees were really not worth tapping but were so close to the sugar shed that there was no point in not doing it, such as Ozymandias. As with his namesake from Shelley's poem, when we removed the lid from his bucket, we "looked on his works and despaired."

The Tree of the Year race was never predictable, though Mad Dog was always a strong contender, winning Tree of the Year eight times out of twenty-five years. Our friend Doug Mayer made a sign that read: Mad Dog: Tree of the Century. We hung this in the sugar shed, along with the plaque Guy made for the award-winning trees.

At the end of collecting the day's sap I read off the numbers of quarts gathered, and Guy recorded the amounts next to each tree's name on the chart posted at our sugar shed; then he added up the total number of quarts produced that day. Every few days he tallied up the Top Twenty Trees to see how the race was shaping up.

We learned that the big trees were not always the biggest producers, though sometimes they could be. We learned — to our surprise — that Voltaire, who was a Tree of the Year, was not a sugar maple. We had the pleasure of introducing

Voltaire to Sumner Williams of the University of Vermont's Proctor Maple Research Center. Sumner knew as much about sugar maples as anyone in the state, very likely the world. We pointed out a large area of rot and proudly announced that despite Voltaire's health problems, he was still Tree of the Year. This astute judge of maples eyed us, a little peculiarly we thought, and said, "I thought you were going to tell me this is a red maple." We blushed.

If I had been sugaring on my own, I never would have thought to track sap per tree per day, nor would I have named all the trees and found a way to make the hard work of collecting sap into a game of suspense. Guy said it was the Tree of the Year race that kept him going. What did he mean by that? I've come to see that Guy's energy came in spurts, in sprints, in sparks, and from inspiration. He could rise up like a rocket, but when his trajectory crested he'd collapse back to earth again. This game with the maples probably served the same purpose as his baseball game keyed to the lines from Milton, or his whistling. By engaging his mind, it staved off the bad thoughts. I saw only the fun, the whimsy in the game. I didn't see what lay behind it for Guy. But there is none of the shaman in me, or charismatic leader, or innovator, as there was in Guy. I was the worker bee — patient, tenacious, and with a dogged streak that made me determined not to let our team down.

But I have to admit that we kept some very silly statistics at Barra.

Perhaps our goofiest one — all Guy's idea — was keeping a life list of blueberries produced per bush. It made sense at the time because we wanted to get a handle on the productivity of each bush. And to give Guy the benefit of the doubt, he didn't know where this was going to lead. For the first few years these bushes were very small — not up to producing quarts — so we counted each individual berry as we picked. Years later, after the bushes were cranking out dozens of quarts per season, we were *still* counting individual berries because we were often just picking enough for our morning cereal or a batch of muffins. But the truth was, we'd *started* this — we'd started counting individual berries, keeping a record by bush, and we couldn't stop. Our minds automatically switched on to count when we approached a blueberry bush with a basket in hand. It was wonderfully meditative work, but we couldn't talk and pick at the same time. Yes, counting blueberries with guests was a conversation stopper. After I was no longer living at Barra, my friend John Saltmarsh told me that when he and Peter Forbes were picking blueberries with Guy, he and Peter couldn't help bursting into conversation. Finally, Peter said, "Oh, Guy. I have to confess, I've lost count."

"Don't worry," Guy said, "I've been counting for you."

We saved our 200,000th blueberry and set it on the front windowsill at Barra, where it slowly dried.

Our friends Sue and Bill Parmenter were along for one of our all-time marathon picking-counting sessions. We were experiencing a stratospheric yield that year and offered to Nancy Frost, who coordinated our town's annual chicken pie supper, to fill a paper cup of blueberries to put at each person's place. The church ladies planned on having between 200 and 250 people for the supper, and each cup held about 100 berries. So, with the help of Sue and Bill, we spent just two and a half hours picking the requisite 20,000 blueberries.

To underline the vital role that statistics played in our homesteading life, it is helpful to look at our organizational chart, drawn up by Guy and called by him "the Administrative Structure." As can be seen, as chairman and chief executive officer, I enjoyed the highest rank in the corporation. I was, in fact, vice president of all categories or operations carried out at Barra: Food Supply, Sugar Bush, Firewood, and Cabin Services. Like all corporate personnel, I had — and rightly deserved to have — a very exalted opinion of myself. But where was Guy? If you let your eye follow down the last column to the right, to the very bottom of the chart in the figure, his name can be discerned in the small print: "Division of Research & Statistics."

Barra Administrative Structure.

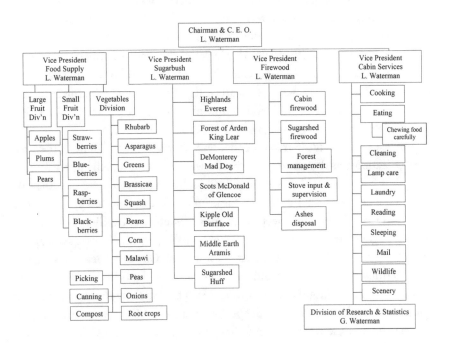

In 1990, in an effort to collect all our records and have the data available on a daily basis, Guy made the Barra Calendar. Each page captured our life for that day tracing back for all our years at Barra. It became our morning ritual for Guy to read each day's calendar aloud before we sat down for breakfast.

On a typical page, Guy wrote at the top, under the date "Today's Birthdays and Historical Events." This included birthdays of friends as well as historical figures we were fond of, like Jackie Robinson (Guy) or Maria Callas (me). "Events" came from history as well as from Barra, marking occasions we wanted to remember, such as when the Empress Pine fell in an overpowering January storm. (That occurred during our first winter, when our tree identification was a little shaky. The Empress Pine turned out to be a spruce, but it remained the Empress Pine on the calendar.)

Next, Guy noted a significant event in our lives for that date, either at Barra or elsewhere. For instance, on March 19, the day I am writing this, we climbed Pinnacle Gully in Mount Washington's Huntington Ravine in 1972. This was my first climb of what was at the time *the* ice route in New England. Technically, we hadn't yet moved to Barra, but Guy felt it was an important enough event to make our calendar anyway.

We had a space for visitors. Some winter days saw very few or even no visitors over the course of twenty-seven years, but during the sugaring season the calendar noted as many as a dozen guests on a given day. Visitors made a point of reading the Barra Calendar, often spotting their own names.

Next followed the weather data. This included the average temperature, as well as the minimum and maximum temperature with the record for that day. Guy noted precipitation: average snow depth with minimum and maximum covers, and the same data for rainfall, noting how many times precipitation had fallen on that date.

The last space on our Barra Calendar was reserved for the Quote of the Day. This quotation was drawn from the books we read aloud together after dinner. After Guy had died and I was at Barra by myself and continuing to post the calendar on a daily basis, it hit me that these quotations, all selected by Guy, often conveyed what he felt most deeply, but spoke about least. Reading them in this new light gave me fresh insight into the man I'd spent thirty years of my life with. I was stunned by my own lack of awareness. Guy had been showing me his innermost self all along through the quotations he had chosen for the Barra Calendar and read aloud each morning. I had been unable to see beneath the quotation's surface down to its deepest resonance for Guy. Awakening to the message behind the words began to happen a few weeks after Guy walked out the door. It marked the first step of my own long journey toward understanding myself and my life with Guy.

There were, of course, many quotations that contained no hidden message and Guy's reason for selecting them was plain. For instance, we came upon this February 25 quotation while reading Sy Montgomery's *Walking with the Great Apes*; it articulated what we both tried to practice with our trail work in the White Mountains.

> Everything else is less important. Career is less important. Science is less important. Fame is less important than doing the right thing when you're dealing with the natural environment.

But here's the quote for April 30. It's from Shakespeare's *Richard III*.

> They that stand high have many blasts to shake them,
> And, if they fall, they dash themselves to pieces.

And for September 25, this one from Kipling's poem, "Certain Maxim's of Hafiz."

> If we fall in the race, though we win, the hoof-slide is scarred in the course.
> Though Allah and Earth pardon Sin, remaineth forever Remorse.

And this obscure line from Shakespeare's *Troilus and Cressida*:

> Modest doubt is call'd
> The beacon of the wise, the tent that searches
> To the bottom of the worst.

Guy had been showing me his state of mind through these quotations for years. Though I was well aware of his sorrow, his pain on losing his sons, I was blind to how hungrily, how eagerly, it fed on his deepest feelings of Blame, Guilt, Remorse, and Regret — his Demons, all tangled under a blanket of immobilizing, suffocating Shame.

For me, now, this calendar holds the threads of my life with Guy together. This morning of March 19, when I read: "1972: L & G climb Pinnacle Gully," a young couple springs into my vision. "The world was all before them." They are not yet married. Barra is only an idea. Someone looking up from the floor of Huntington Ravine would see a team of two, appearing very small, but moving steadily upward, the rope stretched between them. As the lead climber swings his axe, the *thunk-thunk* is heard far below. The leader stops, anchors himself to the ice, and soon the follower is moving up the thick green flow that fills the steep-sided overhanging rock walls of Pinnacle Gully.

I stand and gaze at the calendar page I've just hung on the wall. The "visitors" space is dense. Guy needed to write between the lines to fit them all in, so the years are out of order. We were well into sugaring by March 19. The average temperature was thirty-three degrees, with a minimum of minus twelve set in 1993 (too cold for sap to flow that day) and a maximum of sixty degrees in 1996 (the sap must have been gushing). The Quote of the Day is from Thomas Hardy's *The Woodlanders*. Guy selected it in honor of sugaring.

> . . . a period following the close of winter tree-cutting and preceding the barking season, when the saps are just beginning to heave with the force of hydraulic lifts inside all the trunks of the forest.

CHAPTER ten

They say that "Time assuages" —

Time never did assuage —

An actual suffering strengthens

As Sinews do, with age —

Time is a Test of Trouble —

But not a Remedy —

If such it prove, it prove too

There was no Malady —

— Emily Dickinson, "They say that 'Time assuages'"

During the early years the light in Guy's spirit had the upper hand. At the climbing cliffs in 1969 and during Barra's first decade of the 1970s, he was all April and May. His playfulness, his humor, the pixie qualities that made him so much fun to be with overpowered the damp drizzly November in his soul. I didn't know it was there. In those days he was the sprite who put jelly beans on the handholds of the Bunny on Easter morning at the Gunks. Or who, on a showery day when the rocks were too wet to climb, led us in pied piper fashion to a nearby iron railroad bridge — a perfect jungle gym for climbers. One very rainy afternoon he created a board game called Fiasco that spoofed the hair-raising situations climbers get into, like finding themselves benighted on the cliffs, dropping crucial gear, wandering off route onto hard rock — all of which made for great stories afterward.

We climbed together all the time, and as I belayed him up some wildly exposed bit of rock, I'd hear floating down, "You gotta love your mama ev-er-y night or you cain't love your mama at all," and I'd look up and spot a man with a tam swinging up his hand for a high hold as if he were strolling down the sidewalk.

On April 21, 1981, we awoke to an inch of snow, and the temperature stayed in the thirties all day. We worked inside that morning, me making bread, Guy drafting chapter 4 of a big writing project we'd started — a history of climbing in the Northeast. That evening, as we were finishing up the supper dishes, we heard a step on the porch and looked at each other with alarm. Visitors at this time of day were close to unprecedented. We opened the door to our postmaster, who brought Guy the message to call the National Park Service in Alaska. "It's about your son," Paul said. Johnny, we knew, was climbing Mount McKinley, a solo traverse of the largest massif in North America.

The next morning Guy walked out to call Dave Buchanan, whom we knew slightly. Guy continued to call Dave every few days from the phone at our friend Freda Williams's house in the village. He kept on calling until the Park Service ended the helicopter search two weeks later.

Johnny's body was never found.

Meanwhile, we'd begun planting our garden.

News about Johnny began to reach our friends, and Guy picked up a stack of letters every time we went out for the mail. One evening as I was getting supper I heard Guy sobbing into his hands. I walked over and knelt down where he was sitting on the other side of the cabin and put my arms around him, not knowing how to give comfort in the face of so huge a grief. "He's gone," Guy sobbed. "I'll never see him again." Then he said, as though hit by it for the first time, "And Bill must be dead too."

We knew from Johnny's letters after his Mount Hunter climb in 1978, that he was having a harder and harder time coping with the world. His solo of the 14,570-foot mountain in the Alaska Range by the unclimbed and dangerous central buttress on the south face had earned him a stratospheric reputation in the rough and competitive circle of Alaskan climbers. He was interviewed by *Alaska* magazine and often invited to give his slide show of the climb. *Brilliant* was the word used to describe that route and Johnny's climbing.

In the course of ferrying his loads from camp to camp, Johnny climbed the mountain a total of twelve times. First he led each pitch, attaching his fixed ropes to the mountain; then he made the multiple carries of his gear. When it snowed he had to dig out his ropes and painstakingly clean off the ice and snow so he could climb them safely. The terrain was so steep and dangerous that rarely was he unclipped from the fixed ropes, even when he was in his tent. Afterward he wrote to us about what he had named the features of his route: First Judge and Second Judge. The knife edge of ice-encrusted rock that he straddled and climbed by digging in his crampons like spurs he dubbed the Happy Cowboy Pinnacle.

Johnny's letters were full of the kind of detail he knew his father would relish, and indeed, Guy felt Johnny's glory in a climb that some said had hardly been equaled in the history of mountaineering. But what also seeped out of Johnny's letters, the thing that dogged him every foot of the route, was his aloneness. Johnny was alone as few ever are on this planet. Alone in an inferno of cold and storm and mind-cracking wind. Alone in enervating sun. Alone in whiteout that flips the world into disorienting, dangerous blankness where depth perception is lost. Alone with round-the-clock danger, and alone with his screaming fear. This route on Mount Hunter took Johnny 145 days.

Guy admired this kind of toughness, the test of will, the solitary quest in a harsh, indifferent wilderness. And after his son was gone, Guy was to make this world more and more his own.

Then Johnny wrote: "Doesn't the mere fact that I climbed the mountain diminish my achievement?" Was Johnny saying that because he hadn't died, at age twenty-five, Hunter wasn't the mountain he thought it was? Reaching for an ultimate climb that offers little chance of success is a concept that only the world's greatest climbers endorse, and most of them don't long survive this line of nihilistic reasoning. Johnny had picked this route because of its reputation as "the last great problem" in Alaskan mountaineering, but he was unable to give himself the credit his success deserved. Guy seemed to agree with Johnny's perspective, and I, always too ready to see things from Guy's point of view, kept my half-formed questions to myself. Yet I felt that Guy was disturbed by Johnny's twisted logic; his son seemed snared in a terrible tension between his desire to live and the morbid thought that he had somehow failed by surviving the quest.

After Hunter, Johnny seemed unable to reenter the world of his fellow humans. Despite his fame, at least among climbers, he ended up washing dishes somewhere in Fairbanks. Then, after a fire consumed much of his equipment as well as his journals, in which he had meticulously detailed his daily life, he traveled down to Anchorage and committed himself to a mental institution. He was there just two weeks before he fled, against doctors' advice, to return to Fairbanks. He wrote to us about that, as well as about his decision to run for US president on a platform of feeding the hungry. If elected, he vowed to legalize marijuana. Word filtered back that he had affected a black cape with a star pasted on his forehead, in which garb he delivered his slide shows on the Hunter climb. Toward the end his letters were scarcely legible scrawls with a lot of anguish. He mailed us long fictional fantasies, laced with sex and obscenities, often involving his own demise. Long after Johnny's death, Guy wrote to Jon Waterman (no relation), who was writing an article on Johnny: "One thing he didn't send me, but which surfaced in his effects, was a very controlled and *under*written (in contrast with the grotesquely *over*written fantasies he *did* send) short story describing tersely my receiving a telegram notifying me of his suicide."

As Johnny's letters grew more and more disturbing, we were able to talk about them less and less. I could tell from the way Guy held himself, tense and closed, that he didn't want to discuss Johnny's problems and he didn't want me to talk about them either. Guy thought about going to Alaska, but when? There seemed no good time. It was too expensive. I didn't push it. As it turned out, he never went.

Then Johnny wrote that he was planning a solo winter crossing of Mount McKinley, a traverse from the tidewater of the Cook Inlet near Anchorage to the Arctic Ocean. It would be bigger and harder than Hunter. Guy relaxed. He took this as a good sign. Johnny was back on track; he was headed into the mountains again!

Johnny started at the Cook Inlet near Anchorage in January 1981, with a gargantuan pack. He began walking up the ninety miles of frozen rivers that led to the Ruth Glacier, the mile-wide highway that led straight toward McKinley. We heard from him next about a month later. He was back in Talkeetna. At the two-thousand-foot elevation on the Ruth his stove failed, he wrote, because of the cold. He was so cold he dreaded making camp at night. He lingered on in civilization for weeks, seemingly stalled. Then he had himself dropped off at mile 141 on the Anchorage-Fairbanks Highway and started walking in toward the Ruth Glacier again. By March he was well up the glacier, poised to strike out over McKinley.

The other climbers on the Ruth that spring thought John looked run-down and appeared to be less cautious than usual. He was last seen carrying a small pack with food for two weeks that consisted of powdered milk, honey, sugar, and flour. He had neither tent nor sleeping bag, and he was headed up the northwest fork of the Ruth, taking a straight-line course through an area known to be dangerously crevassed.

By summer's end it was borne in on Guy that his son had not planned to return from the McKinley traverse. Like a wounded, desperate animal, Johnny had walked into the mountains, the only place where he felt at home, to die. What those climbers on the Ruth saw at a glance Guy learned in bits and pieces. Each insight was more painful than the last, and each seemed to hammer a wedge between him and me, sending him deeper into the silent room. Though Guy never tired of talking about Johnny and his climbing achievements, what had happened to his son after the Hunter climb became almost impossible to talk about. I became cautious, even fearful, of moving into this territory, since by doing so I seemed only to keep Guy's wound raw.

Not until years later — during the summer before he committed suicide him-self — did Guy tell me that he didn't think he would have survived Johnny's death, or not for so long, if it hadn't been for me.

The last time Guy had heard from Bill was a letter postmarked May 30, 1973, ten days before we moved to Vermont. This letter mailed from Alaska, where Bill was living, said he was taking a trip, it wasn't in Alaska, and he'd write when he got back.

Bill had been an enthusiastic Boy Scout and achieved high grades in school. Guy told me that when he attended parents' night the young, energetic teachers rushed up to say how much they enjoyed having Bill in their classroom, whereas the older, more staid teachers said they found Bill tough to handle. In high school Bill played drums with a rock band. He was gregarious and well liked. People said Bill had charisma.

During the first few years after that letter, when relatives or friends asked if Guy had heard from Bill, he'd reply, "Bill's off on an adventure. He's always liked to be mysterious. I expect to hear a step on the porch one day soon, and there will be Bill." Bill's Aunt Bobbie liked to recount an old story of how one evening when she was cooking dinner, she turned around and there was Bill, leaning in the doorjamb with a grin on his face, just waiting for her to notice him. Years later our friend Brad Snyder told me that, when he asked Bill what he had hoped to see on that train-hopping trip out west when he lost his leg, Bill waved the question away. He was just headed west. It was the sixties.

As the seventies rolled away, the bolder among our friends and relatives asked if Guy was going to look for Bill.

Guy replied that one of the last people to see Bill told him that she guessed he'd gone to live with the Indians — he was fascinated by their way of life. "Per-haps Bill's living in an Indian village," Guy said. But this didn't really explain why Guy didn't go look for Bill.

Then Johnny died in 1981. With Johnny's death, Guy began to conclude that the chances were slim that Bill was still alive. Not hopeless, but not much hope.

Then, in an uncharacteristic airing of his innermost thoughts, Guy wrote to an Alaskan climbing friend of Johnny's, Kate Bull, who had asked about Bill. But perhaps this wasn't so uncharacteristic. Guy could often talk more openly, more confidingly, with people he scarcely knew. Kate had a right to ask. She had been on the Ruth Glacier and was among the last to see Johnny alive. While east on a climbing trip, she had made a point of seeking Guy out at the Winter

Mountaineering School in December 1981, to tell him what she knew of John-ny's last days.

On January 28, 1982, Guy wrote to Kate,

> I'm glad you raised the question why I've not "gone to find Bill," because maybe if I try to write out an answer it will help me to see whether I've really thought it through clearly. . . . One rea-son I never took off to look for Bill was there was never a single point at which I could say, now I've got to go see.
>
> Another reason has been the selfish one that our life here is very ordered, and geared to not spending money, and very interdependent as between Laura and me. So there is no chunk of time I could easily take off and go to Alaska, or to wherever the trail (if any) might lead. . . .
>
> Mainly, though, it comes down to this: either Bill is dead or he is living somewhere and quite deliberately not making him-self known to me. If the former, it's probably unlikely I could tie down the fact or the circumstances, much as I'd like to. If the lat-ter, then he would not want me to find him. If I were to show up and he was not happy to see me, it would break my heart. If he is alive and happy somewhere, or at least content, he must prefer not to be in touch. . . . There were evenings last summer here at our cabin, the day's work done, when I would stand at dusk and strain my eyes up the wood road that leads to our place, hoping to see a slightly limping form come down through the twilight and the years — before all went completely dark.

Why didn't I urge Guy to go look for Bill? Certainly I had mixed feelings about Guy going away on an open-ended journey. But if he had said, "I want to go look for Bill," I would have helped him find a way. When Bill lost his leg and spent weeks in the hospital in Winnipeg, Guy had gone immediately to be with him. What would have triggered the "single point" Guy needed to go look for his son? A year? Two years? Five years of not hearing from Bill? By then the trail would have turned cold. There is resignation in just letting time slip by. There is a certain inertia. The calendar quote Guy chose for May 30, the date of Bill's last letter, was from Alexandre Dumas's *The Count of Monte Cristo*, the final words: "Wait and hope."

I didn't question Guy about his comment that it would break his heart if Bill weren't glad to see him. Guy's reasoning made sense to me — that is, if I looked at it from his point of view. I didn't want to make him feel guilty about not going to look for Bill. I could see how Guy would be hurt if Bill weren't "happy" to see him. I couldn't see then how Guy's twisted logic seemed to fly in the face of parental instinct. By that time I was living in total empathy with Guy, all my actions geared toward keeping him from further pain. I was in no position to see the similarities to the risk my mother had taken in boarding a plane for Switzer-land to "rescue" me from Moral Re-Armament.

Bill's death was never confirmed. He seemed to have been swallowed up in the wilderness of the Far North. But the question, was Bill alive or was he dead? could not be answered with certainty. Guy had had almost no communication over the years with his first wife, and this did not change with the disappearance of their son. As the years piled up, Guy came to dwell in a netherworld about Bill. Always there was possibility that his son could walk down the path, back into the clearing and into his life at any moment.

It wasn't until after Guy's death that I began to ask myself why he didn't go see Johnny after the Hunter climb, when Johnny began writing those disturbing letters. Some years after Johnny's death, Guy began saying, "There's a lot of Johnny in me, and a lot of me in Johnny." It was obvious to anyone who saw the two together that there was an extraordinary bond between father and son. Guy was very proud when Johnny had written to him once about a climb Guy had done in stormy conditions that, as Johnny put it, no one would have been out in "except my crazy Dad." They shared this love of the wild and the testing challenges it offered. Each needed it for deep inner reasons of his own. Each set big goals that were next to impossible to achieve. Neither could give himself credit for achieve-ment, yet each was painfully desirous of recognition.

Guy could go visit Bill when he was in the hospital in Winnipeg, but he was unable to go look for Bill when he disappeared, and he was unable to go to Johnny when he saw that his son was going mad. Did Guy revisit in memory his own adolescent stay on the psycho ward? Did he relive his old defiant feeling during those unproductive sessions with the psychoanalysts? I am led to think, now, that confronting Johnny's mental problems would have brought Guy face-to-face with what he most feared within himself. He had spent years keeping under control, by prodigious efforts of mental discipline, a debilitating tendency toward anxiety and melancholy. He could not put at risk this hard-won control. But Guy must have known that by not going to Johnny he was condemning him-self to an underworld of guilt and self-blame.

Guy wrote Jon Waterman in 1988 — seven years after his son's death — in an attempt to answer questions for Jon's article about Johnny.

> What I recall of Johnny was an explosive energy and ferocious ecstasy on the rock or ice — a masterfully competent but elec-tric, volcanic, creative vitality. When he — or I — got a hard move, his joy was almost uncontainable. . . . As the years went

by the lows began to match the highs, and he went into these wild swings. I am subject to these same swings. My highs are very high, my lows — usually seen only by the long-suffering Ms. Laura — are very, very, very low. Maybe the reason he's not alive and I am is simply that I found Ms. Laura and he never found his Ms. Laura. Well, more: I found a lot of things along the 49 years that preceded the spring of 1981, and I can be aware of them even in the midst of the lowest lows. Johnny didn't find enough such things before the spring of 1981. . . . I do think Johnny was an exceptional climber on Alaskan mixed terrain, and I do think he had the uncommon vision of reaching for the unattainable which is inherently a defeating objective. To me he belongs with Ahab, Mallory, Prometheus, and the Satan of *Paradise Lost*'s first four books. Do you know what I mean? But he was also mad, in the sixteenth century's usage of that term. When it was that he went from just having unusual ups and downs to being off the deep end, I don't know. I didn't see that much of him after 1974, not at all after 1976, his last visit. . . . At age 18 he wrote, referring to "the incredible barriers in my mind toward meeting people and relaxing, the barriers that only let down when alone in my 'home' in the mountains. I could go on climbing only and try and forget about other things. Only it would have been a very short and hollow life." At 19 he wrote: "As far as John the climber goes, I've already defined my lines. It's John the rest of the time that needs to be found now." It seems like that other John was never found.

On Labor Day weekend of 1981, we drove over to join our Shawangunks climber friends who gathered annually at Lou Cornell's place near Cannon Cliff. We positioned our tent on Lou's spacious lawn so that we looked out on that glorious stretch of alpine terrain that was the Franconia Ridge.

These climbers had known Johnny; most had climbed with him. Johnny had introduced me to Cannon on Labor Day weekend exactly ten years earlier, when he was not quite nineteen. He led me up Sam's Swan Song. Following us from behind, as a second rope of two, were Johnny's dad and our Gunks friend Herb Cahn. I discovered that day that there was nothing like climbing with Johnny. His joy on the rock was unbounded, and he wanted you to love it too. Sam's was in the center of the big cliff. The climb had a reputation for tricky route-finding on sustained, difficult rock. There were no easy pitches on Sam's. This climb was at the top of my level of ability and far longer than any route I'd ever climbed. All the way up Johnny's voice came floating down: "Oh, this is great! You'll love this, Laura." Propelled by Johnny's exuberance, his overflowing zest for climbing, I remember nothing hard that day on Sam's.

At the top the climb peters out into blueberry bushes that grow out of the cracks in the lower-angled slabs. Climbers can make the mistake of unroping too soon here, thinking they're off the hard stuff, only to discover they're making dicey moves that, if they slip, will have nasty consequences. In fact, a party had died a few years earlier from a fall on these slabs. Of course, the specter of what could happen to you on Sam's enhanced the route's reputation.

Johnny and I, and Guy and Herb, kept roped until we were well up into the blueberries, off the tricky slabs. As we unroped and began to sort gear I dropped my hard hat. Johnny leaped down through the bushes after it. It is not easy to catch up with a ball-like object that's rolling downhill, but Johnny sprang over all obstacles and stopped my hard hat before it took its final plunge for the talus slope at the bottom of the cliff. Johnny could do this! Only Johnny.

On this Labor Day weekend of 1981, ten years later, I climbed Johnny's route on Cannon, Consolation Prize, with our friend Bill Thomas. Guy bushwhacked by himself up to less frequented Eagle Crag on the other side of Franconia Notch. He had built a memorial cairn to Johnny a month earlier on Eagle Crag. This cairn was located at the top of a route Johnny had put up on that cliff, and it overlooked Consolation Prize across the Notch. It was the third such cairn Guy had constructed that summer in his son's memory.

That evening, back at Lou's, Guy and I cooked our supper on our camp stove with the other climbers. Then it got dark. There was a party on Sam's that wasn't back yet, but no one was too concerned. People began to drift off toward their tents. At ten thirty I suddenly woke up and knew Guy wasn't beside me in his sleeping bag. I crawled out and began running around Lou's lawn looking for him in my nightgown and bare feet. It was starry, a clear and cold early fall night in the mountains. The grass was soaked with dew. I knew Guy was upset when he'd returned from Eagle Crag, and not wanting to talk much with anyone. It was the first time our climbing friends had seen Guy since Johnny's death, which they knew by now had not been a straightforward climber's death in the mountains. They had heard something about Johnny's problems, and everyone was careful to stay off this subject with Guy.

Where *was* Guy? I began running faster, calling out his name — *Guy! Guy!* — *into* the blackness. I didn't like how I was acting. It was not like me: a little crazy, certainly overdramatic. But I wanted Guy to come back! Headlights streamed across the lawn as a climber drove in and got out of his car. It was Bob Hall. I ran over and asked him what was going on. Where was Guy? He said a rescue party had been thrown together to see about the climbers on Sam's. It turned out they were fine, just slow, and had become benighted. The rescuers had walked up the trail to the top of Cannon Cliff. All they'd had to do was shine lights down for the party coming up. No problem, just the typical story of Gunks climbers being unused to the Big Cliff. Guy would be along in another car pretty soon.

Guy had *left*, and he hadn't *told* me?

I crawled back into my sleeping bag, chilled and teary.

I left the tent flap unzipped.

In a little while Guy slipped in. He saw I was awake, but he didn't say anything. "What happened?" I asked. I was lying in my sleeping bag.

He was silent, unlacing his boots, then peeling off his shirt. I started to ask again, when he said, "Nothing. Just a party benighted on Sam's."

He felt very far away. I knew he didn't want me to keep asking questions, but I said anyway, "Why didn't you tell me you were going off?" I was beginning to cry.

"I didn't want to wake you," he said in this new distant voice that felt so frightening. I knew this wasn't the real reason at all.

He'd been talking with Ken and John after I'd gone to bed. They'd probably left shortly after that.

"I was so upset to wake up and find you gone, Guy." Now I was sobbing. "I ran around calling for you." I was trying to get his sympathy, get him back. I reached up for a hug. He gave me one, but it was like hugging a wall.

A few days later Guy told me that when he was walking up the climbers' trail to the top of Cannon Cliff, thoughts of running up this same trail with Johnny on just such a nighttime rescue came hurtling, smashing back. His memory was of Labor Day 1968. Johnny was sixteen and already so good that climbers three times his age had stepped back and let this boy direct the rescue when they reached the top.

Well, I thought, *this explains why he was so cold to me in the tent*. These memories about Johnny upset him. Johnny had only been dead five months. Guy was still grieving for his son. But really, Guy's grief — or whatever I wanted to call it — explained nothing at all. On some subterranean level I knew this. It was just far easier to placate myself than to push Guy to give me reasons for why he had repulsed me in the tent. That was the frightening thing. Much too terrifying to give words to.

On that Labor Day of 1981, an enormous gulf opened where, it seemed, none had been before. It was wide and deep and hideous. I couldn't understand it. It yawned between us for the rest of our married life. I devoted myself to finding ways to get across, through, over, or around this gulf. At times we caught each other's hands, and the void diminished. But I could never bridge it. For years I thought that this inability to span the gulf had to do with me, that I was doing something wrong that was upsetting Guy. Not until after Guy was dead did I begin to see that to make a bridge that would span the divide, Guy had first to make a journey down, deep down, to the place that hurt to touch, the place he felt it was most important to conceal. Again, I consoled myself by thinking: *This is the thing Guy cannot do.* Or was it that he *wouldn't* do it? It took me a long time to see that this was only half the story. To build a bridge that would have closed the gulf and sealed up all the cracks, I needed to understand why I was so terrified to really talk to Guy.

That first spring of 1970 Guy said to me, "I hurt the ones I love the most." He said this with a serious face and a ghost of a grin. I knew he was telling me something important, but I didn't understand what he meant. I had recently turned thirty, but I'd had little real experience of love. Certainly I had never been seriously hurt by it. Hurting the ones you love sounded a little overdramatic, a little soap opera–ish. In my worldview it didn't really make sense. How could you possibly hurt the ones you least want to hurt? I heard his message: that I was taking my chances by falling in love with him, but I certainly didn't give the risks a second thought.

A few days before he walked out the door for the last time, Guy reminded me of what he had said years before: "I have never forgotten," he said. "And I have never regretted."

I saw that my task, after 1981, was learning to live with this "new" Guy, a changed man from the one I'd married. A light — and a lightness — had been extinguished. Though this light flickered from time to time, Guy never regained the radiance. His world darkened, and though we might be working side by side in the garden, we were often very much apart. Guy was in some far-off country to which I was never invited. Wherever he had traveled to, it had been a solo crossing, and I could see from the lines about his mouth that this other world was a hard and unforgiving land with signposts that read Regret, Remorse, and Despair. At those times I felt pushed aside. So I became adept at sinking into my own tasks and waiting it out. Asking him what was the matter only seemed to cause more pain. I told myself that I could help him most by not adding to his pain.

On the anniversary of Johnny's death — Guy had picked April 1 — he always spent the day up by the rock cairn he'd built in Johnny's memory on a trail-less ridge off the Franconia Ridge. Guy had chosen a commanding spot of wild beauty that looked across the deep notch to Cannon Cliff and the route Johnny had put up in happier times, Consolation Prize. In this cairn Guy had placed Johnny's hiking boots.

We were always sugaring on this date, and Guy was scrupulous about returning home in time to help me collect the afternoon's sap. One year the anniversary fell on a Saturday, and we had eight or nine visitors. The outpouring of sap was enormous, and I sent several people up to the cabin to lug down the washtubs to hold it all. It was exciting, as big runs always are, and everyone was in exuberant spirits.

The afternoon wore on. Four o'clock came and went, as did five. I began feeling anxious about Guy, that kind of nameless fear that came over me when he had gone to the mountains and I had reason to be concerned about his frame of mind. I thought about what I would do if he just didn't show up. What *would* I do? I could never carry that thought any further. Today he knew I had plenty of help, but I kept glancing up the path in the direction he would come. By now all the sap was gathered, people were back to sawing and splitting wood, and there was some conversation about when Guy would arrive. The sun sank lower and lower, and a chill crept into the air. Finally he appeared over the hill, his tam at its usual jaunty angle. Though he was moving along at a good pace, I could tell he wasn't in any hurry to reach us. It was as if he was hanging back, reluctant to leave that shadow world of his own thoughts and Johnny's cairn. Reluctant to cross the bridge into the land of friends who he knew understood the significance of this day. But I was so relieved, so thankful, so glad to see his familiar compact shape, that I just squashed down this hurt. He was back. But from what stony and isolated Mordor?

"Hello, Guy," I said, several times, but he seemed not to hear. And then the sad feelings welled up, and I felt utterly pushed away, as I had in the tent on that Labor Day weekend. I couldn't understand why Guy seemed unreachable, but the way he overlooked me let me know that he didn't want to be reached, especially by me. At the same time I felt my own love go out to him with longing, with a deep awareness of his pain, and with a searing sadness that all I could do was stand as witness to it. Our friends began telling him about the enormous run, showing him all the sap we'd collected, and bit by bit he let himself be drawn back into the circle.

I never told him of my own hurt, because wouldn't that have only caused him more pain? I just kept picturing him sitting beside Johnny's cairn, haunted, hounded by his own punishing thoughts. He must have found that mild day — the benign sky, those zephyr breezes — terribly at odds with his mood, which could only have found its match in a full-blown gale wailing out of the north with winds fierce enough to flatten him.

Life went on at Barra. Over the next nineteen years we wrote four books and many magazine articles. I began writing and publishing short fiction; Guy did the same with baseball research. We climbed, and we began our stewardship on the Franconia Ridge Trail. We constructed a log guesthouse, Twin Firs Camp, and we hosted countless visitors. We continued signing all our letters "Laura and Guy." We sugared, gardened, and collected our wood, the seasonal occupations that ruddered our lives.

If I saw that Guy was low, I would ask him how he was. Sometimes he tried to tell me, but most often he'd say, "Talking doesn't help, Laura."

"But it would help me," I'd say.

So he would try again, this most articulate of men stumbling for words, and would end up saying that talking didn't help, it just belittled what he felt. That was where things ground to a halt between us. Did he mean that talking made his feelings seem less important? I had hoped that by talking he could diminish the pain. Only after his death did I come to see that he needed to keep the pain raw, as a kind of penance for all the things he felt to be his fault.

For May 28, the date on which he last saw his son Bill in 1972, Guy selected for the Barra Calendar this quote from *King Richard III*.

> O, then began the tempest to my soul
> Who passed, methought, the melancholy flood,
> With that sour ferryman which poets write of,
> Unto the Kingdom of perpetual night.

Guy needed to shoulder this burden, more weighty than any pack he had ever hoisted. He needed to carry it alone. He would not allow himself to ease it by sharing it. He was not about to deconstruct it with words. The closest he could come was to say he had let all his sons down. Meanwhile, I stood like Kipling's Dinah Shadd, ready to drop my hand into Guy's "like a rose-leaf into a muddy road. 'The half av that I'll take,' sez she, 'an' more too if I can.'"

Sometimes I would ask how he was feeling if I could see that he was in the clutches of a black mood, but I was always quick to back off when I felt his resistance rising. We seemed to be better off — less at odds, tensions not wound so tight — if I said almost nothing at all. So Guy kept his hard shell intact around his unforgivable self. But as this carapace grew more impenetrable by me, it grew more unendurable to him.

For a long time I thought it was I who had caused this low mood that sprang up so suddenly when we were planting the peas on a mild morning in early spring. "Is it something I've done?" I'd ask. I believed he loved me less because he wouldn't talk.

Finally he said, "My moods have nothing to do with you, Laura." It took years for this to sink in. It wasn't me. It was nothing I had done. And when I thought about it, I felt demonstrations of his love every day. Guy making the trip for water one last time when we watered our young plants on a May evening. Guy pulling out my chair every night at dinner, giving me a kiss, then saying as he began to eat, "I sure do like our Barra meals. Your cooking is just right." Guy writing me these lines in a letter, dated April 18, 1983, that I read in Lawrenceville, where I was visiting my parents. He had just spent the day at Dartmouth's Baker Library.

> I had a *very* productive day at the library, but it was strange being there by myself. I found that all morning I kept carefully using only one half of our table (the one we always use in Special Collections); by afternoon I finally realized there was really no reason I couldn't spill over onto the other half too. Several people asked where you were. . . . Going in and out of the building through the revolving doors, it seemed strangely empty, only one person in a revolving door section at a time. I missed you.

Or in this note penned on a three-by-five card and left on the table for me to find after another trip away:

> Jan. 15, 1987
> Dear Laura,
>
> I love you very much and am so glad we're together again. You are very very good to me and make our life at Barra a world unlike any other place — our world.
> Guy

For a long time — for years — Guy couldn't say he loved me. And I stopped too, until I realized that even if he couldn't say it, I could. I didn't say it often. It was hard to say. Many evenings when he called for me to come in to say good night, I'd find him lying on his back, staring straight ahead, looking sad. I put my hand on top of his, and he twined his rough fingers in mine. If he looked sadder than usual, I'd say, "It seems you had a hard day." I felt it was important to let him know I saw. He might shift his gaze to me, still not saying anything, though he showed me the pain in his eyes, and I saw the way he had pulled the covers up tight against his neck and surrounded himself with Lion on one side and Ben the Bengal Tiger on the other, two of the animals who gave him comfort. Then he might say: "It's a hard world for animals, a cruel hard world." When he was past sixty, lying like this in our bed with the two candles illuminating our small bedroom, he looked like a little boy lost in a bewildering world, just trying to hold on till morning.

It was at those moments that I could say: "I love you." I'd give him a kiss, douse the candles, leave the room, and return to the table and pick up my book. But I would find myself listening. I'd hear him roll over, searching for the right position. After a few minutes his breathing would ease and mine could too and I knew he was asleep.

As I was kneading bread one morning — often a time when thoughts came to me — the words *I could get divorced* flashed across my brain. I tested this. I looked over at Guy, who was writing at our table, drafting a chapter for *Forest and Crag.* He was absorbed. His forming thoughts worked the pencil across the page, without, it seemed, a pause for breath. I realized then that I had no wish to be divorced. But it was a necessary thought. A liberating thought. A feasible option to pass in review across my mind. My mother must have thought it years before. Recognizing that I could leave Guy left me free to stay. I saw for myself that I had no wish to be where Guy was not.

After that, I began to adapt, though incompletely and in fits and starts. It seemed never enough over the course of the rest of our years together.

I learned that he wasn't asking for my help. Since his refusal to want my help was devastating, I had to learn, over and over, not to offer it. I had to learn not to walk into that place where I felt myself pushed aside. I had to learn not to take his dark moods personally, and not to get pulled down into resentful spirits of my own. I felt anger, but rarely, and kept it as well hidden from Guy as from myself. The consequence was that I squashed down my own feelings of hurt. I did not see then what I was doing, and I didn't understand the danger I was putting myself in. But I did know I couldn't lose my own lightness of spirit. If Guy needed anything from me, it was this.

Even though I was learning what I needed to know to be myself and stay married to Guy, I had no objectivity and I continued to live in Guy's world. A world we had built together but Guy had conceived. A world I never would have come to without him, but in which he couldn't live without me, if Barra were to last.

Mostly, during the next nineteen years after Johnny died, I took one day at a time. I was like a fish swimming around and around in her watery medium, unable to see into the larger world over the grassy edges of the pond.

CHAPTER *eleven*

I think we ought to read only the kind of books that wound and stab us.
. . . We need the books that affect us like a disaster, that grieve us deeply, like the death of someone we loved more than ourselves, like being banished into forests far from everyone, like a suicide. A book must be the axe for the frozen sea inside us.

— Franz Kafka, letter to Oskar Pollak

I grew up in a house filled with books. They were an important part of the family. My father directed my reading, although I was unaware of this. When I was nine he gave me one of my most prized books, *Classical Myths That Live Today*, in which he wrote: "Laura Bradley Johnson, from her father, Christmas 1948." Two years later he introduced me to Dickens with *The Pickwick Papers* and *Oliver Twist*. I was swept into Oliver's world of housebreakers, prostitutes, and pickpockets. For weeks I practiced lifting handkerchiefs from my brother's back pocket, just as young Oliver was taught to do by Fagan and his boy apprentices, the Artful Dodger and Charlie Bates. I read this book three times before I was seventeen, in the way children do who make a book their friend.

My mother read many books to my brother and me — Dr. Seuss, *The Wind in the Willows*, much of *Dr. Doolittle*, *The Hobbit*. My father read aloud to me only one, Lewis Carroll's *Alice in Wonderland*. Perhaps it was the only one he needed to read. It worked its spell. "This is a story about a little girl just your age," my father had said one winter afternoon as I sat on his lap in his big armchair, and he began to read. From then on I seemed to fit my stride to hers. Like Alice, I was interested in everything and full of questions. Often I received unsatisfactory answers and in this way I learned the world was full of whimsy and odd inhabitants. I was not put off by the unfamiliar and could accept the contradictions of the gauzy world behind the looking glass, even the irrational that Alice found at the bottom of the rabbit hole. I was unafraid of risk and not overly desirous of comfort. Like Alice, I was happy in solitude, even willing to be lonely if I was learning. I walked through the tangle as a curious observer, and though there was much I didn't understand, I found no murky corners in my world.

I don't remember conversations with my father about any of these books. But he set them in my path. He flung open the door, then stood aside as I began the long walk into a lifetime of reading. It happened as naturally as dreaming, and I was unaware until I was in middle age how well and permanently he had guided me into the companionable world of books, the refuge of a room with an armchair and a fireplace, my book on the little round table where I had set it down, waiting to be picked up again.

In Guy's family too, books held pride of place. When he was living in Cambridge, enrolled at the Shady Hill School, he would walk home for lunch to find that his mother had set out a plateful of peanut butter sandwiches and the Shakespeare they were reading was beside his place. He ate while his mother read aloud, and in this way they worked through all the plays, and, as Guy always added, a lot of peanut butter as well.

Guy told me about staging Shakespeare with the English twins, Kit and Ted, who lived with the Waterman family during World War II. He had kept a dog-eared copy of *Macbeth* in which he'd blacked out many lines and written in stage directions, in this way heavily editing Shakespeare so it could be produced by three young boys.

I, in turn, told him that my parents took me to see the Shakespeare put on by the students at the Lawrenceville School. These productions were staged in the round in the cavernous old gym, the audience sitting on bleachers. In my family this was the equivalent of going to Yankee Stadium. My parents talked about Romeo and Juliet or Katherina and Petruchio for days in advance, and I felt that kind of excitement other eight-year-olds might have felt at knowing they were about to see Joe DiMaggio or Jackie Robinson. In the weeks that followed, I struggled to penetrate these plays in my father's Arden Edition, feeling triumphant when I stumbled on lines I remembered.

> Petruchio: Good Lord how bright and goodly shines the moon!
> Katherina: The moon! The sun: it is not moonlight now.
> Petruchio: I say it is the moon that shines so bright.
> Katherina: I know it is the sun that shines so bright.

The books I shared with Guy formed a cornerstone and forged between us a mind-to-mind connection. Not long after we moved to Barra it became evident that, as Guy put it, I was president of the Slow Eaters Society. His allegiance was to the bolters' camp. So, to save himself hours of downtime waiting for me to plow through my mashed potatoes and allow me to finish eating at my customary leisurely pace, Guy suggested that he read aloud while I finished my meal.

We began this journey in the winter of 1974, with *The Fireside Book of Dog Stories*, and it ended on February 5, 2000, halfway through the second volume of Gibbon's *History of the Decline and Fall of the Roman Empire*. In all, we completed 269 books, an average of 10 a year.

Our writers of choice were nineteenth-century British and American authors. Aside from telling first-rate tales, these books unfolded at a leisurely pace that fit right into the rhythms of Barra, where we lived free of interruptions such as telephones, traffic noise, or even the hum of a refrigerator. In fact, we lived closer to the world of Dickens and Sir Walter Scott, whose characters strode about the countryside on foot and lived with candlelight and privies.

In the course of twenty-six years of reading aloud we worked our way through all but the odds and ends of Shakespeare, Dickens, Scott, Kipling, and Hardy. We read heaping portions of Hawthorne, Melville, Twain, and Cooper; George Eliot and George Meredith; Jane Austen, the Brontës, Trollope, and Thackeray. By no means excluding the twentieth century, we ranked among our all-time great reads *The Great Gatsby* and Robert Penn Warren's *All the King's Men*.

Perhaps our favorite reading-aloud book of all time was *The Count of Monte Cristo*. Or *Beau Geste*. Or *The Scarlet Pimpernel*. (We both could handle embarrassingly large helpings of the swashbuckling.) Or maybe it was *The Wind in the Willows*. A good dog story — heck, even a bad one — could choke Guy up to the point where he had to turn the book toward me so I could read the last paragraphs, silently, since I'd also be unable to get through it out loud.

Both of us contributed sets of Shakespeare when we blended our libraries. Guy brought his Kipling with the inscription "Guy Van Vorst Waterman, 1 May 1935" in the first volume, a gift to him on his third birthday. Our friend Walter Peters sent us the complete sets of Dickens and Scott, which arrived at our post office that first December. We sledded the boxes in from the road and wrote Walter that we couldn't imagine what they contained, but whatever it was it sure weighed like the dickens.

For Christmas 1979, Guy's gift to me came in a slim, orange-colored binder titled "The Most Ultimately Challenging Ever Barra Reading-Aloud Quiz Book." It contained twelve quizzes that Guy described in the subtitle as "Head-Scratching, Rib-Tickling, Heart-Stopping, Mind-Numbing," which were based on books we'd read aloud after dinner at Barra from 1974 to 1979.

The first question in the first quiz was: "What activity had Mole been engaged in when he suddenly said: 'Bother!' And 'O blow!' and bolted out of the house without even waiting to put on his coat? 5 points for correct answer."

This was easy.

The tenth and last question in the first quiz was: "Several books' titles refer explicitly to leading characters within their pages — but not by name. For 3 points each, what was the name of:

> the last of the Mohicans
> the master of Sunnybank
> the bride of Lammermoor
> the merchant of Venice
> the count of Monte Cristo
> the fair maid of Perth
> the prisoner of Zenda
> the three musketeers (name all three)
> bonus point: If you can name any *one* of the seven against Thebes."

This was harder. I was able to answer only five of the eight here and struck out on the bonus point. (For the answers, turn to the last page of this chapter. But no peeking until after you've tried the quiz!)

For Christmas 1992, Guy gave me another quiz book. The hand-drawn card that came with it read: "Blessed are the quiz-takers for they shall inherit 'The Christmas 1992 Barra Reading Aloud-Quiz Book.'" This book contained fifty glorious quizzes, broken down into twenty-five General Quizzes and twenty-five Specialized Quizzes that featured the authors we'd read most: Shakespeare, Scott, Kipling, Dickens, and our favorite category, dog stories. In this quiz book Guy also included a list of all the books we'd read aloud to date — 190 — as well as a score sheet and the answers (no cheating).

These quizzes were *hard*, asking the quiz taker to match first lines with the work they opened and last lines with the work they closed, as well as such brain testers as those that follow:

> Name book titles, and their authors, which mention the follow-
> ing numbers (five points for each book, five for each author):
>
> 1,876
> 31
> 12
> 7 (name one of two titles here)
> 6
> 4
> 3 (name *two* of three titles here)

2
1
0

Guy gave me one other book gift based on our reading aloud. This he called "A Harvest of Shared Memories," the title drawn from our beloved George Eliot. The whole quotation, which comes from *Middlemarch*, reads as follows:

> Marriage, which has been the bourne of so many narratives, is still a great beginning, as it was to Adam and Eve. . . . It is still the beginning of the home epic — the gradual conquest or irremediable loss of that complete union which makes the advancing years a climax, and age the harvest of sweet memories in common.

This was my Christmas present in 1988. It was subtitled "The First 150 Books Read Aloud at Barra: . . . together with some observations, perspectives, and reminiscences thereon." It was a rerembering in the form of lists of all the books we'd read to date. Guy had grouped characters, settings, and scenes together in all sorts of ways in an effort to evoke what we had enjoyed reading aloud together.

We soon discovered that the four candles we used at dinner weren't enough light for Guy when it came to reading on dark winter nights. So he constructed from our own wood the Candlelight Reader, another gift for me. This came with a card addressed to "Laura Guy & Ralph" (who loved dog stories) and read,

> May you enjoy many quiet hours of reading pleasure by soft candlelight down through the years together —
>
> Willy [Shakespeare]
> Scotty [Sir Walter]
> Kip [Rudyard Kipling]
> Chuck [Charles Dickens]
> Emily [Brontë]
> & A.P.T. [Albert Payson Terhune, creator of great dog stories]

The Candlelight Reader was modeled after a reading lectern, with holes drilled along the top and sides for six candles. Very few guests ever saw the Candlelight Reader. During the day it sat on a low shelf beneath our table. If we had guests for supper, we didn't read, though if a guest expressed interest, we were happy to oblige. The Candlelight Reader was as important to us as our crosscut saw and symbolized as much. When Guy had finished his supper he would bend down, pull up the Candlelight Reader, and set it on the table. The book we were reading lay on the lectern, as did a box of matches. Guy lit the candles one by one, taking his time. I felt myself slipping into the world that we had left the evening before and that I had returned to in my thoughts during the day.

Our connection in the world of books remained the sustaining pleasure of our lives. The reading aloud never lost its luster. After Johnny died and much in Guy died also, the solace he took in books never failed him.

We might have endured a difficult day — Guy locked away in his own desperate world, me feeling shut out, my attempts to help rebuffed, no hugs exchanged, our dinner consumed in silence — but when, at last, Guy shoved back his chair and reached down for the Candlelight Reader, immediately the tensions eased between us. I felt myself sink into the comfortable place, as into an enveloping armchair. Guy lit the candles one by one, opened the book, and began to read. We had found each other again as together we entered the enchanted place at the top of the forest and joined Christopher Robin and Pooh, or strode across Egdon Heath with Yeobright on his way to meet Eustasia Vye with passionate embrace, or hopped on the raft with Huck and Jim, heading downriver.

Our last night together, February 5, Guy asks me if I want him to read. He has never before asked this question, but he asks it now because this reading will be our last.

Our books are the glue, the mortar in our lives. Books connected us in the beginning. This shared ritual, more than anything, has helped us bridge the hard times. I look into Guy's face, and I can see that he wants to do what I want. I say yes, a wholehearted yes, to this last reading, and I can feel my own face brighten. We will keep on reading until we reach The End.

So we pick up the thread with Gibbon's lengthy chapter concerning the invasion of Italy by Alaric and Rome's pillage by the Goths. This night I have trouble concentrating on Gibbon's complex sentences. But the music in his phrases calms me, as does Guy's voice, rising and falling, full of the flow of words. He reads half a dozen pages, then closes the book, far from the end of this chapter. He douses the candles one by one and leans down one last time to slide the Candlelight Reader onto its low shelf beneath our table.

This is farewell.

Answers to the quizzes on pages 127–128:

(a) Chingachgook; (b) Albert Payson Terhune; (c) Lucy Ashton; (d) Antonio; (e) Edmond Dantes; (f) Catherine Glover: (g) King Rudolph; (h) Athos, Porthos, and Aramis; bonus point: Oedipus, Eteocles, Polynices, Antigone, or Ismene.

1. *1876 — A Novel* by Gore Vidal; 2. *At Midnight on the Thirty-First of March* by Josephine Case; 3. *Twelfth Night* by William Shakespears; 4. *Seven Against Thebes* by Aeschylus or *The House of Seven Gables* by Nathaniel Hawthorne; 5. *Now We Are Six* by A. A. Milne; 6. *The Sign of Four* by Sir Arthur Conan Doyle; 7. *The Three Mulla-Mulgars* by Walter de la Mare, *The Three Musketeers* by Alexander Dumas, or *Soldiers Three* by Rudyard Kipling; 8. *K2 — The Savage Mountain* by Charles Houston and Robert Bates; 9. *The Once and Future King* by T. H. White; 10. *Much Ado About Nothing* by William Shakespeare.

CHAPTER twelve

So wherever I am, there's always Pooh,

There's always Pooh and Me.

"What would I do?" I said to Pooh,

"If it wasn't for you," and Pooh said, "True,

It isn't much fun for One, but Two

Can stick together," says Pooh, says he.

"That's how it is," says Pooh.

— A. A. Milne, *Now We Are Six*

Our writing collaboration was another part of the mind-to-mind connection where Guy and I could reach each other in that comfortable place high and dry above the turbulent waters of painful emotions. It began on the day we moved to Barra.

I spent my last year in New York City working for *Backpacker* magazine. Its editor and founder, William Kemsley, was a mountaineer and climber who had put up a few first ascents at the Shawangunks back in the fifties.

When Bill conceived *Backpacker*, the backpacking boom of the late 1960s and early 1970s was gearing up into full swing. Bill had a mission and a vision. He wanted his magazine to educate hikers to minimize their impact on their outdoor playground, and he believed this could be done through well-written stories and breathtaking photographs.

At the time I was working for an outdoor store down on Chambers Street in lower Manhattan called Camp and Trail Outfitters. My coworkers knew I was looking for a job more in line with the editorial work I'd been trained for. So when one of the young sales guys heard there was someone in the store who was starting up a magazine about backpacking, he told me about it. I found Bill Kemsley on the second floor, looking at tents. I told him I was a climber and had been an editor for a few publishing companies in New York. We started talking about our favorite Gunks climbs, and it turned out that we knew some climbers in common. Bill hadn't climbed in several years and was interested in hearing about the "clean climbing" revolution: climbers weren't hammering pitons anymore because they saw the damage this caused to the edges of cracks. Instead, we were safeguarding ourselves by inserting nuts, or artificial chockstones, in the cracks. We could slot them in and remove them with our fingers.

When I met Bill I was at a personal crossroads, and it was all because of climbing. And a man I'd met named Guy Waterman. Climbing, when it hits hard, can call into question your marriage, your job, and where you live. Add Guy to the mix, and the upshot was that I couldn't concentrate on the job I had when I first met him, a dream editorial position with Atheneum Books. I started to turn out sloppy work. I'd sit at my desk with the manuscript, pencil in hand, and my mind would drift off to the routes I'd climbed that past weekend with Guy and the routes we'd climb the next weekend. Guy and climbing. Nothing else seemed important. When my mistakes at work were pointed out to me, I felt like I was back in seventh grade coping with math problems that made no sense and, I had a sinking feeling, would never make sense.

I resolved to try harder. It didn't work. Nothing worked.

In the end I was "let go from Atheneum (that is, fired). Suddenly the world of publishing — the only work I could imagine doing — had fallen completely flat. It wasn't that I loved books less, but my interest in being an editor of books had vanished, as had my willingness to go into an office every day. It was embarrassing not being able to turn out good work, but my heart and mind were someplace else, and there was nothing I could do about it. What was important for me now was being outside, climbing, and being with Guy.

But I needed a paycheck, so I stopped in at Camp and Trail Outfitters after one of my weekly visits downtown to the unemployment office, and since the owner knew I worked (*had* worked) in publishing, he asked if I'd put together their catalog.

Then, a few months later, Bill Kemsley walked into the store, and I found out about *Backpacker*. "I'm what you're looking for," I told him as we stood on the second floor among the tents, "a climber with editorial skills."

Fortunately, he bought it.

I was getting smarter too. The agreement with Bill was that I could leave the office at noon on Fridays. Being a climber, he understood. Guy had by that time conceived of the idea of Barra, and we'd picked a date for our departure from the megalopolis: June 9, 1973. I let Bill know I could give him one year.

It was a great year. It was a high note to end on.

As June 9 drew closer, Bill said, "Listen, why don't you and Guy test freeze-dried food for me this summer?" He knew we were going to camp on our land as we built our house. "You can run tests and write up the results for *Backpacker*. You need to eat, right? And while you're at it, you can test tents," he added. "I'll send up some folks to help you with this, and a photographer."

Bill was right. We had to eat. But 174 freeze-dried dinners? It took months to chew our way through the pile at a consumption rate of two out of three nights on backpacker fare.

This job was tailor-made for Guy, whose mind gravitated to imposing order on anything. We came up with fourteen categories. Many, like weight, amount of water required for preparation, and cost per meal, were objective, but the criteria of appearance, smell, taste, and ability to satisfy the appetite were subjective. We assigned each dinner a rating sheet and recorded numerical designations on a scale of 1 to 5, along with written comments (expletives deleted!) about each dish. We checked and rechecked more than three thousand rankings as our rating charts grew.

The freeze-dried dinner evaluation came out in *Backpacker*'s Fall 1974 issue, its seventh, and we soldiered on with evaluations of soups, salads, vegetables, desserts, and finally breakfasts, which appeared in the April 1976 issue.

Backpacker got us started. It gave us a little income. When we quit working in New York offices we didn't know how we were going to earn money, though we were aware that writing was a possibility.

Aside from what we willingly did to our digestive systems, we went on two treks with Bill Kemsley. The deal was that we'd write the story while he took the photographs.

The second trip, a walk from north to south through Maine's Baxter State Park, capped by traversing Katahdin, was a Sunday stroll compared with the first trip — an outing to Newfoundland, trekking through the *tuckamoor*.

Tuckamoor, we found out, is the Canadian equivalent of our furious krummholz, that impenetrable barrier that grows near tree line and presents a boot-to-head defense of stout trunks and branches of interlocking spruce, fir, and birch. Sane people don't tangle with this stuff. They take the trail. But at that time in Newfoundland there were no trails where we wanted to go, so we had no choice but to enter this thicket of gear-ripping, clothing-snatching, skin-tearing tuckamoor.

Nearly a week later we made it out to a greasy motel that had a hot shower. While Bill and I unpacked and hung up the tattered remnants to dry, Guy sat scribbling away on the bed, chuckling to himself. Before long he announced he'd written the article for *Backpacker*.

He read us what he wrote:

The Raucous Raven of the Tuckamoor
   (with apologies to Edgar Allan Poe)
Under a bleak and barren hill
Where cold north winds are never still
And driving rain hath power to chill
We struggled 'round a ten-mile pond
In company of which I'm fond,
Mustachioed gent and pretty blonde.
At end of day we stopped to dine,
Set up our tent on site so fine,
Secured it well with every line,
Wondering what the next day brings;
When above the wind that sings,
We thought we heard great flapping wings.
I opened up the door a crack,
Then suddenly I started back.
A giant awful-looking raven,
With his enormous wings a-wavin'
And a look that made us craven;
Settled just above our door,
Which the north wind rudely tore;
Made our threesome into four.
A sight! We'd never seen one rarer
Inside our Gerry Himalayer
As the steely skies grew grayer.
The sight made Bill and Laura quake,
But I could conquer fear and spake:
"Tell us, bird, if words you fake,
If human language you can borrow,
Of what will we three find tomorrow,
And will it end in joy or sorrow?
What lies out there beyond the shore?
Speak to us above our door!"
Quoth the raven: "Tuckamoor . . ."
Three days we walked and did all right;
At further cove we camped that night

In the dim declining light;
En route our constant boon companion
Along the rim of that dread canyon —
Three musketeers had their D'Artagnan,
We had ours, though more absurd —
Just a black, infernal bird,
Who only seemed to know one word,
Repeated ever, evermore,
As if transfixed from ancient lore —
Quoth the raven: "Tuckamoor . . ."
That night the rains came back again;
Our chance, we feared, went down the drain
With that damn thicket and all that rain.
The wind grew wild, the thunder shook,
And threatened our cold lonesome nook.
But still there sat that brooding rook,
That bird whose look seemed to deplore
Our very being there — and more —
Like some vengeful ancient Thor,
Brooding there above our door;
Causing us to cry out, implore:
"Dratted raven, just once more,
Will it ever cease to pour?
When can we get out of door?
Will we see our homes once more?"
Quoth the raven: "Tuckamoor . . ."
So if you journey to Cow's Head
To find if we're alive or dead,
And whether truth's in what I've said,
Go stand upon a lonesome shore
And listen to that north wind roar,
So shrill you've never heard before.
And drifting down to that chill shore,
Above the storm's eternal roar,
You'll hear those words just as before
Come haunting downward:
"Tuckamoor . . ."

Guy's epic (abbreviated here) was published, along with our article on the New-foundland adventure, in *Backpacker* number 19 in 1977. We continued to write for the magazine until Bill sold it in the early 1980s.

Well before then, in 1975, Lyle Richardson, the publisher of a new magazine called *New England Outdoors*, wrote to Guy about contributing a crossword puzzle on a monthly basis. Lyle had known about Guy's skill with crosswords ever since Guy submitted several to *Appalachia*, the Appalachian Mountain Club's journal, under Lyle's editorship. Guy agreed, and his first crossword appeared in the tenth issue, November 1975.

Thus began our five-year association with this delightful magazine.

A few months later Lyle wrote asking if we'd write a hiking and camping column. We drove over to his house in New Hampshire's Crawford Notch to talk about this. We weren't sure we wanted to make a commitment to a monthly deadline. How would this fit in with our life at Barra? I knew most of the work would fall on Guy. He was the proven writer. I didn't feel like a writer at all, though I wanted to be one. Guy wrote rapidly, and often, it seemed, on the wing of inspiration. He could turn out ten perfect paragraphs to my one in half the time. He thrived on tight deadlines. Guy's story about how to meet deadlines went like this: if he was given three speeches to write, he'd start with the one furthest away, then tackle the second speech, and work on the one assigned first last of all. To Guy this was the technique for making sure you got that first speech written. Logical? Not to my way of looking at it. Once, on a Monday morning commute into the city, after a weekend of rock climbing, Guy said he needed to have a completed speech on the president's desk by noon — the president of General Electric — and he hadn't started it yet. I gasped. He laughed. The previous Friday, as the vice presidents dropped on his desk the material Guy needed to write the speech, they had offered condolences: "Looks like you'll be working this weekend." Guy gave a resigned shrug. Working? Not him. He shoved all the papers in his desk and left for a weekend of climbing.

Guy was my mentor in the writing department. I doubt that I would have become a writer if it hadn't been for Guy. He taught by example, and I picked up on his spark, his prodigious energy, his sense of adventure about the writing game. Writing those monthly columns for *New England Outdoors* proved an excellent training ground.

We agreed to Lyle's offer because it gave us a voice. We were deeply concerned about the changes in the mountains. During the quiet 1950s, even well into the 1960s, there had been perhaps one party a weekend at a backwoods shelter, but now these shelters were filled, and the overflow hacked back the trees to make room for their tents, leaving knee-high stumps, fire rings, and ground compacted into hardpan, never given a chance to recover.

Forest managers knew that education was key. Signs appeared at trailheads and in the shelters about how to soften our impact: please don't cut bough beds, or wash in streams, or trench around tents. "What if we all built fires?" one Appalachian Mountain Club poster asked. The trail clubs began experimenting with ways to protect the trails, many of which had eroded into waist-high gullies from the unstoppable combination of lug-soled traffic and mountain rains.

What was happening above tree line was more devastating and harder to deal with. These tundra plants that could stand a combination of wind and cold that no human could take for long were being trampled out of existence by an onslaught of boots. In an effort to protect them, the hiking clubs and the Forest Service designed a treadway that encouraged hikers to stay on the trails. We wanted to take this a step further and find the balance between protecting the environment and addressing the intrusion on the hikers' sense of freedom of such protection efforts. After all, no one comes to the mountains to walk on a sidewalk. Guy and I felt that if we had to err it should be on the side of wildness. That is, we were willing to sacrifice a few plants to hikers' boots, to underbuild rather than overbuild trails, and to be minimal with educational signs rather than overload with management the wildness that people sought in the mountains.

We plunged into writing about all of this. We had a platform and felt fortunate that our editor, Mike Pogodzinski, liked our ideas enough to print what we wrote. Our first column, titled "A New Ethic," started like this: "A new ethic is spreading through the backcountry camping set. If the woods are to be maintained for future years and generations to enjoy, the old habits have to change."

Writing this column fit right into our life at Barra, where we worked side by side already. In those early years we were hardly out of each other's presence.

Guy thrived on striking out for new territory ahead of the pack, and in the mid-1970s the Northeast's backcountry was at the crossroads of change. Guy was good at beginnings. He believed in commitment to public service, his father's legacy. We found that our column was taken seriously by the managers in the Appalachian Mountain Club and the Forest Service. We felt we had a voice that could make a difference for the mountains that were so important to us.

We planned out our column topics for the year. Then, on our once-a-month writing mornings, we went over the outline Guy had drawn up before breakfast and divided up the topics. We sat facing each other at our square wooden table. We scribbled for an hour or so. Then we "exchanged papers" to go over each other's work, making notes about what else to add. Or, if there were too many scratch-outs, we each read aloud our own piece, the other jotting down points to discuss. We each made a few changes, then Guy took over, writing the transitions that worked my words seamlessly into his. That was it. We could turn out a column between 8:30 a.m. and noon.

Guy often said, as he picked up his pencil, "We'll write the final draft." This was another speech-writing trick. He meant, don't bother to sketch in what you're going to write, just write it. This worked. I found that the initial inspiration of my first thoughts could carry me into a piece of writing. If I put them in note form, those sparks could fizzle.

If our columns required research, we planned for that. Often our "research" was a hike to a place we'd never been before — a section of Connecticut's Blue Blazed Trails, or the Hopper Valley on Mount Greylock, with its huge old softwoods, towering trunks that gave the forest the sacred feeling of a cathedral. We wanted our columns to reflect the whole Northeast, not just the White Mountains, with which we were most familiar.

Mike Pogodzinski covered fishing, hunting, weather, even snowmobiling in the pages of *New England Outdoors*. We always read Mike's column on fishing, not because we had an interest in the sport ourselves, but because Mike was such a darn good writer. By reading the magazine, we learned to be tolerant of what drew others to the backcountry. We became convinced that if we all treated the land with restraint and respect, there would be room for all our varied interests. We came to see that outdoor recreationists were on the same side. We all cared about the woods and streams. Behind the surface differences was deep agreement about one thing: it was the unshirkable responsibility of all of us who loved the land to give something back, to practice stewardship in its cause.

Occasionally we found that a column needed one narrative voice. That was how Guy came to write "Winter above Treeline," a cautionary tale about a father and son who set off with grandiose plans to cross the entire White Mountains in winter. Guy and sixteen-year-old Johnny mushed up into the Presidential Range on snowshoes carrying eighty-pound packs, only to be clobbered by a storm above tree line. They stuck it out for two nights, during which time the temperatures warmed up, turning the snow to sleet. Soaked, they retreated to the valley and fed quarters into Laundromat machines, determined to dry their gear and go on. This time they headed up the Carriage Road on Mount Washington, reaching tree line in time for an appointment with another storm that made what they had just endured look like a light breeze. They spent three nights pinned down while the winds shrieked to well over 100 miles per hour, and the temperatures dropped to twenty-six below zero. Obviously, this was Guy's story.

The column we wrote on winter camping turned into two, since at the end of the morning we found we'd done two columns' worth of work. The one I wrote

I called "Winter Camping Idyll." I was proud of this piece because it was all my own, written out of my own winter camping experience. It was no trouble at all to evoke the joys — uh, miseries — of this specialized branch of outdoor recreation. The winter camper lives with frost feathers that collect around her face as she lies in her sleeping bag, breathing into the frigid night air. The winter camper must keep her water bottle from freezing by taking it into her sleeping bag at night. In fact, the winter camper's sleeping bag bulges with items that must not freeze, like her boots and headlamp batteries, as well as food that must be kept away from inquisitive critters. Then, there is the dilemma of how to proceed when "nature calls" at 3:00 a.m. . . .

Our first column appeared in April 1976. Our last column was published in September 1981, which was the last issue of *New England Outdoors*. Much earlier, Mike had written to us stating that his aim was to publish the best outdoor writing he could. This magazine, which had started out on newsprint and was beloved by a loyal readership for this very reason, expanded with reluctance toward the glossy — mainly to retain its advertisers. Financially teetery in the best of times, the magazine didn't pay us a cent for our columns during the last two years. Every now and then, when we felt the wolf sniffing under our doorsill, we'd write Mike. We'd say, "Hmmm, we know you'd pay us if you could, so things must be tough, but look . . ." Mike always wrote back a very polite and hopeful note reassuring us that they were on the verge of fresh backing. . . . If we could just hold on . . . tighten our belts . . . he promised. . . . Mike wrote very convincing letters, which he signed Chief Rabbit. Other writers stopped sending in their articles; a few columnists dropped out. We were told we were crazy to think we'd ever get our money from this magazine. Just plain stupid. What were we, nuts?

We decided, between ourselves, that we'd keep sending in our monthly column whether we were paid or not. It was that important to us to have a platform to express what we cared about most when it came to the mountains.

One day I picked up a letter from Mike at the post office. We hadn't heard from him in months. I took it home. Guy opened it at supper, our customary time for reading our mail, and a check fell into his hand. I watched his jaw drop, and he silently passed it over to me. Mike had paid us, in full, for every column. We were up to date; we were square. His letter told us that the September 1981 issue was the last.

By way of thanks, we wrote Mike our version of what happened during the final few minutes of the life of *New England Outdoors*: Mike, the sole survivor in an office that's down to a desk and a telephone, hears the creditors stomping up the stairs. They're on the landing, banging down the outer door. He stumbles into his inner office, slams the door, and locks it. Grabs the checkbook off a high shelf, blows off the dust, scrawls a check to Laura and Guy, hammers out a note on his ancient Underwood, stuffs the check and note in an envelope, rummages frantically for a stamp, and dashes to the mail slot seconds before the creditors beat down his inner office door.

CHAPTER thirteen

To say the very thing you mean, the whole of it, nothing more or less or other than what you really mean; that's the whole art and joy of words.

— C. S. Lewis, *Till We Have Faces*

In the fall of 1979, Stone Wall Press published our first book, *Backwoods Ethics: Environmental Concerns for Hikers and Campers*. That same fall the Appalachian Mountain Club wrote to say they'd be interested in publishing a book with us. So the mortar was hardly dry on the first project before we were off quarrying stones for the next: a comprehensive history of hiking and climbing in the mountains of the Northeast. And so began a project that we thought would take a long time, maybe as much as three years.

Thirteen years later it finally ended with the publication of two books. *Forest and Crag: A History of Hiking, Trail-Blazing, and Adventure in the Northeast Mountains* was released by AMC Books in 1989, and *Yankee Rock & Ice: A History of Climbing in the Northeastern United States* was published by Stackpole Books in 1993.

In the end, writing these books proved to be a task neither one of us could have completed without the other.

For about two and a half years we just gathered information. In this honeymoon phase of interviews and research, we traveled around the Northeast to places like the Bangor Public Library in Maine, with its well-cared-for copies of the turn-of-the-century magazine *In the Maine Woods* and its pull-chain johns in the basement, to the Boston Public Library, where we sat side by side in the high-ceilinged reading room at a long oak table with green-shaded lamps. As we ate our homemade sandwiches in the courtyard we told each other about the exciting discoveries we'd made in the last few hours.

Johnny died when we were over a year into the research. I kept expecting Guy to be derailed, to be immobilized by grief. I half-expected to walk into the cabin and find him staring at the wall or to find one morning that he just wouldn't get out of bed. At the very least I expected him to lose concentration. But he was always up at 4:15 a.m. He never stopped working. He said he was glad for this absorbing task. "It occupies my mind," he said.

For December 28, on the Barra Calendar, Guy chose this quote from T. H. White's *The Once and Future King*.

> You may grow old and trembling in your anatomies, you may lie awake at night listening to the disorder of your veins, you may miss your only love, you may see the world about you devastated by evil lunatics, or know your honour trampled in the sewers of lesser minds. There is only one thing for it then — to learn. Learn why the world wags, and what wags it. That is the only thing which the mind can never exhaust, never alienate, never be tortured by, never fear or distrust, and never dream of regretting.

Writing these two books was, at its best, a joyous, headlong journey of learning together. Shortly before his suicide, Guy told me that he had accomplished all he wanted. In a way, he was saying that he had come to the end of learning — that is, all he was interested in learning. There is always more to learn.

By 1983 we were still in the research stage (it lasted five more years) and waking up to the fact that this was an enormous undertaking, *much* larger than we had thought. For instance, we had painstakingly documented every mountain ascent in the Northeast during the colonial period. There weren't many, maybe a dozen. But Guy pointed out that if we went into this level of detail for the entire book . . . well, he'd be working on this project for the rest of his life. "This would be fine if I were a scholar," Guy said, "but I'm not." Neither was I, not in the sense that my father was. We were climbers who were interested in finding out more about how our home mountains came to be climbed. Guy became panic-stricken that, as he was writing a book on climbing, he himself would have no time to climb.

The material flooded in. Guy organized the filing system, which swelled out of the neat wooden files we had built when we constructed our cabin, into cardboard boxes picked up at the supermarket. These ended up piled three deep and encroached on our limited floor space, often serving as tables if we had a houseful of guests.

Occasionally Guy lost track of some key piece of paper. While we were working on *Forest and Crag* in the morning, sitting across from each other at our table, I'd be aware of Guy getting up and going over to the files. If he was back in a few minutes, I hardly noticed he was gone, but if the sound of shuffling paper turned frantic, I knew he wasn't finding what he was looking for. "Do you want a hand, Guy?" I'd ask. Often he didn't answer, or he mumbled and I couldn't make out his words. Either way, I stayed in my chair. I knew from experience that if I walked over to him, he would swerve around me to return to the table, grab his pencil, and start writing furiously, hunched over his pages, forcing a way around the detail-gone-missing.

A misplaced note could really upset Guy, as could his own typing mistakes. Suddenly he would rip the paper out of the typewriter, crunch it into a ball between his hands, and hurl it across the room. These outbursts seemed to rise out of nowhere, and I was always caught off guard. I felt his fury at himself, his self-castigation for a mistake of little consequence, one he knew was of little consequence. His sense of humor had vanished. I was left feeling shaken and helpless, even angry at Guy, while with my whole being I wanted what troubled him to go away. It was the same terror I had felt at my parents' dining room table, though I had no idea of that connection then. What I did know was that Guy knew the minutes were slipping away, the task he had set himself for the morning wasn't going to get completed (though it usually did), and he had jumped from the consequences of the missing note to the worst-case scenario that writing *Forest and Crag* was a lifetime sentence. As I sat there across from him, trying to regain my shattered concentration, he'd break off writing and jerk a three-by-five card out of his shirt pocket. I'd watch him bear down with his pen, then jam the card back in his pocket again. I knew he was making a note to look for the missing note.

This was what Guy had become since Johnny's death. Since I couldn't help him — in fact, all his actions were telling me to keep my distance — I helped in the only way I could: I pulled my focus away from Guy and got back to my own work on our joint project. But when Guy got upset with himself, it upset me as well, and these feelings were slow to dissipate.

At lunch I'd ask him again what he was looking for. By then enough time had passed that we could talk about it. Guy was no longer enraged, and I was no longer afraid — or at least I was less afraid. We talked about where the missing note might be filed. *Forest and Crag*'s topics overlapped, and notes could logically be located in more than one place.

"I'll look this afternoon," I would say.

"You don't need to, Laura," was Guy's reply. "Don't give up something you'd rather be doing just for that note."

But I would be glad he'd agreed to my searching for it, and if I found it (I usually did), I placed it on his side of the table where he'd discover it when he came back from working outside. Often he'd leave me a note on my side of the table.

Dear Ms. Laura,
    You're swell.

Everyone at Barra loves you.
The Committee

To write *Forest and Crag*, we tried the same approach we had used for our columns, but it didn't work.

My attempt to write a chapter bogged down. I could have told Guy I was sticking with it until I learned how. But I didn't. I knew it would have taken time. Guy felt the time pressure from this project, and I knew I would be making it worse if I used this book as a training ground for learning how to write history. "All my life I've written short," he said as *Forest and Crag* kept stretching out. I wasn't about to risk causing more anxiety for Guy — and for myself — so I found other work to do on *Forest and Crag*. It was a disappointment I kept to myself. I liked thinking of myself as a writer. It didn't come easily to me, and I didn't have much confidence. "*Forest and Crag* needs one narrative voice, Laura," Guy said. On the surface this let me bow out gracefully — though underneath I knew very well that I could be contributing to the prose, just as I had with our columns, if Guy hadn't felt so pressured. But that was only half the problem. The part I didn't see was that I was too afraid to talk with Guy about my desire to contribute to the writing of *Forest and Crag*. What I did see was the way Guy drew into himself, and what I heard was the tight and distant sound of his voice, and what I told myself was that I'd be making his life a lot more difficult if I insisted on doing some of the writing. I would only be adding to his pain; ever since Johnny died, this was what I kept trying (and failing) not to do.

What I picked up, what Guy radiated, and what I could not name, was anger. He kept the stopper in the bottle. It must have taken enormous effort of will to keep himself under control like that. What I was feeling was his suppressed anger — at himself. When an inconsequential thing like a missing *Forest and Crag* note gave Guy the excuse to uncork the bottle, his anger was frightening. I never felt physically threatened; that is, Guy was never physically violent toward me. But that made it all the more frightening as I watched him take all his stored-up frustrations — some of which must have involved me — out on himself. At these times, as I watched him trying to contain his actions, trying to do no more than rip a page out of the typewriter, he scared me because I felt what he wanted to do was hurl the machine out the window.

There were plenty of other jobs for me to do on *Forest and Crag*. A big one was putting into note form all of our source materials — books, magazine articles, everything we photocopied on our research trips, our interviews, all the letters we received. These notes went into our files, and Guy used them when he drafted the chapters. I compiled the bibliographic data used in our references. I also served as typist. Guy typed up his handwritten chapter drafts. Then he rewrote, and I typed from that.

Friends asked how we shared this collaboration. Do you both write? they asked. I didn't like this question much and usually answered it by saying that Guy was doing most of the writing. The fact was that he was doing all of it. Then Guy, for reasons of his own, would say something about how we were perfectly suited to work on this together. He was trained to grind out prose fast, he said. I'd been an editor in New York, and it was my editing that honed, pared, and beat his prose into shape. This was far from the truth. While I read his drafts and offered suggestions, I didn't edit in the way he implied. Sometimes during these conversations I said, in a small voice, "It's not like that." But no one picked up on it. I liked being seen the way Guy was telling it, even though it wasn't the truth and it made me uncomfortable.

What we did do well together was discuss all that we were learning as we delved into the rich storehouse of anecdote and fact on northeastern hill walking. Together we analyzed the major shifts in people's perspectives on the mountains over the past four centuries. What were the forces at work that influenced the early visitors who saw the mountains as scary and useless? We tried to put ourselves into the mind of a nineteenth-century traveler, for whom the term *sublime* connoted the rough and uncontrolled in nature. The sublime was tinged, on the one hand, with dread and, on the other, with spellbound rapture. In the chapter "Mountains as Sublime: 1830–1870," Guy wrote,

> The fashionableness of mountains after 1830 reflected a profoundly important change of attitude toward the mountains. To the pioneers in New England, as we've seen, mountains had been difficult, useless, hostile, obstacles to farming and travel, sanctuaries for French and Indian enemies, foreboding shrines of frightening superstition. With the conquest of the wilderness on the eastern seaboard, especially after the flush of optimism that followed national independence, fear of the mountains waned. Wilderness began to attract, not repel.

We ate, digested, slept, and breathed this sort of learning for the decade of the eighties. We talked while eating meals, while working in the garden, while hiking, while in bed. We thrived on making new discoveries and new connections, on watching our theories evolve as we unearthed new facts that led to a shift in our thinking. We asked ourselves the much-debated question: Can we ever know what really happened? How can we, as historians, break through to the gold?

It was in the mind-to-mind connection where we were most at ease, most in tune. Here we could be lighthearted. Guy started a list of the nineteenth-century figures we thought would be fun to hike with. I added to it. We were energized by what we were learning, and we energized each other. I knew Guy listened to my ideas and adjusted his own accordingly. This was where we truly collaborated.

The strength I brought to *Forest and Crag* came from the example of my father. From childhood I had witnessed the countless hours he'd spent in his study with the door shut. I remembered how he'd tacked photostats of Emily Dickinson's poems to the pine paneling so he could examine the changes in her handwriting and date when she wrote them. This kind of scholarship demanded enormous concentration and meticulous attention to detail. It took years of patient work. If the sheer length of the *Forest and Crag* writing project held terror for Guy, it held none for me. I understood the strength of mind it took to keep moving forward on a book that stretched into the unforeseeable future. I understood about pacing and not giving up. But my understanding was all at an intuitive level. I never thought of trying to communicate it to Guy in words.

An example Guy carried was his father's dedication to public service, for which he often expressed admiration. But at a more personal level, Guy labored under an overwhelming sense of responsibility.

One morning he told me he had come very close to chucking the manuscript in the woodstove.

"What stopped you?" I asked.

"The thought of all those people who have helped us."

Even then I saw this was his way of saying he couldn't let them down. After he was dead, I understood that if he had thrown our manuscript into the fire, he would have been letting me down and, worse, himself. Whether it was true or not, he blamed himself for letting others down.

Guy suggested we read aloud a world-class history on a subject unrelated to our own. We decided on Carlyle's *History of the French Revolution*. It's a hefty three volumes, so we agreed we could stop after volume one if we weren't enjoying it. But Carlyle was too good to stop, and we sailed on, picking up many useful historian's tricks. For instance, he uses the words "sea green Robespierre" over and over, the meaning deepening as Robespierre's character becomes revealed. Carlyle uses an extended storm metaphor to evoke the Reign of Terror. It starts as single drops, then enlarges to a ringing tempest with the power to sweep everything away, the good as well as the evil.

The historian Guy felt closest to was Edward Gibbon. He had discovered *The History of the Decline and Fall of the Roman Empire* while in college and often quoted Gibbon or read me selections until I too relished the architecture of his sentences. For Guy one of the great reverberating moments in intellectual history was when Gibbon laid down his pen "just before midnight" in his garden cottage in Lausanne. This marked a pause that was monumental, even heroic, with meaning. Gibbon's enormous manuscript was complete. His labor of years had reached a close.

Often during the *Forest and Crag* years I felt like the ship's keel. I wondered if my mother had felt this way as well. My job was to keep our frail little boat upright in a turbulent sea. Guy supplied the bursts of creative energy, the organization, the writing skill, but I see now that he needed my steadiness to reach the end before he laid down his pen.

In 1993 the Countryman Press released a revised edition of *Backwoods Ethics* as well as *Wilderness Ethics*, a new companion volume, which carried the subtitle *Preserving the Spirit of Wildness*.

With these books Guy and I were back to our old way of working together, as we had been when writing our column for *New England Outdoors*. In fact, much of *Wilderness Ethics* came from these revised columns as we rethought the issues ten years later. But the 1990s saw a major change in our lives that affected my writing in particular. It had to do with my knees.

One morning at breakfast I told Guy I was going to start writing short stories. I was fifty-one. Because my failing knees made climbing no longer possible for me, I needed something to fill the gaping crevasse that had opened in my life. I knew it had to be something as absorbing and important to me as climbing. I'd never written a decent word of fiction in my life. But I'd been drawn to the short story form ever since I was eight, when I'd read Edgar Allan Poe's "The Pit and the Pendulum" and experienced a wholehearted terror that would have propelled me to check under my bed except I couldn't force myself to leave the bed. I didn't know exactly why I wanted to write short stories. I later found out it had something to do with wanting readers to *feel* something — anything, including that delicious, palm-sweating terror that Poe had induced in me. Besides, after *Forest and Crag* I vowed that five thousand words was my limit.

I had never mentioned this interest to Guy. It was a private longing for which I needed a certain amount of confidence — or desperation — to start. That morning at breakfast I by no means felt confident. I didn't think I had the imagination to write fiction. But I was desperate.

That coming winter of 1992, I would often be on my own at Barra. Guy had taken a part-time caretaker's job at a climbers' cabin in the Presidential Range. There was no better time for me to start. Nonetheless, stepping into the world of fiction felt like stepping into the void. This wasn't an unfamiliar feeling. As a climber, I had often found myself on hard rock, my muscles tensing, breathing fast, not seeing where to go next, very close to falling. Guy shouted to me once,

"Relax your mind." I took a deep breath. The tension flowed out of my arms, and my weight was back on my feet, my composure on the rock regained. Although a headfirst plunge into the world of short fiction felt equally filled with risk, I knew I needed to step into this terrain of uncertain outcome.

Guy's writing was also going in a different direction. After the publication of our *Ethics* books, he had returned to an old love: baseball. In the 1970s Guy had written a few articles for *Baseball Digest*, and now he wanted to explore some baseball ideas he had.

So we continued to sit across the table from one another just the same, but we were now working on separate projects.

For three winters Guy was employed by the Randolph Mountain Club to caretake the hikers' cabin called Gray Knob, perched at tree line on Mount Adams, on a week-on/week-off basis. I spent the weeks he was away by myself, learning how to write short fiction. These winters were good for both of us. Guy thrived in his role of genial mountain host and could roam his beloved alpine world. He would return elated, with stories of tussles in the high wind of the Northern Presidentials. "All my life I've felt inadequate," he told me, "but above tree line in bad conditions — I feel good about myself up there."

For me the time at Barra was vacation. A vacation from Guy. I didn't see it then, but with Guy not there, I could relax my vigil. I felt an unnamed relief as I waved him off down the snowshoe path leading from our door, even though, as soon as he was gone, I was aware of how empty the cabin felt and how I missed him. But I became absorbed in my work and settled into my own routine, which varied little from the routine when Guy was home. On the day he was due back I began to look for him in midafternoon — listening for the crunch of his snowshoes as I sawed wood in the woodshed — even though I knew he wouldn't appear until dark.

From the beginning I showed my fiction to Guy, and when he returned from Gray Knob I often had a new story drafted. I learned that the more comments he wrote in the margins, the better he liked the story. So I kept glancing at him when he was reading to see if his pencil was moving. After I had read his comments, we talked, and the discussions left me energized and full of ideas about how to revise.

I was on my own, though, if he read a story in no time flat, dropped it on the table, and went outside. The first time this happened I thought: *he must* really *like this one since he made no comment.* But the way he strode past not wanting to be stopped said something different. When he came in I said, "This seemed all right?" I wanted him to reply: Sure. Send it out.

"I didn't get anything out of it, Laura," he said.

"But you didn't give me any comment!"

"I didn't get interested."

During my first winter of writing fiction, Guy tossed me back a story and said in that tight, careful, reined-in voice, "I don't like seeing myself in your fiction."

I was aware I was basing a character on him, but I expected him to shrug it off because, after all, this was fiction. Nonetheless I was anxious about Guy's reaction. The character I knew Guy would see as himself had communication problems with his wife. But I had made Joe and Alice's problems so different from ours, or thought I had; besides, Guy and I didn't have "problems" exactly. . . .

This story was about two couples who are close friends. Mercy and Steve are visiting Alice and Joe after a long absence. Mercy is fighting cancer. Alice is coping with the disturbing changes she sees in her friend: hair loss necessitating a wig, an unhealthy pallor, physical weakness, a missing breast. Alice also observes Steve's loving care for his wife; in fact, Mercy and Steve, Alice thinks, have drawn closer because of Mercy's life-threatening disease. Alice wishes she and Joe could be the way Mercy and Steve are. In the end Alice makes peace with her grief over Mercy, and she and Joe have reached a comfortable moment, even if she has no greater understanding of the underlying problems in her own marriage.

Guy saw himself in Joe and me in Alice, and what he saw alarmed him. The reader doesn't know what it is Joe can't talk to Alice about, but does see her being shut out by his stony silence. This causes Alice to feel an anger she never voices toward Joe. Since I never allowed the word *anger* to surface in me — I denied all feelings of anger — I wasn't aware when I was writing this story that I was showing Alice as angry.

In retrospect, I remember the feeling of holding back, keeping in check all my unformed thoughts. The censor in my head had Guy's face. Despite this, I had showed enough of what was going on for Guy to pick up on it.

Even in fiction I was not able to look squarely at what was happening between Guy and me. What would have happened if Alice had told Joe how much it hurt her that he couldn't talk? Alice never confronts Joe. In the end we leave them at a tender moment but no closer to solving their problems than they were at the beginning, a recurring scene for Guy and me.

When Guy returned from Gray Knob, I showed him this story, hoping he wouldn't see himself, fearing he would. But I didn't expect that the anger he radiated when he said, "I don't like seeing myself in your fiction," would come close to derailing me from writing stories.

At the time I chalked it all up to his feeling of privacy. His strong sense of his own autonomy, I rationalized, gave him a built-in resistance to seeing himself as a character. But deep down I was angry. I wanted to be able to write what I wanted to write. But I *couldn't* hurt Guy, who hurt so much already. I solved this by telling myself I'd leave him out of my fiction. I had a thick folder of story ideas, none of which included Guy.

I put Joe and Alice's story away for several months. Eventually, I took it out again and revised it. After a while I showed it to Guy. "Send it out," he said. He ended up being as delighted as I when this story was published.

Now I see that even in my revisions I had taken the story no further. Alice's anger and her fear of her husband's reaction — the *real* story, the truth I didn't write — never come to the surface. Guy must have felt he had nothing to be concerned about. I had managed to sidestep our problems, even in fiction.

Guy had been writing fiction for years. He hadn't turned out many stories, but nearly all were published. My foray into fiction writing rekindled Guy's interest. He gave me his stories for comment, and we discussed them. I suggested we try collaborating on fiction. But this never went anywhere. I told myself it didn't interest Guy to labor over stories, to work through revision after revision, the way it did me.

But I think now that it was more than that. Fiction comes from deep within. Guy wrote a father-and-son story. The son has a job — his first — at a garage. He longs to enter into the camaraderie of these guys who live for cars, but his feeling of inadequacy, the risk of looking foolish, keeps him outside the circle. The father sees all this and is filled with heartache for his son, but he is unable even to start a conversation. All the father can do, when he drops his son off at work, is watch the young man get smaller and smaller in the rearview mirror as he drives away.

Guy wrote another story about a man who can make the neighborhood kids laugh but lives at odds with himself and ends up jumping over a waterfall. Guy called this story "Over the Brink." These stories came from painful territory that he didn't want to explore any further, especially not in conversation with me. Though I sensed no outright resistance to my idea of collaboration — he enjoyed talking about his stories — I often felt our discussions ended too soon. After his suicide, friends told me that when they trod on conversational ground that Guy didn't want to stay with — even if he had brought up the subject — he just skittered off, a figurative elf escaping into the deep woods. The friend would be left with the impression that Guy had just played the Ace of Trumps, picked up the deck, and slid out of the room, closing the door on the subject as he left.

Guy began writing poetry in the last few years of his life. If he revealed his inner turmoil anywhere, it was here. Again, he showed me everything he wrote. He showed close friends his poetry as well. He and I could discuss what worked line by line and what didn't. We could talk about word choice and clarity. But we did not talk about what lay behind the words, what the poems meant for Guy. I was pretty numb myself by that time. By the mid-1990s, I too was doing anything to avoid conversations that seemed to drive the wedge deeper between us.

His poems were often about his feelings of isolation and loss, regret, remorse, shame, and blame. Though I saw he was writing about his own darkness within, I responded as if it were a painting on a wall. I'd been looking at this same painting for years. Guy had made it so clear that he didn't want me to do more than look at it, that looking was all I was up to doing now.

He wrote a poem called "Together, Alone" that ended, "So why do you smile? I do not / Understand how you can smile." I read it at breakfast, the time when he showed me his completed poems, and he spoke the last line looking at me: "How can you smile?" he asked.

"I don't know," I said. I understood what he meant: How can life look rosy to you when it looks like hell to me? I remember his face, woebegone, lost, the face of a traveler who's nerved himself to ask for directions one last desperate time for a place he has been trying to locate for years.

"It's just how I am," I added in a bright cheery voice. I remember thinking that I was in some way better than him for being able to smile. That smiling was easy for me and it would be for him too if he'd just decide it was.

I so rarely felt I had the upper hand with Guy. I had it now, and I seized it. I gave a truthful answer that showed no understanding. And oh! what an opportunity I missed. Guy had started across the bridge — he was holding out his hand. This time it was I who remained unbudgeably planted on the other side. By the end I was no more capable than Guy of spanning my side of the bridge.

After Guy was gone I reread his poems. *Then* I felt his overwhelming isolation; I felt too his desire to overcome and connect on a deep level with those closest to him. And I felt as well his inability to do this. And mine.

There was much in Guy that lived to make the world a better place. In Washington he saw himself fighting for rights and justice; through our work on the Franconia Ridge and in our books he fought to preserve wildness for future generations. He felt that he failed in Washington, and he felt that our books hadn't lived up to his hopes for them. In his own eyes he had "let down" his sons. He had warned me when we first met: "I hurt the ones I love, Laura." The quote for January 8 on the Barra Calendar was one that Guy took from George Eliot's *Middlemarch*.

> "What do we live for, if it is not to make life less difficult to each other?"

Here are some of Guy's poems:

Outside the Room
Harsh footsteps echo down the corridor
And round the corner. Shouldn't you assume
That backward glance was meant for you, before
They all withdrew into that other room
And someone closed the door? But that was one
You tried, remember? Do they want you there?
What would you say? Again some feeble pun?
Obscure allusion? Would you really dare
To tell a story of your own — and botch
The point? And shrivel up within. Quick drop
Your eyes from patronizing smiles, not watch
Their cruel kindness, wishing you could stop.
Shriek anger, anguish, tear the place apart!
You know you won't. Does that not break your heart?

Spring 1998

Red Squirrel in the Attic
Tearing up the place. What a mess!
Don't know how he got in or when–or why —
But he must've been in there some time.
Getting into everything:
Bits of insulation scattered about
(Remember how hard it was to put that insulation in?)
Torn corners of old memorabilia,
Old speeches penned for famous men,
Ideas buried in gloom of irrevocable past
In darkened dusty corners of the loft.
Did he seek comforting material for a nest?
I could have told him it won't work for that.
No way to keep him out now.
They don't see the dark corners of the loft.
Maybe we could just leave it alone.
But what a mess!
Of course it'll get worse.

June 13, 1998

Living Will: To Laura on Christmas Day
When time has run his course for me,
When mountains lie beyond my power
And neither woods at twilight hour
Nor charms of garden do I see;
When troubles come too thick and fast
And useful work no more is fun,
And that dark fiend who took each son
Perhaps has come for me at last;
When mind and body seem to rust,
And all my dreams have turned to dust,
And nightmare darkens all my day;
I hope I'll smile once more and say —
Just once, though all my world's awry —
Merry Christmas, with love,
to Laura
from Guy

January 12, 1996

At the last possible moment we were given a chance to collaborate again.

Guy's cousin, John Daniel, ran a small, independent publishing company in Santa Barbara, California. In 1998 John wrote us saying he was sure we must have a lot of material —mountain stories — kicking around, both fiction and nonfiction. Why didn't we put something together and send it to him? He'd act as our agent and market it.

So we sent John a manuscript of twenty pieces. Five were short stories by me written in the last few years. Five were climbing stories Guy had written a decade or two earlier. The remainder was nonfiction pieces, mostly collaborations. John found a home for this collection with the Mountaineers Books. It was published as *A Fine Kind of Madness: Mountain Adventures Tall and True* in the summer of 2000.

We fell back into the rhythm without missing a beat since our last big writing project together in the early nineties. We sat facing each other at the wooden table, its surface scarred from our typewriters. We wrote introductions to each of the pieces. We "exchanged papers" and penned in some suggestions on each other's work. Guy invariably made tweaks that tightened the meaning of my sentences and drove my half-thought-out points right into the bone. We both found this an exciting, energizing few weeks.

By that time we both knew Guy wouldn't be around to see the results or bask in the kudos, if there were any.

Over the years we often told each other that we had created at Barra the perfect writing environment. The ideal writers' colony. Why, we joked, writers would gladly pay to come here and be free of phones, faxes, and email. When we sat at our table on writing mornings we knew we were guaranteed uninterrupted hours. Our windows faced south. We looked out on our garden. We watched it evolve from the end of April, when we planted the peas, until around Thanksgiving, when the snow came to cover the Brussels sprouts stalks; with all their sprouts picked, these had just a tuft of leaves left at the top that turned them into incongruous palm trees. As the snow deepened the Brussels sprouts stalks disappeared.

Guy was always the early riser. Now it is I — the one who considered 7:00 a.m. the only sane rising hour — who is up in the predawn hours, sitting at my desk, a different desk in a different house, my pencil scratching a rhythm across the paper. I pause. I listen. I feel what needs to be said next. I'm writing solo now, but because of half a lifetime of shared thoughts, it can still feel like collaboration.

CHAPTER fourteen

Base men being in love have then a nobility in

their natures more than is native to them.

— Shakespeare, *Othello*

selected by Guy for the Barra Calendar for February 14, Valentine's Day

He woke me every morning at 7:00 a.m., and I knew if his hug was brief and preoccupied that he was in a distant place. I always awoke feeling cheerful, wondering, as Piglet put it, "What's going to happen exciting today?" But if Guy was enclosed in his own world, a helpless feeling overcame me almost before I'd opened my eyes. Suddenly the day was off to a very bad start.

"What's the trouble, Guy?" I'd ask as I stirred our oatmeal on the cookstove. I knew I wasn't going to get very far with this question, but he was so obviously unhappy that I pushed myself to ask it.

He'd continue to grab cereal spoons and bowls with the kind of concentrated energy that told me he wasn't going to talk. By the time we sat down for breakfast I'd be fighting tears. Since Guy didn't like to cause me unhappiness, he'd stammer out a few sentences. This would lead to more questions from me, and by this time I'd have moved to his lap, and we'd be hugging each other, me trying to understand, him choking on words, in tears himself. Then, "Our cereal is getting cold," Guy would say. This meant that we had work to do that day, and I knew how he felt about falling behind. So I'd get up and move to my chair, feeling less cut off than when he had awakened me, though also feeling that too much remained unsaid.

On the worst days, if we were not able to right ourselves during the course of our morning's work, we sat in silence over lunch out at our handmade table and bench under the sheltering branches of the Gabriel Birch. Without words, we picked up the peanut butter jar and the remains of the bread and headed for the house and our ten-minute nap. We lay side by side on the bed, our bare arms not quite touching under the blanket. When we got up I put the mail in my pack and left for the relief of a walk and a brief chat about gardens with Nancy at the post office. As I stumbled, head down, back up our steep hill, my mind was still in disarray. I could turn around right now and hitchhike to New York City and happier days. I imagined myself out on the side of the road, standing in the gravel with my thumb out, arriving at my friend Annie Barry's apartment in the East Village and feeling her warm welcome. I just wouldn't show up at our cabin. It would get dark. I wondered what Guy would do then.

Guy was splitting wood as I regained our clearing. His back was to me, and he had ten pieces set up on his long chopping block inside the woodshed. I paused to watch as he went systematically down the row, splitting each one in half with a precise and mighty crack. He was absorbed in his work, whaling away on the rock maple, and I sensed this gave him some relief from the pressures of his own internal maelstrom. I said, "Hi, Guy."

He spun around and smiled, a somewhat downturned smile, a little shame-faced, but his eyes held mine. He set down his splitting maul and extended an arm. "Moley," he said. "Is that really you?"

When I dreamed about Guy, he was whirling in the center of a group of people I didn't know, and who didn't know me. He was talking, eyes flashing, hands carving points out of thin air. The others' eyes were riveted on him. I held myself to one side. The group revolved past me, Guy in concentrated conversation with a woman who looked at him with adoring eyes. He didn't see me. He didn't glance in my direction.

I think I was afraid Guy would stop loving me if I demanded too much of him. I thought of him as strong. I didn't see then his emotional instability, his brokenness. What I saw was a valiant struggle to come back from the death of one son and the uncertain death of another. That was the side he was showing, the only side he wanted people to see.

Guy hated to dream. He told me that he had nightmares about his sons, though he never gave me details. Still, I knew he was preoccupied with how his sons had died. Or, if Bill was alive, what had happened to him? He went back and forth about Bill. Had Johnny died in pain? He wondered about the last thoughts of both his sons, and in the next moment he would say, "But I don't know if Bill is dead."

The calendar quote for April 1, the day Guy had chosen to mark Johnny's death, was from George Eliot's *Middlemarch*.

> Intense memory forces a man to own his blameworthy past.
> With memory set smarting like a reopened wound, a man's past

is not simply a dead history, an outworn preparation of the present; it is not a repeated error shaken loose from the life; it is a still quivering part of himself, bringing shudders and better flavors and the tinglings of a merited shame.

And what about his youngest son? Guy had set money aside for Jim's college education before we moved to Barra. When Jim came to draw on this fund, tuitions had skyrocketed and Guy's contribution was meager. The fact that he could not have foreseen this was, as Guy saw it, no reason to let himself off the hook. Later I would wonder: If Guy blamed himself on the practical matter of Jim's education, which he could talk about, what kind of self-blame did he put himself through over Bill and Johnny?

Not until Guy himself was dead did I come to see that he needed to feel the pain, to keep it throbbing and alive. Pushing his pain to the limit and beyond was a self-flagellation for transgressions he could neither atone for nor forgive himself. For January 16, Guy chose a quote from T. E. Lawrence's *Revolt in the Desert*: "There can be no rest-houses for revolt; no dividend of joy paid out. Its spirit is accretive, to endure as far as the senses endure, and to use each advance as base for . . . deeper privation, sharper pain."

A couple of things happened to help me.

First, Guy kept on telling me that I had nothing to do with his moods. It wasn't me, he said. It wasn't about me; it wasn't my fault. It wasn't anything I had done. *I* wasn't making the problem for him. It took years, but finally I let that sink in.

And second, by 1983, two years after Johnny's death, I woke up to the fact that my parents needed me more than once a year. In the late 1970s my mother had gone off the road on her way back from a cocktail party and ended up in the hospital. Guy and I came down to be with my father and help my mother when she got home, and it was on that visit that I discovered she hid her liquor in the clothes basket and stashed her empties in the dryer.

Since Johnny's death, I had been concerned that my parents' problems would only add to Guy's difficulties. I thought he would regard them as another troublesome interference to the smooth running of his daily life. But the truth was that he could handle the shameful — and to me terrifying — drama of my parents' alcoholism much better than I could. The Christmas when we arrived on their doorstep to be welcomed by my father falling down the stairs didn't put Guy off. Nor did the scenes at the family dinner table, my father's long pauses filled in by my mother's neon-bright conversation as the great man slid into slurry inarticulation, his interior castle now fallen into ruins. "I'm just sorry I only caught flashes of that superb mind everyone talks about, Laura," Guy said.

But my own coming to grips with my parents' problems gave me something to focus on other than Guy. I needed his support; Guy saw this, and it no doubt helped to pull him out of himself. My parents liked him. I had known that from the beginning. Guy had a firsthand knowledge of alcoholism, so theirs was familiar ground. Most important to me, the scary, emotionally charged territory of my family had nothing to do with him. He couldn't blame himself for this.

I stepped up my trips to Lawrenceville to every three or four months. This gave us a break from each other. I was aware that I needed the break from Guy, but I didn't want to admit it. Thinking of it as a break implied there was something I needed to get away from. This was a wayward thought, tainted with disloyalty. I sensed on some unadmittable level that Guy wanted to keep the cracks plastered, so this was what I wanted too. This allowed no room for thoughts about taking a break from Guy.

If it was spring, something was happening that I didn't want to miss, like the progress of the snowmelt or the first crocuses. If it was summer, I would return, only gone a week, to find the squashes filling in the garden with their tangle of sturdy, tube-like vines. If it was winter, Guy had my snowshoes in the car when he picked me up at the bus station, along with my windpants and the ice axe I used as a walking stick. On the drive back he'd tell me about the flock of chickadees that greeted him at the entrance to the woods when he went down for water every morning. "They always asked me: When is Laura coming home?" he said, with a glance at me from where he sat so solid in the driver's seat, knobby hands on the wheel.

Guy parked in the winter spot and turned off the headlights. I was back in the kind of darkness that revealed the stars. The air felt cold, fresh, and clean against my face. Such a contrast to New Jersey. We strapped on our snowshoes and mushed the mile home, unable to stop talking.

As we crossed into the clearing, I'd see our cabin sitting there, secure and bathed in moonlight. I opened the door. "The house smells so good," I always said as I breathed in the wood smoke, the dill and basil I'd dried that fall, the unnumbered loaves of bread. I could only smell this when I'd been away. I was home.

Often my trips allowed Guy to accomplish some special task, like cleaning out the cellar or building a new set of shelves. Or reorganizing the books, relocating the references to a handy spot near our table. Or putting up a new display of pictures sent by friends of a recent climb in the special frame he'd built from our wood.

I always found something. Some unexpected surprise he had kept a secret until I walked in the door. "Your trips away give me the chance to do these things for you, Laura," he said.

On one of my visits to Lawrenceville, three years after Johnny's death, I decided to talk with an old family friend, Sheila Morgan, who was a therapist. Her husband had taught in my father's English Department, and Sheila had known me from my childhood. I wanted to tell Sheila — a professional, yet a friend — about Guy losing his sons and how his deep despair was affecting me.

"Take a walk. Visit a friend," Sheila said. She helped me to see that I could best help Guy by taking care of myself.

I was already doing this with my afternoon mail runs and brief chats with Nancy at the post office. Just walking to the village brought me back to myself. Village life proceeded along, winter or summer, rain or shine, with a sweet monotony I found reassuring. I felt the contrast with my own life, where I maintained a twenty-four-hour vigil, silently checking in with Guy, feeling a surge of relief when he was fine, and something close to despair when his world was awry. On these walks out with the mail I could let down my guard. As I reentered our clearing I knew just by the way Guy was splitting wood — whether the sound was clean, even, and methodical or carried a frantic, jerky energy — how he was.

I never mentioned my half-hour talk with Sheila to Guy. For that brief time in Lawrenceville I had stepped off the Barra campus. A few times after Johnny had died I asked Guy if he wanted to talk to a therapist, but he remained dead set against seeking professional help. Perhaps this had to do with his unfortunate experience as a teenager with the psychoanalysts, but Guy's feelings on this subject — that therapy would do him no good whatsoever — never wavered. Not telling Guy about my talk with Sheila felt enormously disloyal. I had put myself in the position of keeping a secret. But I preferred not telling to telling him. I was sure he would disapprove, perhaps heap scorn on what I had done. It would have been his view that I had shown weakness by seeking outside help. Moral weakness. I couldn't reveal to Guy that I didn't have the strength of character to handle my problems single-handedly. He would have been only too aware that he was the source of those problems. I couldn't risk putting him in the painful position of thinking he'd become such a problem for me that I needed to seek professional help. Every day since Johnny's death I'd seen the evidence of Guy's mental discipline. I knew the strength of will it had taken to overcome his drinking problem. By sneaking off to a therapist, I had broken some code that had hardened into unstated law between us. The last thing I could do, because his reaction was literally too terrifying to think about, was tell him what I had done.

Guy wrote in his memoir, "If there is one strain in my make-up that has always been uppermost, it is my passionate insistence on my own (and anyone's, if they want it) individuality. I will *not* be placed in any pigeonholes." As Guy saw it, doctors of the mind turned you into a "type" and pasted on a label that placed you in a category, a box. But it went deeper. Guy could explore with no one the painful place within. He was unwilling to reveal the source of his shame and self-blame. Yet he was aware of how self-destructive this was. He knew that by holding tight to his worst secret thoughts he was in fact piling on more shame and digging deeper into the dunghill of blame. No wonder I sensed so strongly that he could not have stood to hear about my conversation with a therapist. This was a mirror he didn't want to look into. But if I had been able to hold it up, if I'd been able to be honest and tell him, what might have happened then?

Jim and his wife Kathleen came to visit us in mid-October 1994. We hadn't seen them since attending their wedding in Colorado nine years earlier. There had been little correspondence since then, and in fact very little contact between father and son. I knew this distressed Guy. Part of Guy's wedding present had been money to hire a professional photographer for the wedding. He had never seen the pictures.

Although Guy saw his first wife at Jim's wedding, he had had almost no other contact with Emily after the divorce — not over whether to look for Bill, or over Johnny when it became clear he was in an unstable mental state. Guy made a point after Jim's wedding of putting something in the mail to him about once a month. He rarely heard back, and after a while his notes decreased to a handful of times a year. Jim suggested that his father phone because he didn't like to write letters. Guy phoned a few times when we were staying overnight with friends and there was access to a phone. He found these conversations difficult. So Jim wouldn't write letters, and Guy didn't like to use the telephone. But Jim and Kathleen did finally come to visit in 1994.

They had brought the wedding pictures, and we spent all that first afternoon looking at them, as well as showing Jim and Kathleen our pictures, especially albums Guy had made of the Waterman family and taken down to the big family reunion held at his sister Bobbie's house in Connecticut in 1989. Jim hadn't come to that, and there had been much speculation as to why. Guy had been hoping up to the last moment that Jim would show up.

But at Barra in mid-October of 1994, everyone was trying to let bygones be bygones and just enjoy this visit. The four of us picked apples, walking up into the part of our land we called The Highlands, where we had three or four big old apple trees that could always be counted on to produce good cooking apples. Over the next few days Kathleen and I made over four dozen quarts of applesauce.

Jim and Guy worked on Twin Firs Camp. Jim had been a carpenter for six or seven years after he moved to Colorado and before he went to college. At supper Guy told Kathleen and me how Jim had figured out a way to get a key supporting log in place. Guy's face was radiant. Jim looked pleased too. I felt a surge of relief. There was a lot riding on this visit.

The last morning Jim and Guy talked about John and Bill, which they never had done before. Guy had not seen Jim since Johnny's death in 1981, except at Jim's wedding in 1985. They talked about early family life, when all the boys were small. Kathleen and I listened, taking turns grinding apple pulp through my Foley food mill.

They left later that afternoon.

I wrote in my journal after they had gone: "Hard to describe the last two days, but enough to say this visit was GOOD for G + J, for me, for K, for all of us together."

"I'm glad you and Jim could talk," I said to Guy as I started the woodstove for supper.

Guy began pacing, nearly sprinting back and forth across the cabin, and I knew something was very wrong. "The other two must have felt the same. Oh, God, it's worse than I thought."

"Felt the same . . . ?" What had I missed?

"The hikes and the climbing. The part I thought I'd done right."

Then I remembered: Jim had said that he felt the only way he could have a relationship with his father was to go hiking and climbing with him.

"I let people down. Don't count on me." Guy was shouting, waving his arms. "I let everyone down."

He ran to the piano and threw himself into heart-wrenching blues. I worked on the potatoes, tears leaking onto the cutting board. I had seen it all wrong. I had so much wanted this to be a happy reunion of father and son that I had made it be that. I had blotted out the twinge I felt when I picked up that their conversation had turned hard. Guy's voice had been clipped and metallic as he kept himself, for better or worse, from saying the things he was thinking — what he had just told me. Jim's voice pushing, emphasizing, growing stronger, making his points clear, in his logical, lawyerlike tone.

They never saw each other again.

My brother Tom also made infrequent visits to Barra. After graduating from Williams College, he had moved back into his old room in our parents' house. He found a job in nearby Princeton working with a computer. He took me to meet this machine he was spending most of his waking hours with one weekend when I came out from New York. It occupied one windowless room and was as large as a factory boiler. As we circled it my brother explained how it worked. I saw only its blinking red, yellow, and blue bars, the pinpoints of light, but Tommy saw into the potential and the mystery — he was an acolyte at the altar. He had wanted to go to Princeton and study engineering, but Dad had allowed him to apply to only one college, Williams, his own alma mater. For the first two years Tommy got by on what he had already learned at the Lawrenceville School. The last two years he spent checked out with alcohol.

His job with the fledgling computer company couldn't save him. The police picked him up for drunk driving, and my brother lost his license for two years. He spent some time on Payne-Whitney's psychiatric ward in New York, and when I went to visit him he was wearing his red plaid bathrobe, which I remembered from home. He introduced me to his new friend, an older, bald guy with pale, fleshy arms who didn't talk above a whisper. The doors were locked, just as Guy had said. A month after Tommy got out he came to visit me in New York and downed my best bottle of Cutty Sark when I was at work.

But back home one evening he overheard my mother talking on the telephone to a friend about her husband's decision to join Alcoholics Anonymous. My brother made the decision to do the same. As he put it to me later, "I didn't want to end up like Dad."

He pulled his life together and moved out of his old bedroom to an apartment in Princeton. Then, in the late 1970s, he jumped to southern California, where he worked with computers for the University of California for most of the next twenty years.

"Did you love Dad?" I asked him after our father was dead.

"No," he said. "I respected him, but Dad scared me."

Tommy had long periods of sobriety, he told me, then would nearly lose his job, or lose it and be granted time out to get himself together again.

After my father died in 1985, and I had helped my mother move to a retirement home in the New Hampshire town near where we had spent many summers, Tom and I had taken to meeting there about twice a year. It was easier for both of us. It was easier for Guy.

When Tommy visited us at Barra he arrived with his medications, vitamins, tinctures, ointments, and salves — and more every visit — which he spread out on the shelves in our guest quarters. On one of these visits Guy said, "I want you to see something, Laura," and he took me around to look at the pharmacy. "Your brother told me one entire bag was filled with this," he said, gesturing toward the shelves. This self-help stuff of my brother's I knew Guy lumped in the same category as therapists.

Over supper Tommy gave us the details of what he was doing for his baldness. He had spent a lot of money. I knew Guy was disgusted by this conversation. Guy's distaste for makeup on women amounted to phobia. My experiment with some fancy three-step face cream a New York friend had sent me precipitated the most serious disagreement we ever had because I refused to give in. But I finally did. I ended up mailing back the cream.

"In southern California you can fix anything you don't like about how you look, if you're willing to spend money," Tommy said.

Guy didn't reply to that. I managed a weak smile, but I wished Tommy would just stop talking about this. It was making Guy uncomfortable. I imagined him thinking that Tommy's "pharmacy" and self-help schemes were a waste of money, showed a distortion of values, and implied a lack of willpower and mental and moral fiber and that talking about this at Barra was just plain inappropriate.

Tommy moved off baldness and onto astrology, which he treated as a serious science. Guy pooh-poohed planting by the phases of the moon and dismissed the age-old connection of late frosts with the full moon. None of this had anything to do with astrology, but astrology was in the same vague, speculative ballpark. Guy asked a few questions, though I heard in his tone that he thought Tommy was wasting his time. Astrology was incapable of solving anyone's problems, and Guy would rather be out splitting wood.

Tommy changed the subject and asked Guy to give him a list of the top-ten classics. He wanted to improve his reading, he said. My heart rose at this, and Guy launched into talking about authors and titles, pulling out a three-by-five card to write things down. As Guy was talking, Tommy reached a book down from the shelf and started thumbing through it, glancing up from the pages, then down again. Guy scribbled out a few more titles and tossed the card over to my brother, who reshelved the book with a guilty look.

On the first morning of one of Tommy's visits, Guy woke me and said, "I don't know what I'm going to do."

"About what?" I was alarmed. He sounded so desperate.

"Tommy came in at five thirty and asked for a cup of coffee." I knew what this meant. Guy would have had to start the cookstove and get water boiling — a half-hour interruption of his work.

"Then," Guy went on in the same at-wit's-end tone, "after the fire had died out, he wanted hot water for shaving." He looked at me as if Tommy had moved in and this was going to go on forever.

I had heard their voices. Guy had perhaps sounded a little too controlled, not relaxed, but I had heard nothing alarming. Nothing that had prevented me from dozing off again. Now I realized that Guy's morning had been completely disrupted — all the correspondence or book work he had planned didn't get done — because of my demanding brother. Somehow I felt responsible for this. I should have been able to prevent this.

When Tommy brought up memories from our childhood — the *Green Avenue Bulletin*, for instance, the newspaper he and his friend Martin put together by riding their bikes around the neighborhood ferreting out stories, such as old Mrs. Satterswaite getting bitten by her cat — I kept thinking that these conversations were probably boring Guy. I saw how I was acting toward my brother and felt disloyal and mean. Yet Guy's mental comfort came first; I would do whatever it took to ensure his peace of mind, even if it meant cutting myself off from my brother.

So my brother and I began meeting at my mother's retirement home in southern New Hampshire. I hoped we would find again the easy pleasure in each other's company that we had enjoyed as children when we played on the Oriental rug in our parents' living room, constructing card houses as high as skyscrapers while *The Magic Flute* blasted out of our father's hi-fi system. But too much had changed for Tommy, and though I did not see it, I had aligned myself with Guy.

The fall after our mother died, in 1997, my brother returned to Barra for a visit.

His letters preceding this event had told us he was taking early retirement. He didn't have anything lined up — maybe he'd take a trip, he didn't know — but he hated his situation at work.

"I don't understand what's going on," I said to Guy. Tommy's letters were often full of how much he liked his job.

The other news was that he'd just been handed a cancer diagnosis.

When he arrived I could see that he wasn't doing well at all. He had been putting on weight for the last several years. His face was puffy. He would fall silent, as if it was just too much effort to speak.

Our twin cousins had joined us for this visit, and immediately they picked up that Tommy was in bad shape. I asked him about his cancer. Well, he'd probably made it sound worse than it was. It was slow-growing.

"Awful, Tommy," someone said. "The radiation. Losing your hair." His hand shot up to his hair that he'd spent a fortune on. He sent me a stricken look.

The last evening he broke down in the restaurant. I had Guy, he said, the twins had each other, and he had no one. "I'm concerned for my future," he sobbed into his hands.

We all hastened to assure him we loved him. We encouraged him to seek help. He said he'd tried that route too many times. Most of his life. Nothing helped.

He left the next day.

I wrote him right away. I wanted to know if he'd made it back to California. I wanted him to know I was thinking of him.

He forgot my birthday later that month, and that was a very bad sign.

Ten days after that a neighbor walked in with a message for me to call the state police. They told me that my brother had been found on the floor of his condo, dead a week. The police asked if he'd had an alcohol problem. "Yes," I said.

"There was strong evidence he'd been drinking," they informed me.

CHAPTER fifteen

A man who decides to commit suicide puts a full stop to his being, he turns his back on the past, he declares himself a bankrupt and his memories to be unreal.

— Boris Pasternak, *An Essay in Autobiography*

On July 3, 1998, Guy asked for my help, though not in words.

That afternoon our friend Mike Young showed up unexpectedly. He and I were sitting on the porch when Guy appeared at the bottom of the garden, home from a hike to the White Mountains. He unlatched the lower gate and walked slowly up past the rows of beans and corn. He took his time closing the upper gate, then proceeded up the path as if he were in no hurry to reach the porch. As he drew closer I saw that he had that squinty look about the eyes, a sign to me of his reluctance to engage with an unexpected guest. I was surprised, and a bit upset with Guy. Why should he be holding back? Mike was a dear friend whom he hadn't seen in several years.

The three of us had supper on the porch in the warm summer evening. We chatted with Mike about his plans. He was moving back east after years of being away. Around ten o'clock Mike went out to sleep in Twin Firs Camp. I was sitting at our table, reading for a few minutes before going to bed, when I became aware of Guy pacing back and forth beside my chair.

"I tried to jump off Cannon Cliff today," he said.

My eyes leaped to his face. *It's as though a kitchen knife has slipped, the blade drawing itself across your fingers, slicing deep into the flesh. You stare at your fingers, but see no blood. So it's not so bad. But the blood wells up, beading along the edges of the wound, spilling down your hand, which begins to shake. This cut is deep, deeper than you thought.* I went numb.

"Just take one big step." Guy's voice. He was standing in front of me. "I thought this would be easy."

This is crazy, but this is Guy talking, and I know he isn't crazy. So I know he is serious.

"I was at the top of the cliff before eight."

"Near which route?"

"The Whitney-Gilman."

The narrow arête we've climbed many times that looks across the Notch to the Franconia Ridge and 600 feet down to the talus, a rock-strewn slope with boulders the size of cars.

"I sat down to eat my ice cream . . ."

"A pint?"

"Vanilla. A last treat. But I heard voices down on the talus and didn't think I had much time, so I ate fast and ended up feeling bloated. Then the voices stopped."

"Where did they go?"

"I don't know."

"I'm sorry you had to bolt your ice cream, Guy," I said. I couldn't make what he was telling me seem real. He was standing within touching distance of my chair.

"I sat staring at the Franconia Ridge and thinking about our trail work. All the years. The sun was so warm I took off my shirt. I think the sun had something to do with why I couldn't jump."

Good sun, I think.

"I stood up and propped the sign I'd made against my pack."

"Your sign?"

Guy dug a piece of cardboard out of his pack and showed me.

> to whom it may concern:
> this is a deliberate jump.
> it is not an accident.
> please notify:
> Laura Waterman
> East Corinth, Vt.
> The Car Keys are with
> Identification Cards in Top
> Flap Pocket of Pack

I stared at Guy's handwriting: black lettering made with a thick magic marker.

"I walked to the edge. I fully expected to make this last step. Just walk off." His voice turned high-pitched. "I couldn't do it. The space. I couldn't step into that nothingness. So I tried lowering myself onto the rock face. . . ."

It's all loose. . . ."

"Yes, on the Black Dike side. I started dancing from foot to foot, to break off a hold so I would fall. I kept telling myself to let go. A foothold broke, but my hand gripped."

Guy was reliving this. One half of my mind listened as if this were a climber's story about a close call. *Plenty of adrenaline, but it ends up fine.* The other half of my mind was collapsed in fear. I stretched my hands across my thighs and squeezed — the cold sweat on my palms penetrated the fabric of my pants.

"I pulled myself back up over the edge. Then I stood on top, right on the edge, and swayed back and forth. I couldn't make myself fall." He keeps pacing in front of me. "When I left this morning I wasn't planning on coming back."

I can't imagine him not back. "When you woke me to say goodbye you seemed upset," I said. "I watched out the window, and you flung a look back. I thought about you all day."

"You did?" he said.

I nodded.

He shrugged. "I packed up my signs and came down. Listen, Laura, I've heard that after an unsuccessful suicide attempt you can feel glad to be back in the land of the living. The world looks like a rosy place again. I didn't feel this way. I felt utterly defeated. I don't want to be here, and I don't see any way out. I passed two people on the way down. The last thing I wanted was to talk with anyone."

Guy came to rest where I was sitting in the chair at the table. He looked at me with pleading eyes. "In a few days I want to try again. But I don't know if I can do it. I'm terrified of making that big step."

I thought about standing up and giving him a hug, but kept feeling that kind of numbness I'd heard about when you cut off your foot with an axe. It lies there, detached from your leg. You just can't take it in. I didn't feel anger. I never thought of stopping him. I just jumped, as I always had, into wanting to help him do what he wanted to do. And deep, deep down, at the level of instinct, I felt the jolt a small animal feels in the desperate search to save its own life. "Guy," I said, looking at his face, "if this is what you want, I have to be in a better position."

He nodded.

Before going to bed, I wrote in my journal, "If he really feels this way we should plan for it. This is awful. Guy feels totally uninterested in life."

The next morning, when Guy awakened me with a hug as he always did, I said, "I didn't sleep well."

"Neither did I." We smiled at each other.

Something in me had shifted, lifted. What he had tried to do yesterday had pried things open. Not that I questioned his decision to take his own life. Guy seemed so sure of this. Only, since this was his plan, the next logical step was to make sure I would be all right after he was gone. My own future, one without Guy, was what had opened up.

We had breakfast with Mike, who got into a conversation with Guy about the senators he had known — Lyndon Johnson, Everett Dirksen, Robert Taft, and Jacob Javits. Guy talked, telling stories with his usual animated energy. *On some level*, I thought, *he is enjoying this.* Then he and Mike began speculating about what makes for great leadership. I kept thinking: *To Mike this is like any other visit on a summer morning at Barra.* It never crossed my mind to talk to Mike, who knew about Guy's unnamed moods and was a doctor. Guy had come back. He had told me everything, and I had forgiven him without even thinking about it.

As I kneaded my bread, half-listening to Mike and Guy, I knew that Guy and I had started down a new road together. The renewed closeness I felt — and I sensed he felt it too — came from this complicity, though I saw it then as only a continuation of all our years of working side by side. This would be our last side-by-side walk, and at the end we would go our separate ways. On this road we would not meet any fellow travelers.

As soon as Mike left, Guy strode over to his desk and picked up some folders stacked in the upper-right-hand corner. He carried them over to the table.

"Did you see these yesterday, Laura?" he asked.

"No," I said.

"I was worried you might have found them before I got back."

The top one contained notes he'd written to family members and friends, with a note to me asking if I would deliver them. He showed me the items that would help me to carry on, such as our schedule for the rest of the year and the finances. He left directions for wood collection that summer, noting which firewood stacks I needed to bring in and which areas in the woodlot I should take trees from next.

Then he said, "Look at this." From his shirt pocket he pulled *one* card. It was his schedule for yesterday, July 3. I felt myself grow cold. Gone was the card on which he kept the list of birds seen and heard each day; gone was the grocery list card and the card for hardware and clothing purchases. The weather card was gone, as was the card for wood. Guy was down to *one card.* More than anything else, this let me know that he had not intended to come back.

He didn't stop there. He showed me his shelf by the table where he kept items for reading: clippings friends sent us in the mail, magazines, anything that we set aside to read later. It was empty. I hadn't noticed this. Not that I could have concluded anything from it; Guy could get caught up with this reading. But not often.

He showed me the three-by-five schedule card he made up at three-week intervals and posted on our bulletin board by the door. I frequently referred to this, just to remind myself when I was baking bread next or when our next visitors were due. It ended with July 3. But this also would have signaled nothing to me. Guy made up a new card and posted it on the last day of the old card, which he then took down. Still, Guy was showing me in every way he could that he wasn't planning on carrying his life beyond July 3.

He showed me next the page in the three-ring notebook where he recorded our schedule for the year, penciling in events as they became firm. Across the top of the page containing May, June, and July, Guy had written "final page." The last entry in the July column was: "Fri. 3 — G to mts." Near the bottom of the page Guy had penciled in, in capital letters, "NO MORE."

It wasn't likely I would see this. I rarely looked in these notebooks. Guy kept them over by his side of the table, and though he frequently pulled them out, I only needed the schedule cards that he posted for me.

"Why July 3, Guy?" I asked him.

"I didn't want to leave before we'd planted the garden," he replied. "I wanted to help you get a good start on wood."

It was true; we'd had more wood days than usual this spring. "I thought then you'd have the rest of the summer to get set up for continuing on without me."

I wrote in my journal for Saturday, July 4: "He'd really worked this out, as he always has attended to detail. But the world does not look rosy to him. He doesn't want to go on. It was after Johnny died that these demons acted up again. Mentally, he's never been very happy since April 1981. Though I don't regret one day."

That evening at supper on our porch, Guy talked about trying again later that week, on Wednesday or Thursday. I told him then, if that was what he was set on, I wouldn't stand in his way. But at the same time I couldn't imagine him walking out the door just four days from now. He was back, and I was going to keep him here.

We sat close to each other on the bench at the porch table and looked out over our garden, at all we had built. I had fixed a salad supper, but our appetites were gone. We couldn't eat, but we could hug each other and shed tears. Guy told me he loved me. He said he should have said this a long time ago.

"I know you love me, Guy," I said. "But why didn't you tell me what you wanted to do?"

"I thought you would try to keep me from doing it."

"It would have been awful if you hadn't come back."

"You're a survivor. You would have been all right."

"I would have been furious at you."

"You would have?" He looked surprised.

The next morning, Sunday, July 5, Guy was up at 4:15 a.m. His unvarying routine was to tramp up to the outhouse and, when he came back down, pull out his typewriter until it was time to start the woodstove for breakfast. I always slept through all of this, until I heard him lifting off the iron rimmers to build the fire in the stove, crumpling up paper, shifting wood around. Comforting sounds that eased me back to consciousness.

But this morning I was wide awake. I gazed out the window. The sky was filling with a pearly light. Twin Firs Camp stood nestled under the sheltering double evergreen for which it was named. Suddenly I saw what I needed to do.

I remembered that Guy had asked me several times during the last months if I saw myself continuing to live at Barra when he was gone. I knew he didn't want to live to be old. He had often told me this. But what was "old?" To me old was *very* old.

"Do you want to move back to Lawrenceville?" Guy had asked.

"No."

"Or New York?"

"Heavens, no."

"How about the village?"

"I don't know."

We'd left it that I'd remain at Barra. We talked about how I could put in a road. Get local loggers to help me with the wood. I'd keep planting the garden.

Early that morning of July 5, I knew I couldn't remain at Barra. I didn't want to be there without Guy. Suddenly I could see myself in a house within walking distance of everything that was familiar: the post office, the general store, the library, the church, and our health center. I felt this surge of energy as I lay there on the bed. I would propose this to Guy. It would be his last big project, and we would work on it together.

I heard the wooden latch fall into place on the outhouse door and Guy's steady stomp as he descended the steep log steps. I heard his boots crossing the porch. He opened the door and eased it shut.

I said, "Guy?"

He came into the bedroom that was filled with the soft gray light of dawn. He put a knee on the bed and leaned over me.

"I have an idea," I said and began to talk. He lay down beside me, propped on his elbow, and listened. As the light turned golden we worked it out that together we would take the practical measures that would allow me to carry on by myself.

All that day we talked, and as had happened the day before, we ate little. We discussed the timing and manner of Guy's ending. He concluded that going to the mountains in winter might be the easiest.

This winter?

I'd been planning a trip to Australia with my friend Carolyn Hanson for January 1999. I offered to forgo this. "If you leave this winter, Guy, I want to spend every day until then with you."

"No, no." Go with Carolyn. I can put it off for a year."

I knew that he would be here when I returned from Australia.

So it was settled. We had a year and a half left together. I felt elated with myself for my idea. Eighteen months seemed like another lifetime.

My journal for Sunday, July 5, read: "He wants to go. I am not fighting this. He has made it so clear this is what he wants. I am deeply grateful to him for hanging around to help me because of course he thinks of all the important steps, financially and otherwise. His mind breaks it all down systematically. . . . Now we have come to grips, and I think it will work out all right. I feel much better today. Guy rearranged our books to make more room for my published short stories. He is wonderful! We worked outside — garden, yard, flowers — all afternoon."

For Monday, July 6, I wrote: "We are talking about the future — mine and G's — and ours together for the present. When he leaves, I will be ready — in all ways. Meanwhile, we will try to keep him from difficult situations and too many trips away from Barra. We should have done this years ago, but as G says, he doesn't like to be unsociable or rude."

And on Tuesday, July 7: "It feels like a new life together — or it feels like we stepped back to how we were together years ago, but with all our past life's experience to enrich this present. Worked in the garden (weeding), and G in the yard (scything, mowing, raking). We stop in our work to admire Barra's beauty."

Guy picked up his life again. He went back to making up the schedule cards he posted on the bulletin board near the door. He began keeping track of birds seen and heard, garden yield, blueberries picked, and all the rest. He carried his three-by-five cards in the left-hand pocket of his shirt, his glasses in the right.

In many ways those last eighteen months were happy months. We had visits from a few friends we hadn't seen in years. We attended a reunion of Guy's five siblings at his sister Bobbie's house in Connecticut. These occasions, though often edged with sadness, gave Guy a chance to say goodbye — a one-way goodbye. Later, after he was gone, a friend pointed out that those months gave us both a chance to say goodbye to "Laura and Guy."

Guy's bad times seemed less oppressive, less frequent, perhaps because he knew he was so close to stepping across to the other side. When we were down to our last few weeks Guy's spirits grew even brighter, as if he were anticipating a voyage. With the end in sight, his pain eased. At the time I didn't see the irony.

We began talking to our friends about our plans: buying land, building a house closer to the village in anticipation of when Laura would be without Guy. For several years Guy had been outspoken that he was "going first." But these plans raised questions. When would we (or just me?) move in? Would Guy stay at Barra? Guy was clear that this was my house. What would happen to Barra? In the mid-1990s we had begun talking with the Good Life Center, an organization that advocated sustainable living and ran Helen and Scott Nearing's homestead in Maine, about taking over Barra when we were no longer living on the land. Barra fit into their plans. They wanted to keep on running it much as we had: as a working homestead. We told our friends of our decision to give Barra to the Good Life Center.

But what is the timing? our friends asked. Would we live in two places for a while? Guy always came back to saying that he wasn't planning on living in the new house. It was Laura's house.

As the months slid away we talked over whether to tell certain family members and close friends about Guy's decision to take his own life. He decided not to. If he confided his plans, he said, he put friends and family in the position of talking him out of it, or at the very least urging him to seek medical help, which he wasn't going to do. I offered no opposition. He was so dead set on this course that it never occurred to me to try to change his mind. Perhaps he was thinking about the time his parents had taken him to the appointment with the psychoanalyst and he'd been left there, locked in the psycho ward. Perhaps he was thinking about Johnny, whose mental difficulties led him to break with reality. "There's a lot of me in Johnny, and a lot of Johnny in me," Guy often said.

Guy did not want to cross the line Johnny had crossed, so he was not about to let himself drift anywhere near it. For me, right then, the main thing was that Guy was alive. We were still together. I knew his plan, but he was going to stick around long enough to make sure I'd be able to carry on without him. I couldn't see any further into the future than that.

It was a strange bargain we struck. But in the context of our world — our life at Barra — it made sense. It grew out of how I'd been acting toward Guy, especially since Johnny's death.

Guy had kept his suicide attempt a secret. But he had been unable to pull it off. He had returned, and he told me about it. Somehow the fact that he told me erased my anger.

If he was to pull this off, he needed my help, though this wasn't something I reasoned out at the time. Just as, at the time, I didn't conclude that he was unable to jump off Cannon Cliff because, well, he just couldn't *do* that to me. Maybe I'm reaching here — maybe I'm just trying to comfort myself — but the fact remains that Guy couldn't commit suicide that first time around. He did not have to reveal his secret. He could have come back and said nothing, then left a few days later, as he said he wanted to do. Or he didn't have to come back.

But he did. The sinews of our life were too closely entwined to allow him not to come back and not to tell me. We were too much of a team. We had built Barra together. He couldn't leave me, and leave everything that Barra had come to mean to both of us, without bidding a proper goodbye.

CHAPTER sixteen

How gladly would I meet

mortality, my sentence, and be earth

insensible! how glad would I lay me down

as in my mother's lap!

— John Milton, *Paradise Lost*

I lived that last year in two worlds. Our daily tasks went on as always, as if they would never end. Yet I knew a full stop would close the book of our life together in the winter of 2000. I had no idea of how I would get from here to there. When I tried to imagine Guy walking out the door for the last time, then what I would do after that, I found myself thinking: *Maybe he will change his mind.* Even on that last morning as he darted about the cabin packing, talking quietly about how he was going to stop and get a paper to see how the Dartmouth women's ice hockey team did in their game the previous day, I half-expected his next sentence to be: "I've changed my mind."

The only way I could handle the fact that my husband was going to commit suicide was by keeping on living the way I was living. The work at Barra had always sustained me. I found comfort and purpose in the routines of making bread, tending the garden, sawing wood in the afternoon in the woodshed with Guy. Telling Guy about an encounter with a chickadee, him telling me the temperatures at 7:00 a.m., 1:00 p.m., and in the evening again at 7:00. Nevertheless, our last year together was a conscious process of saying goodbye to the life we'd created and lived in this seasonal round, each step evolving out of the one just taken. By saying goodbye to the land, we were saying goodbye to each other.

I could not see what lay ahead, but I knew I could rely on myself. I had begun to learn this lesson when I was twelve and realized I couldn't count on my alcoholic father. This lesson continued to be driven home when I started climbing. I could see how the hard move would start but not always how I'd get through it. The sequences became clear only by committing to the rock, only by starting upward. Reaching the summit was a matter of trusting myself, my strength of body as well as of mind. The difference with the climb that lay ahead of me now — the exit cracks aswirl in mist — was that when we reached the top and untied the rope, instead of walking back down the mountain together as we always had, Guy would turn in one direction and I would head in the opposite.

That March of 1999, we were engaged in sugaring the same as ever, and we were both keenly aware that it was our last time. I wanted to let myself feel the finality of each day, but in such a way that thoughts of what I was about to lose would not overwhelm my pleasure in the work. I wanted also to enjoy our many visitors, who, as they mushed about the sugar bush on snowshoes, bringing in pailfuls of sap, had no thought that they too were doing this for the last time.

During this last sugaring, Twin Firs Camp, with bunk space for six and room for children in the tiny loft, was rarely empty. Our guest quarters had been ten years in the building. We'd spent over half that time taking down the softwood for logs: white pine, spruce, hemlock, and balsam fir. We stripped off the bark in spring, when peeling logs is as easy as removing your winter underwear. We looked for logs with interesting twists in their branches and for trunks with burls — anything that would be both decorative and functional. In the early 1990s, even before it was finished, Twin Firs Camp opened its doors to our overnight visitors.

During this last sugaring season friends piled packs on the bench under the sign that read Twin Firs Camp: Dedicated to Our Welcomed Guests. They spread their sleeping bags on the bunks and hung parkas, shirts, and snowshoes on the branch stubs we'd left on the logs to use as handy hooks. After supper, as the heat of our cabin, full stomachs, and a good day's work began to produce more yawns than conversation, Guy slipped out and lit the candles, the two by the doorsill lighting the way up the low granite steps. As the snow melted and this last sugaring season wore on, the sight of the candlelight mellowing the log walls and the spurts of laughter coming from Twin Firs became more and more precious, and we gazed from our bedroom window until the last candle was snuffed and all was silent.

When Guy and I were by ourselves and weren't too busy, we often alternated mornings at the sugar shed. This gave Guy a chance to work up wood at the cabin, for me to make bread, or for either of us to put in a morning of writing. We had located the sugar shed, an open-front log structure we'd built in the mid-1970s, on a gentle knoll in the middle of our sugar bush about a tenth of a mile from our cabin.

Whenever I was working down there by myself, I was conscious of storing up how everything felt so I would never forget: the slant of April light as it glanced off the flat needles of the hemlocks; the smell of bubbling sap thickening to syrup and sweetening the air; the rasping sound the bow saw made as I worked it through the piece of rock maple across the sawhorse. I took note of the snow as it pulled back from the trees, revealing a widening circle of damp leaf mold. I marked the long vertical frost crack in the trunk of a nearby yellow birch and heard the pileated woodpecker drumming on the decaying beech seventy-five feet downhill from me. Always my eyes returned to the sugar buckets hanging from our maples. Most of all, I wanted to etch in my memory each of our faithful trees — Speckled Red, Athos, Porthos, Lady Walshingham, and Dame Quince — and all the others I could see from the sugar shed, proud with their buckets that we had painted green. I was aware of the snow melting, the quality of the sap changing as the season moved along. These things that in the past had only marked the turn of the season were now imbued with the passage of time itself. Time ticking, time moving toward conclusion, each stroke louder, more insistent than the last. The only way I could keep in balance was to let myself be caught up in the process of syrup making, working with Guy as we always had for the past twenty-six seasons.

Guy, whose daily presence felt like an extension of myself. As for missing him, that would be with me for the rest of my life. Though deep down — too deep to pull to the surface then — was that feeling of relief, the same kind of relief I felt when he was away on a solo mountain trip and I was alone at Barra.

On the last day of boiling, April 2, 1999, as we walked away from the sugar shed carrying the last of the syrup, we impulsively turned and looked back. Only a small stack of wood remained. The fire was down to coals, and the air smelled heavy with the damp smoke of a dying fire. We looked into each other's faces, and I saw that Guy's eyes were wet. Of all our tasks at Barra, sugaring went the deepest. It required that we give our hardest work, our strongest care. Once again we had made our syrup for the year. We were saying goodbye.

Two days later we washed up our buckets at the stream. The afternoon was cold, in the forties, and blustery. The path between the sugar shed and the stream was slick with ice, and the water was a degree or two above freezing. Later that afternoon I found an envelope addressed to me on my side of the table. It was from Guy (of course!), and upon opening it I read that I had received the coveted PITFOCH Award — Perseverance in the Face of Cold Hands. The award's committee included the Antarctic explorers whose spirit we admired and whose books we enjoyed: Scott, Shackleton, Amundsen, and Cherry-Garrard.

At the end of April we put in the pea trellises. We planted lettuce, spinach, arugula, chard, kale — our favorite greens. In early May we moved on to the onions, broccoli, cauliflower, cabbage, and our beloved Brussels sprouts, three twenty-foot rows of them. These last were a staple of our fall diet; I steamed them with heaping amounts of garlic and ginger that had even the confirmed Brussels sprout haters among our guests asking for seconds. The secret wasn't in my recipe but in the fact that these sprouts were picked a half-hour before we ate them. The carrots and beets followed, then potatoes planted from our own seed crop. We finished off with the "freezables," as we called them: cucumbers, summer and winter squash, pumpkins, corn, beans — pole and bush — as well as dry beans (for which we used our own seed) and the annual herbs, dill and basil. Marigolds, nasturtiums, zinnias, and cosmos we sowed along the borders as companion plants. We ended by setting out transplants of melons and tomatoes, the only plants we started indoors. Guy dug the hole, and I planted the final seedling. Then, down on our knees, we mulched it with grass clippings pushed close around the slender stem. Our garden, this on-the-ground mosaic that took seven weeks to plant, was complete.

We cleaned off our tools. In fall we would again fork in wood ash and manure and plant the cover crop of winter rye, but this was the last full growing season at Barra for Guy and me. I let the finality of this fill my thoughts. I felt it was important to look it in the eye, then to place it to the side — not out of sight, but far enough away that I would have to turn my head to look at it.

Collecting our wood for the year began in May and ended just before Thanksgiving. The trees we felled — sugar maple, hop hornbeam, white ash, beech, and red oak — wouldn't be burned until 2001 and 2002. But during 1999 Guy spent many afternoons in the woodlot by himself adding to these stacks and creating new ones. When Guy split and stacked wood on a daily basis at the house, he stockpiled more than usual, though I didn't let myself take in the full meaning of this until the summer was well along. "There's so much wood in the shelter, Guy," I finally said.

"It should take you well into March after I'm gone," he replied.

One day late in the fall, when we were working in the woods, Guy hung up a spruce. As it fell its branches became entwined in another tree, making it very difficult to pry free. This can happen to woodsmen now and then, and often we could work together with the peavey, axe, and saw to get the tree down. But on this day Guy seemed compelled to attack the spruce with everything he had in him. I stood by, ready to be helpful, but the way Guy handled his axe, the strokes pelting down, the muscles in his forearms standing in cords, let me know there was no room here for me.

That awful morning I felt such anger at Guy — all unspoken, all pushed down. *The next time he acts like this*, I said to myself, *I'm walking off the job.* I mulled on this for several days, wondering if I could actually do it. It was a thought loaded with disloyalty. One of the team members refusing to play the game. But deep down where I didn't want to look, it was a liberating thought as well.

A week later Guy hung up a branchy white pine. He became distraught and whaled away at it with his double-bit axe. I kept on limbing the tree I was working on, but Guy's anger at himself crowded me out; it made me feel so miserably helpless that the work I was doing felt useless to me. *He's out of control.* I said these frightening words to myself for the first time. *This is no place for me.* I reached for my axe and saw. Then stopped. I couldn't do this. We had work planned for this morning. I knew how important, how driving, this was to Guy. I would be sabotaging everything by walking off the job. I would be adding to Guy's pain.

He was so horribly in pain. Chips from the white pine were flying in all directions. His violence was terrifying to me. Why did he have to withdraw into this awful place? It made me angry that he couldn't get a grip on himself. I grabbed my axe and saw and strode back to the house.

After a while Guy found me sawing wood in the woodshed. He slowed his step as he came in, ducked his head, and looked at me with bleak eyes. I saw the pain, the sadness, the shame, the blame, and as always my heart went out to him. All my anger dissolved. He offered me no explanation. I didn't ask for one. Yet I had acted. Though nothing changed between us, nothing was any more out in the open — I was glad I had done what I did.

A day or two later Guy said, "I know my moods are hard on you, Laura." He had said this before.

And I answered, as always, "No. It's all right."

Why didn't I leap, this time, for the opening Guy was giving me? I could have said, "Yes. Your moods are horrendously hard on me. Your rage is frightening. All you'd done was hang up a tree. Anyone can make a mistake like that. But something snapped; you went berserk. It made me angry to watch you act like a four-year-old in the throes of a temper tantrum. Why are you so hard on yourself, Guy? It feels so self-destructive."

I didn't say any of that. I didn't even think it. Always foremost in my mind was: *I can't tell Guy that his moods hurt me.* For nearly twenty years I had schooled myself not to cause Guy pain. Even though Guy had opened up the subject, my reaction had become instinctual. I was mired in the useless habit of silence, of acquiescence.

More and more he spoke to others about his "moods."

"Laura has to live with my bad moods. Laura's the only one who sees my bad moods," Guy said.

"Bad moods" was Guy's term for something much worse than a spell of ill humor or the blahs or simply a bad day. Was there no way out of the tormented pathways of the mind?

To keep out from under his "bad moods," he needed to keep himself under control. When Guy hung up those trees, I saw what happened when he lost control. He had developed an arsenal of tactics — his three-by-five cards only one of them — that effectively kept the demons out and himself organized, ordered, on track, and reined in.

Counting the blueberries. It was a joke. Guy knew it was silly, and he made the most of it, played it for laughs. It showed a charming eccentricity. Everyone who came to Barra during blueberry season entered into the whimsy: this counting of individual berries Guy had turned into a game.

I see now how dead serious Guy was. Counting berries wasn't just about keeping a life list for each blueberry bush. It was about keeping within bounds the thing that lurked below the surface, trying to break the chain. "The amazing thing about Guy," our friend Doug Mayer later said to me, "was that the mechanisms he used to control his demons were the very same he used to turn work at Barra into play."

All the record keeping, all the routines, were something I needed to buy into if I was going to make a life with Guy. It was easy for me to do that. It happened as soon as I saw (without *seeing* anything) that if I wanted to be with Guy Waterman — no question about that! —I needed to get up in the dark so he could be climbing in the dawn's light, *every* weekend. I was willing. It was fun. But if I had wavered, I believe our budding love would have died then and there, right at the beginning. Guy needed to be in this kind of climbing routine that had less to do with climbing than with feeding the rats that lived in his basement. The ones that he let no one see but that could drive him into a blind rage, like the rage I witnessed against the white pine. Or over a lost *Forest and Crag* note. Or over the typing errors, when I feared he was going to pitch the machine through the glass. Or over a carpentry project gone amuck, when he just needed to hit and keep on hitting the goddamn nail until the board was pocked with hammer blows.

A few years after we moved to Barra, I lost my temper over some carpentry job the way I'd seen Guy do. I kicked the board and shouted "Fuck!" two or three times. I was copying him.

"*Never do that, never say that again.*" Suddenly Guy's face was in mine, his voice low but very, very insistent. I got control over myself. Acting like this felt self-indulgent, even childish. It was unfamiliar territory, but now I was mad at

Guy. It didn't seem fair to ask me not to lose my temper if he couldn't keep control of his own. Yet I never questioned him, even though in the way he'd said "*Never do that . . .*" I heard something I didn't understand. Instead, I made sure I never lost my temper like that again. Years later I came to see that my behavior was frightening to him because it was so like his own.

Observant friends no doubt saw how Guy used his three-by-five cards to keep order in his life and may have wondered whether I felt controlled by this or just entered into the spirit of the thing, or did a little of both.

The part nobody saw — and the part I told nobody about — was Guy losing his temper, losing control. I mentioned to a few very close friends that Guy couldn't talk about the things that troubled him most. I always said "couldn't." I never said "wouldn't." And I never mentioned that I felt abused by his temper or by his silence, because I had never said *that* word to myself. *Abused.* It began that night in the tent on Lou Cornell's lawn in 1981. If you don't talk, the other person will never know just how filled you are with blame, shame, anger, regret, remorse. How crammed with self-hate. In fact, what a terrible person you really are. This was what Guy had to keep under wraps. No matter what the cost to himself or to others, he had to never, never let those thoughts out.

I pushed against this, but not too hard. After all, I knew how to live with what I was living with. I knew how to keep silent. On some inarticulate level, I understood complicity. I knew how to exist in an atmosphere of terror caused by the people I loved most. I was an expert at keeping the waters smooth. I knew all this because I had graduated summa cum laude from the rigorous school of my alcoholic family.

What everyone saw was that we were a united couple — idyllic, really — who lived in a kind of Garden of Eden. Guy and Laura. Laura and Guy. At the beginning the idyll was really true. For a long time after that I could convince myself that it was true. Near the end I saw how important it was to Guy to keep the cracks plastered, and I was willing to help wield the trowel. What no one saw was how my shit, as they say, fit perfectly with Guy's. This was the other side (the murky underside) of our perfect match.

Not only were we saying goodbye to Barra, but Guy was saying goodbye to friends and family. None of them knew this.

In the heat of summer, when I could talk myself into thinking these days could never end, it was easy to put these thoughts aside. But as the months wore away I became acutely aware that we were often with friends for the last time.

For me the most symbolic goodbye came on New Year's Eve 1999. We had long celebrated the turning of the year with the same three couples, and always at Barra. It was our tradition to end the evening with "Auld Lang Syne," Guy at the keyboard, the rest of us standing in a circle, hands joined, singing this simple Scottish air we had all learned as children.

> Should auld acquaintance be forgot,
> And never brought to min'?

> Should auld acquaintance be forgot,
> And days o' auld lang syne?

Guy's face was in shadow as the rest of us swayed to the music under the glow of the kerosene lamps. Our eyes met and held as we gazed back and forth across the circle. If our friends saw emotion in mine, I saw the same in theirs. This was, after all, the turn of the millennium. There was a palpable feeling of time passing, which carried for me a layer of meaning the others could not know. I could see into the future. One member of our little band was leaving soon. This was the last singing of "Auld Lang Syne" at Barra. The last time they would hear Guy play. Dan and Natalie were leaving in a few days for an eight-week hike on the Appalachian Trail; they would work south from where Dan had left off the previous winter, deep into North Carolina. Dan and Nat would not see Guy again. But even so, I took pleasure in this gathering of friends who were held together by countless days spent in the mountains and at Barra. I knew my friendships with all of them would continue into the new millennium, even as I was conscious of Guy pouring his soul into the keyboard, "Auld Lang Syne" ringing out into the starry winter night.

CHAPTER seventeen

It is a fundamentally insane notion . . . that one is able to influence the course of events by a turn of the helm, by will-power alone, whereas in fact all is determined by the most complex interdependencies.

— W. G. Sebald, *Vertigo*

During that last year we came to grips with my transition from Barra. We found a piece of land, six acres, with a field and a strip of woods separating the field from the river. This would give me room for a vegetable garden, flower beds, raspberries, highbush blueberries, asparagus, and a few rhubarb plants, though I didn't need the quantities we had at Barra. The land came with eight wild apple trees and was on a dirt road a half-mile walk from the post office.

I told Guy that I intended to enter the twenty-first century, which coincided with this turn in my life, at the level I'd left it in the early seventies. That is, I'd use electricity for specific items like lights and a record player. But I had no need for a dishwasher or a microwave. Computers were an unknown world I didn't feel tempted to explore, despite the encouragement of friends. "I have to ease into this," I told them. My situation seemed similar to that of a nun who's about to step out of the cloister, or a convict whose thirty-year jail term is coming to an end — each is on the threshold of rejoining a world she knows has changed.

I said yes to a refrigerator, but to retain the useful and familiar I planned a root cellar. I acquired a washing machine and a dryer to use in winter. In summer I'd hang the clothes in the sun. I conceded to a telephone, but didn't want an answering machine and opted for an unlisted telephone number. I couldn't imagine living without wood heat, though I backed this up with a heating system that would keep pipes from freezing if I went away in winter. I debated about cooking with wood but decided it would bring more heartache than joy. Our woodstove meals belonged too much to Barra. I vowed I would recycle, compost, or burn all my waste, just as we had done at Barra. In fact, because I would be living "on the outside," where tossing was so easy, being careful about waste felt even more important.

We got lucky with our builder, John Nininger. We knew John from the White Mountains and had originally gone to talk to him about steering us to a log home builder we could afford. John told us that he wanted to build this house himself. He asked us to sketch a floor plan, and he set the delivery date of the log shell for October 1999.

Delays pushed this to November. In December the house still sat, partially assembled, in John's yard. Guy told me he wanted to see my house set on its permanent foundation before he left — in the winter of 2000. He didn't want to pinpoint a date, but I knew he would leave before mid-February. After that time the weather was less reliably cold. I didn't need anything more specific than that. I fell into a pit of the unknown every time I thought of what it would be like — the hour, the moment, of his leave-taking. It felt as unfathomable as Milton's "illimitable ocean," as "without bound / Without dimension, where length, breadth, and height, / And time and place are lost."

I knew that Guy would leave. I felt this with the kind of inevitability one feels about night following day. But so that I could go on with daily life — baking bread, working up wood, seeing friends — I placed his final goodbye in a separate part of my mind. Since I was not challenging him, since I had elected just to watch my beloved husband walk out the door to his own death, I had put myself in the position of spectator, gazing from the bleachers as the fateful game played itself to the end. Yet I was not a spectator to my own life, and that had something to do with why in early December, on a once-a-year trip to Lawrenceville and New York, I told my friend Annie Barry what was going to happen, over a bowl of soup in a Chinese restaurant near Lincoln Center.

Annie was an old friend from my New York days. She had watched me fall in love with both rock climbing and Guy. She was in my wedding. When she married David, Guy supplied the music. She had made three special trips out to Lawrenceville for the memorial services of my parents and my brother. She had first visited Barra when it was not much more than an idea and a clearing surrounded by woods stretching up the steep hillsides.

Annie and I arrived at the restaurant around 6:30 p.m. It was a large, impersonal place where diners could grab a plate of noodles and be off again. Yet it was also a place where one could linger. We sat on the second floor at a small table for two near the stairway. Several times during that bowl of soup I had started to say something but faltered. I hadn't come to see Annie for this specific purpose, but it had crossed my mind I might say something if the moment felt right. After a while there were only a few diners left. It was late. This would be my last chance. But I kept thinking of Guy. Even though he hadn't asked me not to say anything, I knew I was stepping across a line by telling Annie this huge thing that was entirely between Guy and me. I knew also that she was the only person in the world I could talk to.

"Guy is going to take his own life," I heard myself saying. I watched Annie's face across the table. I saw some shock, but Annie knew about Guy's demons, so I saw also a deep concern. I began to talk, filling in the background of Guy's suicide attempt on July 3, 1998. Right at this moment I was telling Annie something I wanted her to know, and I felt the risk slide into relief and went on talking. I was telling her what was going to happen, I said, because I wanted to give her some advance warning. If she knew, it would make it easier for me to tell her when it *did* happen. I assured Annie that this was what Guy wanted, and that I would be all right.

Annie kept staring at me as I jabbered on. I heard her say, "Now I understand why Guy called your new house 'Laura's house.'" And later she broke in to say, "You've reached a level of acceptance that I haven't reached yet."

I began talking faster, harder, intent on explaining why it made sense for Guy to commit suicide. I expected Annie to start nodding as she began to understand. But she just kept staring at me in a way that told me she was unconvinced. Since I had never questioned Guy's choice and had never questioned my own role in standing by while he carried out his plan, I thought I wasn't explaining it well enough.

Finally, she asked if she might write me about this. I hesitated. Why would she want to write me? I was brought up short by what Guy might think. I was afraid he would be angry, and I was suddenly plunged into my old childhood fear — the deeply buried but overwhelmingly familiar fear I experienced nightly at the family dinner table. I knew Guy wouldn't want me to be telling any of this to Annie. Above all, I had to protect him from Annie's interference, which would, I told myself, cause him pain. As for Guy's anger at me, in reality Guy was never outright angry with me, but he was often angry at himself, and it was this anger — the unrecognized fear of it — that connected me right back to the terror of the family dinner table. That was where the camera focused and held, and I was stuck, without any idea that I was stuck, in the freeze-frame of the stop-action. All I knew was that I had to avoid this — the immobilizing terror — at any cost. So I asked Annie not to write. I explained to her that Guy and I shared all our mail, reading letters from friends at dinner. I didn't want to be in the position of withholding Annie's letter from Guy, finding a moment to read it to myself, then tucking it away to answer later without Guy's knowing about it.

When we left the restaurant I thought Annie understood everything. Even accepted it. Of course she would write me, but it wouldn't be about this.

A few days after I returned to Vermont I picked up a thick letter from Annie at the post office. I had a strong feeling that I should read this to myself as soon as I returned home. She also sent a book by Terrence Real called *I Don't Want to Talk about It: Overcoming the Secret Legacy of Male Depression*. It was about how our society shapes the male persona, and she wanted me to read it and to show it to Guy. I knew that Guy was going to be very put off by this book, which I could see had words like *mental illness, dysfunctional* — an overused, jargony word Guy scoffed at — *workaholic, rage, self-destructive behavior*, which Guy was all too aware he exhibited. He was not going to like any of this. I was in a bad situation of my own making, and I knew I had to tell Guy what I had done.

When he came in from splitting wood I showed him Annie's letter. "I told Annie what you are going to do. She wrote me about it," I said.

"What did she say?" His voice was tight, and his eyes were fixed on my face.

"She thinks I should encourage you to seek help. Get the information I need to help you. She sent this book." I pointed to the book lying on the table. He threw it a glance, and I watched his jaw grow rigid, like stone. I felt awful for causing him this problem and anger at myself for my weakness in confiding in Annie. Now that I was back at Barra with Guy, what I had done was backfiring.

"Here's her letter," I said, holding it out to him. "I wish I hadn't told her, Guy." The last thing Guy wanted was interference from Annie, but even as I said this I was not sorry that Annie knew.

"I'll read it later." He strode over to the table, seized the book, and flung it up into the loft, out of sight.

"Right now I'm going to work on my baseball article," he said and headed over toward his desk, his usual routine in the half-hour before supper.

I was relieved that Guy wasn't outright angry with me, but the way he drew in all his feelings was even worse. I was painfully aware of the problems I was causing him, and I saw also that he was keeping himself, only by a supreme effort of will, from flying apart. I began building a fire in the cookstove. If anyone had opened the door at that moment, all would have appeared calm — under control and in order — in our cabin.

After supper, after our reading aloud, after doing the dishes together, and after Guy made the run to empty the vegetable scraps in the winter compost and read the 7:00 p.m. temperatures, he sat down at the table and pulled Annie's letter off his shelf. I was dreading this moment and couldn't help watching him as he read it. He moved through the six pages quickly, with an impatience that told me he was reading this only because I had asked him to.

He tossed the letter across the table. "I couldn't have expected you not to tell someone, Laura, but you picked the wrong person." I wasn't so sure, but I wished Annie had not written.

"Do you want to talk to someone, a doctor?" I said.

"No," he said, then added, "If Annie writes any more letters, I don't want to see them."

Annie herself had grown up in an alcoholic family, and what she wrote me came out of her own understanding of the dynamic. At the time, I thought her letter, written on December 19, showed little or no understanding of what was going on between Guy and me. "I can't think of one good thing secrecy did for me or my family," Annie wrote. And I thought: *There are no secrets between Guy and me. I know exactly what he plans to do.* "Why are you keeping secrets now?" Annie went on. "Who is it helping? Was it Guy's idea? Did he ask you to keep his secret? Why did you say yes? Or was it your idea? Why? Who does it serve?" Guy had not asked me to keep secrets. I had told Annie this. Didn't she understand? "You said our friendship had reached a new level. Well maybe. Surely our complicity has reached a new level."

Complicity? I had never been called complicit. Being honest was extremely important to me. How was I being complicit? Annie saw it wrong. She didn't understand. Annie urged: "If you feel over your head in helping Guy live (as opposed to helping him die), get help for yourself, not him." Come to New York, she wrote. "Don't have the money? I'll lend it to you. Don't dare leave Guy? Well, what's the alternative? If you're right, and all is lost already, will it make it that much worse to get some help for yourself?" Couldn't she see? Guy didn't want help, and I was fine. I didn't need help. She said that I could stay with her and that she knew a good therapist who had experience with suicidal people. "Whatever came out of a conversation with Chris, you'd get support and help for yourself. As a good child of alcoholic parents (as one myself, of course I never even questioned your doing this) you pitched in without complaint, without telling anyone, and worked hard to keep Guy alive and as happy as he could manage to be, for decades. All by yourself. Rejecting all help. You and I were brought up to act like this—all these years later, why are we still acting this way? I think somewhere inside you know you need some support in this, and that's why you told me." *Again, wrong,* I thought. I didn't *need* to tell her anything. I had only told her to make it easier on myself later, after Guy had committed suicide, and I would have to write to her about it. Besides, my parents' alcoholism hadn't caused problems for me; I was left with a few bad memories perhaps, but nothing that I hadn't long ago gotten over. She just didn't understand, and by telling her I'd provoked this big reaction that was putting pressure on Guy in our last days together, which I so much wanted to be as smooth for him as possible.

After Christmas, after our New Year's singing of "Auld Lang Syne," I knew we were into the countdown. I was taken over by the inevitability of what was a foregone conclusion. As the revolution of each twenty-four hours blew another day off the calendar, I was palpably aware of the end point looming. What had felt so distant the previous March during sugaring was now nearly upon me, bearing down as unstoppably as a tidal wave.

On the weekend of January 14 and 15, 2000, Guy accompanied a jazz singer at a local talent show. When they had begun rehearsing, Guy told Danuta Jacob that he made his debut as a jazz pianist on New Year's Eve 1949. He was seventeen. He had hoped to play someplace this New Year's — fifty years later.

On Friday the fourteenth, Guy changed into his rented tux at the library, where we spent three afternoons a week as volunteers. He emerged pulling at his jacket, grinning, and needing help with his tie. We drove over to the town hall. It was a below-zero night, and the stars were sharp pricks of cold light. Most of the audience that evening had heard Guy's music from when he gave concerts at the church, or for the Trail Foliage Ride dinners in October, or at the chicken pie suppers in August. Tonight there were twenty acts. The finale featured Danuta and Guy. Three weeks later, after Guy was gone, Danuta told me she had seen this as their debut.

All our life together I loved hearing Guy play. Much of what he could not speak came out in his music. When Guy and Danuta came on I found myself blinking away tears when everyone else was tapping feet and clapping. It was dim enough so that no one could see me, but this was just too hard. I didn't want to put myself through that again, so I told Guy that unless he really wanted me to be there, I would stay home for the second night.

He burst in around midnight telling me how "on" he'd felt. "I'm so glad I got the chance to accompany a really good jazz singer," he exclaimed as he stood by my chair and stripped off his tux.

"Danuta's going to take it hard, Guy." Their duo had lasted only six months.

The next weekend, January 21 to 23, we spent with our friends Tom Simon and Carolyn Hanson in Burlington. The weather was frigid, with a ferocious wind, the most arctic weekend of the winter. Guy wanted to see one last women's ice hockey game with Tom and Carolyn, a sport we had shared with them for the last few years.

Guy and Tom had been working on a book on baseball, profiles of all the major leaguers born in Vermont, thirty-five in all. *Green Mountain Boys of*

Summer was due out in the spring of 2000. Guy was working on the index and had brought along his typewriter, packing it out from Barra. The proofs had just arrived, and he was going to have to scramble to complete it in time.

The next morning we found Guy downstairs, his work spread out on the dining table. Carolyn's cat reclined on top of his typewriter, her tail dipping in and out among the keys. What Tom saw was Guy doing his best to meet the publisher's deadline. What I saw was Guy determined to finish this index for Tom within the confines of his own personal deadline.

Guy left at 9:00 a.m. for Hanover, New Hampshire. He planned to spend a day doing baseball research at the Dartmouth College Library, then attend the women's ice hockey games on Saturday and Sunday. He had been following this team for the past three years. We would meet again back in Burlington at the Flynn Theater for *Macbeth* on Sunday evening. We stood in Tom and Carolyn's hallway, and Guy hugged them goodbye. They had other plans for Sunday evening. They would not see Guy again.

I felt like a spectator who has read this sad play before going to the performance. I watched Guy walk toward the car and saw what the others could not see, a man doomed in his self-imposed aloneness. He had been marked in this way for a long time. But because he was so near the end now, and I knew how it was going to end, I could see more clearly how he had wrapped himself in an invisible cloak of isolation, pulling it tighter year by year. I stood inside the house, peering out the bay window, and watched him drive off into the solid January cold. What were his thoughts? I could not imagine. He didn't wave.

Carolyn and I spent that Saturday in Montreal. "I thought it would be fun to go someplace warm," Carolyn said as we strolled through the greenhouses at the Botanical Garden. They overflowed with lush tropical vegetation, and we chatted about how similar it was to what we had seen in Australia's rain forest just one year ago. On the car ride, in the greenhouses, in the café where we had coffee and cake layered with whipped cream, I had in my mind what was going to happen. It took up enormous room. I was bursting with it and expected Carolyn to ask me what was wrong. On one level I wanted her to ask, but on another I was terrified that she would. If she had, I would have told her because I knew I couldn't lie. I couldn't look her in the eye and say, "Why, nothing!"

But I was not going to "prepare" Carolyn. I had learned from my experience with Annie that this was a bad idea. This time I wasn't going to weaken, so I put it on a back shelf of my mind. There was, after all, no point in letting it interfere with this wonderful day in the tropical gardens of frigid Montreal.

That Sunday evening back in Burlington, I had dinner with our friends John Dunn and Linda Collins before the play. Again, what Guy was going to do kept pushing, but I held on to it even though I knew I was deliberately not telling them something they would want to know. They had been at Barra for New Year's. We had known John since he was seventeen. Now he was a doctor and married to Linda, who was also a doctor. They had named their young daughter after me with the hope of forging a grandparent connection, especially with Guy in mind. I could have confided in them as friends and professionals. Guy had talked with them about his demons. They knew he wasn't interested in seeking medical help, either counseling or medication. But I said nothing. I was not going to repeat the awful situation I'd gotten myself into with Guy when I told Annie.

We walked the few blocks to the Flynn Theater, and as we approached the group of theatergoers I scanned for Guy. He was there! Instantly I was shot through with a lightness, an unbounded joy. I knew that he had had a good trip just by the way he was talking with our friends Reidun and Andrew Nuquist and Priscilla Page. Everyone was laughing, their faces close together. Guy looked so like himself. The isolation was gone. On the surface everything appeared normal. Yet I had that dizzying feeling of a foot in two worlds, because I knew what no one else could see. If anything, *I* was the one who felt isolated, holding a secret that was going to shock all these dear friends when it came out. I didn't like supporting this weight that got heavier with each friend I knew Guy was seeing for the last time. But I knew I was going to go on holding it. I was going to go on keeping the secret.

On Tuesday, January 25, it snowed.

John Nininger dropped us a postcard changing house-framing day to Thursday, January 27.

It snowed all day on the twenty-sixth.

Meanwhile, that morning, Guy had come down with a full-blown case of the flu.

Thursday the twenty-seventh was cold and clear, with a 7:00 a.m. reading of minus four. Guy and I snowshoed out to the car and drove the mile down to the house site. The truck with the huge logs was there, as was the crane. John and his crew were already a few courses up. The sky was that intense dark winter blue above the rim of hills to the south that would form the view from my kitchen windows. The fresh snow, moved by the plow, was mounded above our heads.

Guy felt lousy. He stayed only a half-hour; when he left he told me he hoped he'd be able to make it home.

As I stood in the snow and watched him walk back to the car and drive off, I felt myself testing the feeling that this was how it would be for me. I wouldn't be "Laura and Guy" anymore. Just Laura. The kind of connection Guy and I possessed I knew I would never have again. If we spent an hour apart on separate errands in Hanover, my heart surged in joy to see his compact shape as he stood waiting for me at the bookstore. It was as though, as I reached for his rough and callused hand, we were meeting for the first time. It was as though we were the only two people in the world.

Perhaps it was right that Guy should leave me here to watch my house be set in place. He probably felt relief that he didn't have to stay and play a role. He had told me he felt more and more like Canio in the opera *I Pagliacci*, the traveling player who is forced to act the clown onstage while his heart is breaking. Canio hates himself for this and in the end tears off his mask before the audience, singing: "No, Pagliaccio non son" (I am a player no more). Guy never tore off the mask, but on this house-raising day his flu gave him a good excuse to bow out.

I stayed. I watched each log slot in, knowing that after the log shell was in place, Guy was free to leave. That made up the background of my thoughts as our friend Ned Therrien snapped pictures from his tripod set on the slope above the house. A few friends from the village arrived to watch, as did Maureen, John's wife, and their two daughters, who made a sliding hill out of the snow piles.

As the sun dipped and the air turned even colder, John had all of us help set in place the four huge log pillars that divided the front living space from the back, where my bedroom, writing area, and bathroom would go. These pillars were Guy's idea. Yet this was "Laura's house." He had made no room for himself. No room for his piano.

That evening I wrote in my journal: "Guy was out finishing up wood when I returned. He wants to leave me well supplied. We talked about our life together at Barra — the climbing, the books — reading and writing. It makes me teary just to write this. But I am not fighting what he has to do. I just want what he wants. It is good to say goodbye to Barra together. We're down to just days now. G went to bed early, and I hope he sleeps well."

The next morning I woke up with the flu.

We spent the next week taking care of each other. Guy, who was a few days further along the path to health, fixed me bouillon and cups of tea. During the mornings we worked on our various writing projects. Then, as we ran out of steam, we pulled out the camping pads and took naps on the floor in front of the Ashley, soaking up the wood heat, trying to remember if we had ever both been this sick at the same time.

Sick as I was, this week was a gift. Each day was crystal-cut, and each day felt numbered. I could only think about the day itself. The hour. Not how few or how many were left. I still could not imagine the last day.

That evening Guy played all the songs he knew I loved — "Just a Closer Walk with Thee," "The Tennessee Waltz," "The Maple Leaf Rag," to which he gave the soulful dignity and deliberate pacing of a New Orleans funeral procession. From where I stood at the cookstove I couldn't see him, but I knew exactly how he sat on the piano bench, leaning over the keys, elbows held away from his body, hands grabbing bunches of notes at either end of the keyboard. His mouth turned down in his customary absorbed expression. He was giving these songs everything he had, and the thought of what I was about to lose overwhelmed me. All the years of pleasure I had taken in Guy's music — the deepest and best part of him — were about to go silent. When he finished he came over to where I was cooking, and we stood there in the lamplight, looking at each other. He saw that my eyes were wet. "Please don't play again, Guy," I said. "It's just too painful."

On Saturday, January 29, our friends Jon Martinson, Rebecca Oreskes, and Brad Ray mushed in on snowshoes with their dogs Echo and Tuckerman. The plan was to head down to Hanover to watch Dartmouth's women skaters play Princeton.

We stood in the bright morning sun in front of the woodshed and watched the dogs poke around in the snow. The others joked about Guy's flu, saying they'd make him drive separately and at the rink sit way at the end of the row.

I opted out on the grounds of illness, and I felt an unnamed relief as everyone headed down the path without me. Though I did not see this at the time, the flu gave me an excuse not to put myself in the situation I'd been in with Tom and Carolyn and the others during that weekend in Burlington.

The next day, Sunday, I wrote in my journal: "G's nose and eyes run. He feels wretched. He slept all a.m. I did some correspondence and napped. We worked on wood for an hour or more in the p.m. It was warm — so pleasant out. I came in and napped again. Then worked on Eleanor's novel while G finished up his Index project for Tom — and 'laid down his pen,' like Gibbon in the garden cottage at Lausanne."

On February 1, I wrote: "We try to have the days be like normal, but nothing is normal now. Tonight Guy played the piano when I was getting dinner, and I feel torn apart inside. As if my heart is being pulled out. I think I can't stand it, won't be able to stand it living without Guy. But Guy has not wavered in his decision. He's been writing our dear friends notes for me to give to them. He wants to go, is eager to go."

Those notes included one to his surviving son, Jim. We had not talked about Jim in a long time. In that restaurant near Lincoln Center, Annie had asked me how Jim was going to take his father's suicide. I mumbled something about how we hadn't been in touch. I found conversations about Jim and Guy hard. Right then, I couldn't imagine that Jim would be that much affected. In the last few years friends had asked me if Guy and Jim were estranged. "No." I had always replied. "Just out of touch."

"He'll probably find my death a relief," Guy said in a tone that did not invite dialogue. If that was how Guy felt, I told myself, then that was how it was. I had reached the point of listening only. I wasn't processing in a critical way, and I was hardly reacting. The train was speeding along much too fast. I wasn't about to interrupt the engineer. Jim was Guy's son, and I had never interfered with decisions Guy made about his sons. Pushing Guy into a painful conversation about Jim was out of the question.

On Wednesday afternoon, when Guy came in from working on wood and I was starting supper, he said, "I was thinking of leaving tomorrow morning, but I can't leave while you are still so sick."

Tomorrow morning? That's too soon. I felt a wave of relief that it wasn't going to be tomorrow morning. Gratitude to my flu. Now I knew he would leave as soon as I was better.

On the fourth I wrote,

> Worked on getting the marketing package ready to mail to the Mountaineers Books. On the outside things look like every day. We both go into the PO this afternoon. Say a casual goodbye to Nancy's "Have a good weekend." As we walk across the road to the library, we look at each other: this is too painful. We do a little work for Janene who walks out the door with us without a thought that she won't see Guy on Monday. We drive to our village house. John and his crew are finishing up. We make a little ceremony of giving each of them a copy of our books, standing in the long shadows near the porch.

And finally, on the fifth I wrote,

> This is the last day together. So many familiar routines have been happening for the last time. G just brought in the Ashley wood. I watch him kneel and fill the wood boxes, slotting each piece into the right bin according to size. Everything makes me cry. We walked over to the sugar shed this afternoon with scrap wood for kindling he and I will never burn and noticed that our maple Kinkapot had broken off around 20 feet up. We talk about this change in the forest, just as we always have. This AM I finished reading Eleanor's novel and drafted a critique. G completed a baseball project and I'll make five copies for him for his five notebooks he wants me to give to his baseball friends. Sawed

a little wood. Had supper. G asked me if I wanted the reading. A question he would never ask except this is the last one. We continued on with Gibbon, G closing the book in the middle of the long chapter on the invasion of Italy by Alaric. It was a short reading since it was a bath night and G helped me wash my hair.

Before we go to bed Guy says, "Maybe I am depressed." He's standing sideways, throwing back his head and looking me in the eye. I hear defiance but also confession. It's a statement. Not a question. I have the feeling he's telling me something, some last-minute thing he wants me to know.

I gaze at him. *You're not depressed* flashes across my mind, though I say nothing. His words catch me by surprise. He has never mentioned depression. Neither have I. Certainly, he has never applied that word to himself before. If he is asking for my help, I am unaware of this. I am on my own train now and cannot slow it down.

The next morning he is gone.

CHAPTER eighteen

As for suicide: the sociologists and psychologists who talk of it as a disease puzzle me now as much as the Catholics and Muslims who call it the most deadly of mortal sins. It seems to me to be somehow as much beyond social and psychic prophylaxis as it is beyond morality, a terrible but utterly natural reaction to the strained, narrow, unnatural necessities we sometimes create for ourselves.

— A. Alvarez, *The Savage God: A Study of Suicide*

Guy leaves at eight o'clock on Sunday morning, February 6, 2000.

I follow him with my eyes as he walks away from the cabin, then turns right on the winter path around the garden and into the woods. I catch a final glimpse as he climbs the slope on the other side of the stream, his solid shape shifting among the tree trunks dark in the shadow of an early winter morning. He moves upward at a steady pace, his father's ice axe in his hand, his pack on his back, his form fading to a soundless silhouette, not looking back.

I follow him in my mind as I knead my bread. Where the slope eases he can look down on the sugar shed. Then he will pass our maples — King Lear, Kent, the Fool — everything already steeped in memory. I know when he arrives at the car and how long it takes to unlash his snowshoes, stow his pack, and drive away.

I follow him as he drives to Crawford Notch to get the forecast, then back to Franconia Notch. The weather is clear and cold, so I'm sure he has started up the trail toward Lafayette's summit. Guy and I have walked the Old Bridle Path several hundred times on the way up and down to do our trail work on the Ridge. We know it as well as our own walk in and out of Barra. So I know how long it takes him to move from the trailhead to Dead Ass Corner, a lookout one-third of the way up where one encounters the first sweeping views of Mount Lafayette,

its summit cone scored by slides now filled with snow and ice. My mind casts
back to the day when Guy and I stood at the base of a slide we called Gateway
Gully because of how it narrowed between rock walls, then shot straight up to
the summit. There was a biting wind. Guy hung the thermometer on his ice axe.
We had had an agreement that we wouldn't do such hard climbs when the temperature was below zero. We were above tree line now, and I looked down Walker
Brook to where our tent lay in the trees far below and out of sight. Guy read the
thermometer, then put it away.

"How cold is it?" I asked.

"One," he said, and grinned.

After our climb, as we warmed up on hot chocolate in the tent, Guy said he
had a confession. The temperature had been one, yes, but one *below* zero. That
was the second time Guy had gotten away with that.

I continue to track Guy in my head as I saw wood that afternoon. The sun
streams into the woodshed. I look up from my work many times, half-expecting
to see him striding into our clearing. But I know that if I see his figure, he will
be approaching with his head down, leaning on his ice axe, his shambling pace
radiating a weariness that will reveal to me his dejected state of mind. I don't
want to see Guy returning like that. But my mind keeps jumping back and forth
between wanting to see his familiar shape and knowing that if I see him it will
only be because he has been forced to come back.

I picture Guy seeking a resting place near the summit. He will be very cold.
He will have to suffer in the cold and wind as he seeks this passage from life to
death. As dusk fills our clearing I hang up the saw and stand in the woodshed
door, gazing at the webbed print of his snowshoes leading away from Barra until
I can stand my own thoughts no longer and retreat to the warmth of our cabin.

I don't go to bed until I'm falling asleep over my book. I want to avoid lying
awake with my mind coursing through images of Guy in the wind, Guy in the
dark, Guy in the cold and the wild. Orion shines in our west-facing bedroom
window. This constellation has defined our winter night-time landscape, and
tonight he gives forth an appalling brightness reserved for the coldest nights. I
know Guy sees Orion too.

I'm warm in bed, but I can tell that the temperature is dropping in the
cabin. Whenever a gust of wind hits the window, I spring awake with thoughts
of Guy crouched among the rocks. I know about strong wind in a cold place.
How quickly it numbs the body. How its roaring obliterates thought. How one's
instinct is to flee a punishing wind.

The next morning the temperature at seven o'clock is three below zero, and as
the time moves toward noon I am certain he isn't coming back. If he changed his

mind, or if he just couldn't go through with it, he would have returned by now. I am sure that he has taken his own life. His agony is over. As I look around, the cabin feels suddenly empty. Guy's place across the table is vacant and in its stead is a throbbing silence that echoes and spreads and seems to stop time. I am hit by the overwhelming thought that what we created at Barra is truly over.

That Monday I continued revising a short story I'd started when I'd first begun writing fiction. My childhood is in this story. The central character is a man with the power to draw others to him, yet he holds himself apart, and in the end he walks down his own hidden path to his own destruction. Though I hadn't seen Guy in this before, I did now. I felt my vision enlarge as Guy merged with this character and expanded into myth in a great jumble of images: Guy as Prometheus in his need to help mankind; Guy as Ahab living with the daily torment of his soul; Guy choosing the mountaintop — from such places are heroes raised up by the gods. Guy, the man of vision — wild places are the terrain of visionaries.

As I worked on this story I felt myself possessed of an insight more penetrating than we are given in the dailiness of our lives. It was exhilarating, yet tinged with wrenching sadness. My sadness for Guy's life was honest, but even as I mythologized him I knew he had been too filled with a sense of his own failure to have listened to me go on like this. On the other hand, he had been egocentric enough to have been glad I was. At this moment I was in an unreal place, and by letting my mind turn Guy into the Classical Hero, I was writing my own wished-for redemptive ending to his story. I wanted him, after his trial, his suffering in wind and cold, to find peace of mind before the final darkness overtook him. I couldn't bear to think that his last moments in life on Lafayette's home-like but indifferent summit might have been full of the kind of anguish I'd seen on his worst days at Barra. With all my heart, I wanted it to all come out right for Guy in the end. With no clear knowledge I was doing so, I was attempting to justify his suicide, to make sense of it. Suicide as atonement.

During those four days I was alone at Barra I took comfort in the grounding of our simple routines: fetching water and reading the temperatures, bringing in wood, keeping the fire stoked, sawing wood in the afternoon. Since writing in the mornings was part of the routine, I kept working on that short story. I could have taken a walk or even read, but these activities would not have occupied my mind so fully. Without realizing it, I had put myself in an entirely other place — the land of fiction — so that I could leave behind the hammering thoughts that collected when I was sawing wood or doing anything that didn't require my full concentration.

The rub came when I went out for the mail. Beth, who was at the post office filling in for Nancy, always inquired about Guy. She knew we'd been struck down by the flu that past week. I wanted to avoid conversations about Guy, so to Beth's well-meaning question I replied: *fine.* In a way Guy was fine. But by coming down to the village, I was placing myself in an awkward situation.

We had talked over when I should notify the authorities responsible for search and rescue in the White Mountains. Guy asked me to wait until Friday to give him plenty of time. We both thought that the state police would contact me first about the car left in a trailhead parking area.

Shortly after Guy had walked away, I had doubts about this plan. The state police wouldn't become concerned about the car until the end of the week, and by that time the search and rescue effort would be backed up against the weekend. I felt it was essential to get Guy's body down before the weekend hiking traffic headed up Mount Lafayette on Saturday morning. I decided to walk out to the village on Thursday.

My next problem was deciding where to call from. Guy and I had discussed this also, and we concluded that in the event of no one notifying me directly, I could call from Sarah and Dick's house in the village. When Sarah's mother, our dear friend Freda Williams, was alive, we had used her phone for the rare emergency.

But as the time drew closer I began to feel uncomfortable about throwing myself on Sarah and Dick. What was I going to say? Guy left for the mountains on Sunday. He isn't back yet. May I use your phone to get the search and rescue going? This wasn't the truth of what happened. I knew I had to tell the whole story.

Wednesday night, when I went to bed, I didn't know what I was going to do. But I had to make the call early Thursday morning.

During the night it came to me to go to our village pastor, Holly Noble. I knew that Holly's view of her role extended to nonchurchgoers like Guy and me. I felt that, if I could use anyone's phone, it would be Holly's. As I strapped on my snowshoes and mushed out through the woods, I rehearsed in my head how I would phrase what I needed to say.

The previous days had marked the beginning of my life without Guy. I stood on the threshold, and I could feel myself begin to gain a perspective on our life together. In part this came about because of the words Guy left me. His note — four short paragraphs — began, "The one impossible note to write is this." But Guy had found the words that told me what our life together meant to him. I kept his note, along with the other notes for friends, in the folder beside me on the table as I worked. His last paragraph seemed to steer me into my future: "One part of me will never leave one part of you. But you will also build your own life from now on, and I know you will do it well." Even though, at that moment, I felt very far from building my own life, something in me lifted every time I read his words.

When I shut the cabin door behind me on Thursday at 8:00 a.m., I knew that I was going to shatter the quiet. At Barra I was living in the eye of the hurricane, in the calm spot. By making one phone call, I was going to set the winds of storm churning in the counterrotation, hurling myself into them. I was about to open a door that would lead I knew not where, and the territory ahead felt full of obstacles I could sense but not see. But I couldn't remain in the buffer of Barra any longer. I had to walk straight toward whatever was out there, eyes open, hands in pockets.

When I walked up Holly's front steps, it was 8:45 a.m. I was shaking from not knowing how I was going to say what I had to say.

"Hello, Laura," she said. This was the first time I had knocked on Holly's door, but she showed no surprise at seeing me. She asked me to come in.

I stood in my snowy boots in her hallway. "I'd like to talk to you." My voice was so constricted I thought I was going to suffocate.

"Take off your coat, Laura."

After I was seated on her couch, Holly leaned toward me. "How can I help?" Her face showed concern, and her voice was calm.

I forced out the sentences I'd been practicing on my walk out: "I have tough news. Guy left for the mountains on Sunday, without the intention of coming back."

I watched Holly's face as she took this in. "Oh, Laura," she said.

"I knew what was going to happen," I added. I explained, telling her about Guy's suicide attempt on July 3, 1998, and what had happened since.

"How can I help?" she asked again.

I had made the right decision in coming here. "You can help me make some phone calls," I said.

Right away I ran into difficulties. My hope was to reach Rebecca Oreskes, who worked for the White Mountain National Forest and who I knew could put in motion the search for Guy. But Rebecca wasn't in her office. No one seemed to know where she was.

When Guy and I had discussed this, we both thought I'd call the Fish and Game Department, the organization responsible for search and rescue in the White Mountains. But when it came down to it I couldn't call the Fish and Game.

I knew no one in those offices. I needed to work through a friend. Rebecca was a close friend who had plenty of experience with search and rescue.

But how to get ahold of her? I called Ned Therrien, who had been Rebecca's boss. Ned had last seen Guy when he came to take photographs of the log house set in place a little over two weeks before. When I got Ned on the phone, I spoke the same words I had said to Holly, adding that I was trying to get ahold of Rebecca. There was a silence on the other end of the line. Then Ned said, "I'll track her down for you, Laura." I could hear he was fighting tears.

About ten minutes later Holly's phone rang. It was Rebecca. She had last seen Guy twelve days earlier, when she had sat beside him at the hockey game. We talked a little about Guy, about what he had done. About how I was. Then the line went silent. I could feel Rebecca trying to pull herself together. When she could speak again she said, "I'm sorry, Laura. Guy was my friend." Then she said, "It's almost noon, too late to send a search team up by foot. A storm's coming in tomorrow. We need to get Guy's body down before then and before the weekend." She paused. I knew what she was going to say next. "I hate to ask you this, Laura, but would you agree to a helicopter search for Guy?"

"If you think it's absolutely necessary. But what an irony! Anyway, I doubt it will work," I said. "Guy was wearing navy and forest green. He'll totally blend in."

Rebecca almost laughed. It was a relief for both of us to make a small joke about calling out the helicopters for Guy, who felt so strongly that these noisy contraptions were overused in the mountains. "Did Guy say where he would be? I'd like to pinpoint his location as close as we can." I replied, "I know he didn't want to make this difficult. I think he's very close to the summit of Lafayette, probably just off the trail as you turn north."

Though the helicopter made a dozen passes that afternoon, the flyover was fruitless.

Meanwhile, Rebecca had reached our friends who were active in mountain searches — John Dunn, Mike Young, Doug Mayer, Jon Martinson, and Mike Pelchat. They decided to go up early the next morning, storm or no storm, and bring Guy down. I asked Rebecca to tell them not to take risks, but I knew also that they would not come down without Guy's body.

That evening, as I snowshoed home in growing darkness, I tried to step in a way that left Guy's track visible. I couldn't bear to obliterate his webbed print, the last tangible part of him. I had been doing this every time I'd gone out for the mail, and by now his track was so faint, and I had to concentrate so hard to make it out in the stormy light, that I was unaware that I was crying. I was thinking that if it snowed tomorrow, I would lose this last trace of Guy. But I preferred that — the soft sifting down of snow flake by flake — to my own crude crushing of his print now faded to suggestion.

After dark, around seven, I heard a step on the porch. John Dunn, on his way over to the White Mountains, had tramped into Barra with his dog Brutus. We held each other in the doorway, and John's face was wet with tears. "I had to come see if you were all right," he said.

The next day, Friday, while the searchers were up on the mountain, I made calls to Guy's family from Holly's house. Then, in the early afternoon, Holly and I walked into the village to tell some key people about Guy: our postmaster Nancy Frost, our friend Polly Stryker, and John Nininger, who was building my house. Holly and I knew that each of these friends would help us let the community know about Guy.

John was at work in the basement when Holly and I arrived. I leaned down and said, "When you have a moment I'd like to talk with you, John." In a few minutes he came bounding up the cellar steps with his usual expectant grin. Holly stepped aside, and I stood alone in the snow facing John. I braced myself, trying to control my shaking voice, willing my mind to speak the same sentences I had said many times in the last two days: "I have bad news, John. Guy went to the mountains on Sunday, without the intention of coming back."

John's eyes bulged. "Laura," he said. "Oh, Laura."

He put his arm around me, and I stretched mine around his shoulders, and we began striding up and down in the snow beside the solid log structure John was building. We couldn't stand still. We paced away, and then turned about again. John flung out his arm toward the house and cried, "Guy won't see this. He won't see the house finished!"

It was past midafternoon by the time I returned to Barra. I had just lit the fire when I heard a knock on the door. It was Ginny Barlow, whose aunt had taught me eighth-grade English back in Princeton, New Jersey, one of the best teachers I had ever had. Ginny was in tears. "I was afraid, when you heard the steps, you'd think it was Guy," she said.

The next day, Saturday, was cold and sunny, a classic winter day. Seventeen people and four dogs found their way to Barra, friends who lived nearby as well as ones who had driven up from Massachusetts or over from New Hampshire. The three who had brought Guy's body down off the mountain came to tell me the story. "Guy picked the perfect spot, Laura," Doug Mayer said. "He was a few hundred feet from the summit on a shelf of rock, a big boulder behind his back."

"I can picture it. Just before the trail dips down toward North Lafayette."

"Guy was lying on his side," Mike Young picked up the tale, "that long wooden ice axe of his father's planted in the snow behind him. His body was curled in such a way that he faced north, where his sons had gone, and west toward Vermont and Barra."

The sun was warm on my back where I sat on the window seat, listening. I could hear people sniffing. A few were sitting on chairs, but most were spread out on the floor. I knew Guy and I had formed strong friendships. But I felt the depth of it for the first time that afternoon. I couldn't have felt this before, because Guy couldn't. He couldn't allow himself to feel how much he was loved. He had blocked himself, and I had placed myself in his lengthening shadow. Now he was no longer here, and he had taken his shadow with him.

Guy's leaving had swung open a door that for me led into a sunny room. Indeed, in our cabin that Saturday the sunlight streaming through the windows seemed unstoppable. I looked around at the faces of our friends as they told stories about hikes with Guy. I watched the tears in the men's eyes squeeze out in drops that contorted their faces. They didn't like to cry. They had tried to be the sons that Guy had lost. He knew this. But he would not let it heal him.

I had a story of my own to tell. One I knew they didn't know: Guy's suicide attempt of July 3, 1998, and what came out of that.

"Now I understand about 'Laura's house,'" Doug said. "We knew he might do something like this, but we thought it wouldn't be so soon. I wish I'd tried harder to let Guy know how I felt about him."

"Me too," Rebecca said. "I wish I'd let him know I understood about his demons."

"Would it have helped him?" Doug asked, looking at me.

I didn't know.

"Guy was at bottom such a private person," Jon Martinson said. "I thought about talking with him, but felt he'd find such a conversation an intrusion."

Mike said, "Guy told me once: people come to Barra to see Laura."

"I know, Mike," I said. "Guy said that to me too. I couldn't understand why he should think that. All I could say was, 'And you too.'"

The tears I shed that day were for all that love Guy had cast himself adrift from. The enormous sadness of that. But on another level my spirits soared. Then it hit me: Guy wasn't here. My life was growing lighter without that self-imposed vigilance. I expected to feel a wave of guilt, but I didn't. *It's just me now*, I told myself, feeling a shift. I seemed to be righting myself. Something within was opening. I was rejoining my old self, the self I had been when I first met Guy and during Barra's early years. Then I remembered that final morning, only six days before. Guy had said: "I want to get out of your way." Prospero had indeed freed his Ariel.

As the sun lowered and the light in the cabin dimmed, people began to say goodbye. I was hugged many times, hug piling on hug, infusing me with lightness.

A week later Guy's pack was returned to me. In it I found a small plastic bag containing his eyeglasses, three pencils, two pens, and a copy of the map of Barra he had spent years making. He had colored it in greens and yellows, the stream a blue line, the paths that led into the heart of our woodlot traced in brown. He had penned in the names: Chipmunk Hill behind the house, the Forest of Arden with the maples named for characters in Shakespeare. In the northeast corner was our cabin with woodshed attached, Twin Firs Camp, the garden, the orchard, and the circle of sixteen highbush blueberries. This map had more in common with the map Tolkien had sketched for his world in *The Lord of the Rings* than a surveyor's land map. Guy had always carried a copy of it in his pocket, along with his three-by-five cards, and now, as I stood in the kitchen, holding it in my hands, I saw how creased it was at the folds, how soiled the edges were. I remembered how he had pulled it out for visitors. Guy had placed the map in the plastic bag so I would be sure to see what he had written on the back. "For who would lose . . ." I began to read, and my mind jumped ahead to the following lines. I could have recited them myself. They were from *Paradise Lost*, a last message from Guy.

> For who would lose,
> Though full of pain, this intellectual being,
> Those thoughts that wander through eternity,
> To perish rather, swallow'd up and lost
> In the wide womb of uncreated night,
> Devoid of sense and motion?

His handwriting was jerky and stiff, the words running together, and I was aware of the enormous effort it had taken, with freezing fingers in the hammering wind, to keep his pen moving across the paper. Was Guy questioning his own action: "*For who would lose . . . ?*"

It seemed to me Guy was saying he'd taken the hard work of living as far as he could. Like Ahab, like Milton's Satan, Guy had been led to this final isolated spot on a cold mountain by who he was. He felt the sadness and felt as well the inevitability of his own death.

There was much of the Romantic in Guy. There is much in me. This was Guy on the brink, sending back a message at the last possible moment. This was the postcard we had talked about on that last morning. It was as close as he could come to telling me how it all came out. I saw that there was no redemption here for Guy. No apotheosis. Instead, he was losing everything. "Swallow'd up and lost / In the wide womb of uncreated night, / Devoid of sense and motion."

As I stood in Barra's kitchen and read these lines I was overwhelmed by the continuing marriage of my mind to Guy's. Right then I was living in the spirit of accepting. I had not yet begun to ask the questions. But perhaps it began then as I stared at Guy's familiar handwriting, now so changed by cold. I knew I had to find out what had happened to me. If redemption lay anywhere, it was there. And because my mind could not resist the literary turn, I knew that, like Ishmael, I was the one left to tell the tale.

CHAPTER *nineteen*

We are each inevitably and terribly and forever personally responsible for everything we do.

— Guy Waterman, from a speech written for the president of the General Electric Company

February 17, the day of the service for Guy at the church, was cold and clear, a picture-book winter day in our Vermont hill town. The river behind the buildings clustered on the bank cut a channel between upturned blocks of ice. The snow was heaved along the sides of the road by the plow. The white church, whose sign out front pronounced it Congregational, kept cheek-by-jowl company with the general store on its uphill side. The library, a red brick building, overlooked the store and the church from its knoll across the road. Up the street, in a white cape with a bank of sunroom windows facing east, was the Valley Health Center, its name in raised black letters above the entrance on the porch.

A worn double yellow line snaked down the center of the road. The village had no sidewalks, except for a short concrete strip that spoke more to whimsy than to purpose in front of the gray shingled house that faced the Health Center. Next came the post office, a government construction with a low-angled roof and in need of a coat of paint. But its dowdy looks were no indication of the post office's importance as the pulse of village life. Here neighbor greeted neighbor, passing up and down its four wooden steps. Inside, conversations moved through the seasons, from sugaring to late frosts to woodpiles.

I had gone to the post office six days earlier, when it was time to get word out about Guy. I knew that by asking Nancy to mention that Guy Waterman had died, the village would learn this news as effectively as if the town crier had galloped through on horseback. Friends and neighbors would hear well before the first headlines. "Writer, Outdoorsman Guy Waterman Dies on Mountain," proclaimed New Hampshire's *Manchester Union Leader* on Saturday, February 12, the day after Guy's body was carried by his friends down out of the winds of the

Franconia Ridge. "Nature Writer Dies on Mountain" ran the *Denver Post*, and a similar headline, also picked up on the AP wire, appeared in the *Los Angeles Times*. The *New York Times* obituary appeared on February 20. That reporter got through to me by calling Holly, as had the reporter from the *Boston Globe*. There were reporters at the service. One from the Associated Press waited at the tail end of the line to speak to me. I gave her a hug, thinking she was a friend I was drawing a blank on.

A few nights before he left Guy said, "I doubt I'll have an obituary."

"Probably the *Journal Opinion* will run something," I said. This was our local weekly. "Or the *Littleton Courier*. They cover accidents in the mountains."

Several years before Guy had written his own obituary. He saw this as an exercise in assessing his accomplishments as well as a reminder to fill in the blanks while there was still time. As Guy put it, "Do the words *after* the comma fit with how you want to see yourself?" The words he put after "Guy Waterman, . . ." were "conservationist-homesteader, author, musician, and authority on baseball history."

He had compiled a folder of suggested readings — poems, excerpts from our own books, in particular *Backwoods Ethics* and *Wilderness Ethics* — that could be read at his service. Then, about a month before he left, Guy threw this out. "Too pretentious," he'd mumbled.

"Leave something in there, Guy," I said. "It will make it easier."

When I came to pull that file off the shelf, it contained only a few poems — Emily Dickinson's "My Life Closed Twice before Its Close," Elinor Wylie's "Wild Peaches," and Robert Frost's "The Road Not Taken."

Guy had also been clear about Bible readings. He wanted the passage from Ecclesiastes — King James version *only* — *that* begins,

> Vanity of vanities, saith the Preacher,
> Vanity of vanities; all is vanity.
> What profit hath a man of all his labour
> Which he taketh under the sun.
> One generation passeth away, and another
> Cometh: but the earth abideth forever; . . .
> For in much wisdom is much grief; and he that
> increaseth knowledge increaseth sorrow.

I wondered if these words would reveal that hidden side of Guy when read aloud by Holly in the church. Reading them to myself less than a week after he died — letting them sink in — raised the shade on Guy's despair in a way I had not seen.

As for music, he'd jotted down names of a few hymns: "A Mighty Fortress," "Abide with Me," "Once to Every Man and Nation," and "The Battle Hymn of the Republic."

But Guy wanted more than just hymns. On February 14, 1998, Doug Mayer and Rebecca Oreskes had come to Barra to record Guy playing music for his own service. I had asked then if, while he was at it, he could play music for my service as well. Guy's mention of my request only added to the general nervous joking of this occasion. No one, me included, knew what Guy had in his mind. But Doug and Rebecca weren't too surprised. Everyone knew how well organized Guy was, how he planned ahead. As Doug recorded, Guy played four pieces: the slow movement from Haydn's Quartet Opus 54 in G Major, which he had played as a young violinist at Greenwood, a music camp in the Berkshires; Scott Joplin's "Maple Leaf Rag"; "Lament for the McLean of Ardgour," a Scottish song that was played at his father's memorial service and had great meaning for the family; and the hymn "Just a Closer Walk with Thee," which he knew I liked and which he played with the compelling beat of a jazz piece. When we listened to the tinny playback I had my doubts as to how this would come off in the church. It seemed somewhat controlling, if not borderline gruesome. Guy pulling the strings, insisting that people sit and listen to his music. He was aware of his self-absorption and therefore bent over backward not to inflict his piano on anyone. He almost always had to be asked to play. This often led people to see him as selfless. Since these thoughts felt disloyal, I kept them to myself.

(After the service our friend Lou Cornell wrote to me: "I was deeply moved by Guy's service. A high point was, to my surprise, the scratchy recordings of G's music — I thought, when Linda and John told me what he planned, that it was a bad idea, but in a haunting way G's voice came through and lingered on after the music ended.")

Then Guy got the idea that it might be nice for people to walk in to his music, and he asked Doug and Rebecca to pay a return visit. This time I knew Guy's plans, but I allowed myself to feel only a nagging discomfort as we listened to Guy play and I watched Doug's and Rebecca's faces. I kept squashed down the question that fought to surface: *How will they feel when they discover what Guy has in mind?* This time there wasn't any joking, nervous or otherwise.

Later Rebecca told me what Guy had said during a walk in the garden that November afternoon. "'We've had some wonderful times here. I wish it could go on forever, but it can't. Nothing can.'"

"He was telling me something for which there was no argument," Rebecca said. "I knew his words were true, but there was something behind them I wasn't ready for, so I stayed silent."

I walked with Guy's family, all from out of town, from the parsonage to the church. The sun was blinding as it struck the snowbanks, and the high sky behind the hills shaded to indigo. Already, a half-hour before the service, a long line of cars stretched on both sides of the road.

It seemed that everyone we had ever known was in the church. They were seated in the balcony and stood against the walls. Holly sat in her high-backed chair behind the altar. The readers sat in the choir stall to Holly's right. Guy's family occupied the front two rows. I sat next to Guy's surviving son, Jim, who had come from Colorado.

Guy had told me he thought just his tam on the altar might be fitting. Nothing else. I wasn't so sure. I thought the gesture was a little morbid, perhaps even show-offish. But Guy was inexorably connected with his tam. Does he take it off to sleep? friends often kidded. I had asked my friend Polly Stryker to do the flowers. "I'll do boughs, Laura," she said. I mentioned what Guy wanted with his tam. "Can you get it to me?" she asked.

Later Polly told me that items for the bough arrangement just appeared on the seat of her truck: deer antlers, several birds' nests, one with eggs. The tam fit right in, and the church was permeated with the aroma of evergreens.

Danuta Jacob, the jazz vocalist Guy had worked with for the past six months, sang "Over the Rainbow," a song Guy associated with his son Johnny.

Tom Simon, Guy's baseball friend, read from an essay by Bart Giamatti, the Yale president who had become commissioner of baseball and died in office after only 154 days. "It breaks your heart," Tom read.

> It is designed to break your heart. The game begins in the spring, when everything else begins again, and it blossoms in the summer, filling the afternoons and evenings, and then as soon as the chill rains come, it stops and leaves you to face the fall alone. You count on it, rely on it to buffer the passage of time, to keep the memory of sunshine and high skies alive, and then just when the days are all twilight, when you need it most, it stops. Today, a Sunday of rain and broken branches and leaf-clogged drains and slick streets, it stopped, and summer was gone.

Guy's niece, Laura Cooley, read Milton's "Song on May Morning," which, weighing in at ten lines, was a bit easier to take than Milton's twelve-book epic.

Rebecca read a reflection she had written on Guy and his literary heroes: Milton's Satan, Ahab from *Moby-Dick*, and Prometheus, stealer of fire. All three were consumed both by journeys of one kind or another and by fire in various forms, and each one was painfully human.

A few days later my friend Lou Cornell would write me,

> Despite the affinity Guy felt for Ahab, Satan, and Prometheus, I can't really identify him with any of them. He wasn't cruel like Satan, or monomaniacal like Ahab, though he did want to help mankind like Prometheus, at great cost to himself. I thought instead of Hamlet. To me Hamlet has never been the wishy-washy intellectual that the Romantics wanted to make him: rather, a Renaissance prince, a formidable swordsman, a brilliant and witty mind addicted to wordplay but afflicted with depression, a questing imagination haunted by self-doubt and tempted by the thought of death — by far the most interesting of Shakespeare's tragic heroes, the only one you could imagine talking to. I thought of his friends carrying Guy's bier down the mountain, as Fortinbras's soldiers carry Hamlet off the stage, and Horatio's wonderful lines of farewell ["Now cracks a noble heart. Good night, sweet prince, / And flights of angels sing thee to thy rest"] kept running through my mind.

Sally and Tek Tomlinson read poems they had each written about Guy, neither knowing the other was doing this. As did Art Kirn, whose poem began, "Elfin giant of the mountain ways."

Twelve-year-old violinist Hannah Meier and her cellist father, Larry, played a J. S. Bach piece that Guy had heard them play before. Ida and Nancy Nininger, my builder John's daughters, played a four-hand piece that they'd performed on our Steinway at Barra a year earlier.

Near the end of the service Holly read a piece sent by village friends Sue and Bill Parmenter: "Guy Waterman was a 'counter,'" they wrote. "He counted virtually everything that affected his life — the crops that he and Laura raised, the number of blueberries they picked, the amount of sap produced from each tree in their sugar bush, the many visitors who came to Barra to see how they lived, hockey and baseball statistics — and so much more that we never knew."

Earlyn Dean, a friend from our rock climbing days, spoke.

> I hiked and climbed with Guy and Laura in the Gunks. While I was on the Appalachian Mountain Club's nominating committee, Ralph Waterman was proposed for membership. Ralph had completed all the major eastern peaks. He was well mannered, red-haired, and a good hiker. The committee had almost passed the application when one person said, "I thought Guy had only three sons: Bill, John, and Jim. Who is this fourth son, Ralph?" Guy's dog was out of the bag, so to speak, and membership denied.

Doug Teschner, who lived across the Connecticut River, had this to say.

It was always a fairy tale adventure to visit the Watermans. You walked deep into the woods and suddenly came into a clearing with a small house. If you were lucky and they weren't out hiking or climbing, you would be warmly greeted by Laura and the elflike Guy in his ever-present tam-o'-shanter. Guy had a wonderful mischievous personality, and he loved kids. He told Ben and Luke about trolls in his root cellar. Once he gave them a little ceramic elephant, no doubt a leftover from his political days. And he often entertained us with ragtime on the piano. ("How did you get the piano up here?" the boys would ask.)

On the last page of the program I wrote: "All his life, Guy felt that Ariel and Caliban represented the two warring forces within himself." Then ran the words with which Guy ended his memoir.

> *Closing Words* —
> In *The Tempest* Prospero calls Ariel:
>
> > . . . my industrious servant,
> > . . . my tricksy spirit
> > . . . my diligence.
>
> He speaks thus of Caliban:
>
> > A devil, a born devil, on whose nature
> > Nurture can never stick; on whom my pains,
> > Humanely taken, all, all lost, quite lost;
> > And as with age his body uglier grows,
> > So his mind cankers. . . .
>
> And in the play's Epilogue, these are Prospero's closing words:
>
> > Now my charms are all o'erthrown,
> > And what strength I have's mine own,
> > Which is most faint . . .
> > . . . Now I want
> > Spirits to enforce, Art to enchant;
> > And my ending is despair,
> > Unless I be reliev'd by prayer,
> > Which pierces so, that it assaults
> > Mercy itself, and frees all faults.
> > As you from crimes would pardon'd be,
> > Let your indulgence set me free.
> > (*Exit.*)

That last evening, as we sit at supper, Guy says that soon the voices will be still. He puts his hands to his head. Stupidly, I just look at him. I don't say: *What*

voices, Guy? What are the voices saying? I think I know what he means — the "voices" telling him he let his sons down, that our *Ethics* books fell on deaf ears — but I see now that I have no idea what he means. He has never spoken to me of voices before.

The next morning, as we stand together at the table, Guy hands me the last three pages of his memoir.

"Please don't read them until I've left," he says.

This is what I read a half-hour later.

> The transition away from deep involvement in the mountains and in the issues of preserving wildness in the northeastern backcountry has been painful, associated with a sense that we were retreating, defeated, from the field. A few people have said some very nice things about our books, but on the whole they and our ideas about eastern wildness seem to be sinking into oblivion unnoticed. All this is accompanied by a feeling that I could have done better.

> To be retreating from that arena is to remind myself that I retreated from others at other times in my life. I left jazz piano playing without ever finding out whether or not I might have had something important to contribute there. I walked away from an amazingly promising start in Washington politics. In many ways, thinking of the public service aspects of my work in Washington, I think the most useful thing I could have done with my life would have been to remain in the center of staff work there. . . . There are people who would say that the example Laura and I have set in living as we have for 27 years is a shining beacon to others. But we are not cut out (as Helen and Scott Nearing were, for example) for a leadership role in this arena. For one thing, we really have shaped a life relevant only for the two of us, not a pattern for others to imitate. If you look closely at almost anything we have done, it doesn't stand up to scrutiny as a model for others.

> Considerations like these have left me with a sense of dissatisfaction about what I've accomplished all my life. When this feeling first became uppermost, as we pulled away from our mountain involvements, it was very depressing. The year or so before and after my 60th birthday [May 1992] was particularly depressing. The years since have not really been much better, only more numbed. I play the role of genial host and wit as best I can, so that few of even our closest friends are likely to be aware of how I feel. The opera *Pagliacci* seems to me particularly poignant as a result: that's what I seem to be walking through these days, trying to provide sparkling company for everyone but ready to give up otherwise. Laura is the only one subjected to the blackest of my moods — an intolerable burden for her, which she bears with inexhaustible patience and sympathy.

I could add that the physical process of aging appalls me. I have been uncommonly lucky physically, all my life, have sailed through with no major broken bones, no serious illness, not even significant pain. But now I find all kinds of minor aches and pains and physical limitations I never knew before, harbingers of advancing age which are only bound to become much more evident, more limiting, more uncomfortable. As I look at people in their 70s and 80s, even those who are cheerful and uncomplaining, I see they put up with many things I hope I never have to. I'd not be cheerful and uncomplaining. So longevity has ceased to be an objective of mine.

I have used — probably to excess — the metaphor of Ariel and Caliban to describe the warring tendencies within me all my life, the constructive and positive versus the negative and destructive. I think of my father and my son Johnny as embodying these two impulses.

My father — Hawee, as all the family called him — stood for everything positive, a deep sense of public service, an "Olympian calm" (my sister Anne's apt phrase), always in control, upright and strong, though always gentle and reserved. If this sounds like hero worship, let me add that he was never, for me, a warm father or able to be close to me, or to help me with my childhood, teenage, or young adult problems. I do not revere his memory. But I see in his dedication to public policy a side of me that has always struggled for expression.

Johnny, on the other hand, poor Johnny embodied those impulses in me which have been destructive, as they were so finally for Johnny. He was always at war with the world, never knew calm, always teetered on the verge of being out of control — and frequently was. As Hawee seemed to dwell in a world of sunshine, in the service of his fellow humanity, Johnny struggled always in a world of darkness and storm, alienated irretrievably from his fellows in this life.

Both in me. I know that the same high positive impulses of Hawee's have been prominent in me at times — wonderful tendencies. But the same demons which drove Johnny to destruction have always intervened — where, after all, did Johnny get them from? And though I've grown a protective covering of smiles and talk, I, too, am alienated from my fellow humanity and dwell in a private world of storm and darkness.

Ariel versus Caliban. Prospero's options — the world was all before him, where to choose his place of rest. As I look at where I have come to, after 67 years of struggling, I see that Caliban has won.

❀ ❁ ❀

CHAPTER twenty

"All the privilege I claim for my own sex (it is not a very enviable one, you need not covet it) is that of loving longest, when existence or when hope is gone."

— Jane Austen, *Persuasion*, Anne Eliot speaking

When the time came to leave Barra and move down to my new house in the village, it was clear to me that the best way to execute a stress-free move was to put into practice what I had learned from Guy. He often joked that there were two positions at Barra: the chairman of the Board and chief executive officer, who was me, and the head of Research and Statistics, him. While chairman of the Board was the high-visibility title, companies can be run by the statisticians. And this was how Barra worked. Now I see that, as chairman of the Board, I was responsible for providing stability, a rocklike grounding, for our frail little company. Barra's statistician knew he needed that. At any rate, after three decades of living with the brilliant statistician, this chairman of the Board had witnessed what could be accomplished with good planning.

I began my own sorting and packing job at the end of February. This gave me four months to go through more than thirty years of files, letters, and accretive memorabilia from both our lives. I wanted to live with the transition as it unfolded day by day. My life was going to change. I felt it was important to take a deliberate, thoughtful leave of our years at Barra.

That winter of 2000 my routine was to snowshoe out in time to pick up the mail when Nancy got back from her lunch break at one thirty, and then go down to see how my house was coming along.

The Monday after Guy's service, I walked into noise and sawdust and a four-foot stack of lumber in the middle of the floor. There was no plumbing, or wiring, and the only heat was from a large old Fisher woodstove John had hooked up to the cinder-block chimney in the basement. He was feeding it hop hornbeam and rock maple that Guy had brought down from Barra late the previous fall, anticipating that John would have an immediate need for wood. Whenever I went into the basement, I threw a glance toward the woodpile. It was shrinking. I wanted it to sit untouched forever where Guy had stacked it. Finally, it was down to just a few scattered logs lying on the concrete floor, a pile no longer, and I bid it goodbye.

"How do you like this, Laura?" John said one day. He held up a round pine stick between the windows, a bank of four, over where my kitchen sink would go.

"Oh! You're looking for wood like that? I've got all kinds of pieces left over from building Twin Firs Camp."

I began packing out one- to six-inch-diameter softwood sticks with interesting angles and stubs all weathered to a silvery gray. The carpenters turned these pieces into drawer pulls, dividers for the bookcases, and railing posts that contrasted with the golden-hued pine.

My friend Helen Whybrow offered to come help me pack my books. We lifted the sets of Dickens and Scott, Kipling and Shakespeare down off the shelves, carried them out to the porch, and dusted each one before we laid them in boxes. That evening I wrote in my journal: "If anything can make me feel I'd like to leave Barra, it is looking at the bare shelves. I'm making the house unlivable for myself. If the books are gone, I don't want to be here. So I follow my books to Page Hollow. Guy is gone. It remains only for me to be gone as well."

I'd set moving day for June 17. Kate Botham, Barra's first steward in a room-and-board arrangement worked out with the Good Life Center, the organization that would carry on the homesteading tradition at Barra, was arriving two days later. We had met Kate when she was a sophomore at Dartmouth College, and she had helped us with garden jobs and wood over her years there.

On the seventeenth, nine hiking friends helped me pack out 192 boxes, 76 of them books. We kept track of the numbers for Guy. After everyone had left, I stood in the middle of the floor of my new house and confronted the boxes stacked up to the window ledge. I was alone. I listened to the house. It was silent. I wanted Page Hollow to be a silent house, just as Barra was. The late afternoon sun slanted in beneath the overhanging roof, striking the log walls and spilling a yellow glow.

I unpacked a box on which I'd written open soon: it contained my toothbrush and towel, a pot to boil water in, and a few tea bags. I began unpacking books. Guy loved arranging books. Once he'd arranged them all by color: reds together, the greens, the blues, and so on. A few months earlier he had said: "You'll enjoy arranging your books."

"Not without you," I'd replied.

Now I stood in front of the empty bookshelves of my new house and stared at all the boxes of books. *How* was I ever going to organize them? Guy's mind handled this kind of organization. I opened a few cartons looking for the sets: Dickens, Shakespeare, Scott, and Kipling. I told myself I didn't have Guy, and I wasn't at Barra now, and I felt my own mind kick in. I decided to place them in the corner bookcase in the living area. Next came our own books, and my father's.

I carried boxes upstairs for the shelves Guy had designed at either end of the built-in guest bunks. I pulled out the old set that had belonged to Guy's grandfather on ancient Greece and Rome; Guy's collection of *Iliad*s; history, including Churchill's history of World War II; the Macaulay that Guy read on the commuter train when I met him; Carlyle, whom we'd read aloud when working on *Forest and Crag*. Next came the fiction, mostly nineteenth- and twentieth-century European and American authors, a collection that cast a wide and unsystematic net. Many were paperbacks, dog-eared and yellowed, dating back to the 1960s and my book-buying New York days. Many of the children's books came from my childhood bedroom in Lawrenceville, except for a complete set of *Dr. Doolittle* that had belonged to Johnny. I kept stumbling across all the books we had read aloud. The spines had darkened, and some were nearly illegible from twenty-seven years of wood smoke. I opened *The Count of Monte Cristo*. It smelled of Barra.

This job took me close to a week. I worked on it at night, after spending the day at Barra helping Kate get the garden planted. It felt strange — indulgent and wasteful of resources — to work after dark in a house electrically lit. Guy and I had placed only a single lamp on the table where we wrote and read in the evenings. The rest of our cabin was plunged in shadow. We each carried a flashlight, which wore holes in our pants pockets. Here at Page Hollow I kept reaching for my pocket flashlight, forgetting to turn on a light when I went up and down stairs.

That first week I became aware of something else. More subtle, and impossible to capture in an electrified house, was how Barra filled up with darkness at the close of day. I had found this crepuscular turning from day to night calming and indescribably peaceful. I had become a participant in the process myself. Electricity banished twilight and erased as well the easy connection to the night I had felt at Barra.

That first night at Page Hollow I kept putting off going to bed. It got late. Midnight. Finally, I made myself get into this new bed that snugged into the log wall. I turned on the electric light, settled myself with two pillows at my back and a book in my hand, and looked around at my life from this new angle. I heard myself say out loud: *This is going to work out.* I set down my book and picked up a thick three-ring notebook, my journal: "I don't like to think of Barra being dark, as it is tonight," I wrote, "and I couldn't bring myself to take a shower. I certainly needed one. I went in and looked at its white tiles, then came back out. It's a lovely shower, but no leafy bower of green. I'll sleep in Barra's sweat and grime tonight and take one on the first day of my new life tomorrow morning. My bed is perfect. I sit here and gaze in wonder, surrounded by wood, by this house that Guy designed, and by the beautiful dresser and shelves John and his carpenters built. It makes me feel very good. I hope I can do good work here."

Afterword

I want, by understanding myself, to understand others.

I want to be all that I am capable of becoming. . . .

This all sounds very strenuous and serious.

But now that I have wrestled with it,

It's no longer so. I feel happy — deep down.

All is well.

— Katherine Mansfield, *Journal*

Near the end of the summer of 2000, six months after Guy's suicide, I attended a local production of Strauss's opera *Ariadne auf Naxos*. In the climatic moments Ariadne and the god Bacchus evoke in a duet of musical flight the *transformation*: the step across from life to death.

Strauss's soaring outpouring of golden notes transports me up to the Franconia Ridge. The temperature plummets below zero, and the air turns jagged as the sun's warmth flees the earth, lifting last of all from the high mountain ridges and leaving behind an unsurvivable arctic cold. I see Guy, crouched among the hoar-frosted boulders in the alpenglow, the sole audience in the front-and-center seat, star in his own performance witnessed by no one.

At that moment, in the grip of Strauss's music, I feel Guy's transformation.

During the past month I had tried to imagine what embracing death was like for him. I had hoped that at the end, as the unstoppable cold seeped in, he achieved a oneness, a final revelation that his mind, attuned to the nineteenth century's perception of the sublime in nature, could grasp. Especially I had hoped he sensed that absorption into the wild that meant everything to him in life.

In the course of writing this book I have come to see that I wanted more. I wanted Guy's burden — the grief and guilt and blame, all the shame — to lift like mist on a summer morning. I wanted Guy to forgive himself.

On the heels of Guy's death I received hundreds of letters. Most of them were from friends, but some came from people I had never met who had read about Guy's death in the newspapers and magazine articles. I answered them all. I wanted to respond to everyone who was reaching out to me. His suicide provoked a spectrum of reactions. "Guy was my hero," a friend wrote. "I hope I can be that brave when the time comes." Another said: "Oh, Laura, his death was such a waste. He was so talented, with so much still to offer the world." The big question — "How could you let it all happen?" — was never voiced. At that time I could not have guessed that was what everyone was asking themselves but did not dare to ask me. Back then I was very far from asking it of myself.

In the first month of 2003 I traveled to Boston to visit a Shady Hill School classmate of Guy's, Gil Murray, who I knew wanted to talk about Guy. After I returned home I received a note from Gil, dated, by coincidence, February 6, 2003 — three years to the day after Guy walked up the wintry path to the summit of Mount Lafayette. Gil wrote: "Yes it helped so much to talk to you about Guy's life and your ongoing life. I think part of my dilemma was in feeling alone with my questions. Was I being disloyal — too critical? I think now I can put Guy away with fondness for his humor, drive, and style, and sadness at his vanity and egocentrism contributing to his death."

This conversation with Gil had helped me too, though even three years later I was surprised, and a little disturbed, that Gil would use words like "vanity and egocentrism" in describing Guy. But I was willing to pass them over for his description of feeling fond of Guy's "humor, drive, and style." Those were the words I entirely agreed with, the words I wanted applied to Guy.

So I was especially grateful for my friend Lou Cornell's letter of May 27, 2003

> Guy's nobility of spirit, combined with an extraordinary force of character, gave him the power to lead a good life — something that many of us resolve to do but fail to accomplish because we lack the qualities that Guy so eminently possessed. We muddle through taking life as it comes, and, if we're lucky, succeed to some degree in inhabiting the world without messing it up too much. Guy was different. He planned his life carefully, carried out his plans with force and deliberation, and took responsibility (too much truthfully) for what he considered his failures. His end was therefore much closer to tragedy than anything I've ever encountered.

Though Lou wasn't exactly saying it, I liked thinking of Guy as the tragic hero. Others had written me along these lines, and I had taken comfort that people were saying such nice things about Guy. I told myself that he would have liked being seen this way and would have handled it with appropriate modesty. It wasn't until much later that I began to realize that while a part of Guy might have relished being called a hero, he would have turned the phrase against himself because he, unlike everyone else, knew that it was utterly false.

In 2003 Chip Brown published a book on Guy's life and death called *Good Morning Midnight*. Chip's visits and our conversations about Guy had all been very positive, even moving, experiences for me. The year before, an ardent group of mountain friends had established a memorial fund for Guy that continues his vision and work of stewardship in the alpine world of the Northeast — the Guy Waterman Alpine Stewardship Fund (www.watermanfund.org). The Good Life Center, the group that Guy and I had donated our land to, was ready to take over at Barra, and as soon as I got settled in my new house I began work on this book. I'm trying to find out what happened to me, I told friends who asked why I was writing a memoir.

As I worked I thought about my friend Annie Barry. I had betrayed Guy's confidence by telling Annie what Guy was going to do. She elbowed her way rather dramatically onstage at the last moment. I was still mad at her for this, and I still thought she didn't understand. If she had understood, I repeatedly told myself, she would never have acted as she did.

Finally, I finished writing. After I decided to look over the manuscript for the last time before turning it in to my publisher, I pulled Annie's letter — the one I asked her not to write — out of the file and reread it. I had already read it twenty, maybe fifty times and always ended up stuffing it back in the folder, feeling certain once again that Anne was wrong, just plain wrong. She had urged me to think about why I was keeping Guy's secret. She had wanted me to get help, if not for Guy, who didn't want help, at least for myself. At the time, I didn't understand what Annie meant by secrecy because, after all, wasn't Guy, by telling me his plan, being honest with me? And I didn't need help either, I told myself, certainly not from a psychiatrist, a breed Guy thought the worst of, and right then I was living entirely in Guy's world. This time, when I read her letter, I had reached a point in my own process of discovery when I understood what Annie was saying. Through the journey of writing this book, I was at last able to answer for myself that burning question: How could I have supported my husband in his plan to commit suicide? I had finally reached this point, the destination, the last stop where I could step off the train.

But before I could properly savor this victory, another question appeared. If I had known then what I know now, could I have helped Guy? Could I have made a difference in the outcome? First, I told myself, I would have had to come to grips with that underlying terror of my father's alcoholism. This was the same terror that I could feel around Guy and that could hold me immobile. Perhaps, I told myself, if I had been able to understand that terror before Johnny's descent into craziness and death . . . then . . . But Guy would have had to want my help. He would have had to ask.

On July 9, 2004, I received a letter from my friend Doug Mayer, a letter he had written to someone else who had written with questions about Guy. Doug wrote,

> Guy was extremely tough about taking personal responsibility for one's actions. I found that admirable, in an era when everyone seems to be passing the buck. This is an especially interesting aspect to his personality, because I think it was also his downfall. He was unable to open up to Laura and friends, and never really found true love in this sense. In the end, that inability endears him to those of us who knew him best, creating a permanent sense of loyalty and protectiveness. In a sense this quality makes him a tragic figure, which only creates a tighter, sadder, more heartfelt bond.

Doug, a close friend, had helped to carry Guy's body down off the mountain, and I knew he had been struggling to make sense of Guy's suicide. Reading Doug's words, I was reassured that some of us had come a long distance toward understanding this complex and intriguing man who had kept so much of himself beyond our reach and about whom much, we knew, would remain mysterious. I knew also that in spite of these personal struggles with the meaning of Guy's death, we still loved him. I, for my part, would have married him all over again.

How do I feel now about how we lived at Barra? This was a life that embraced an extreme. Most people, I imagine, saw us as living with a degree of privation that was probably not necessary. And I can see now that our life, so stripped as it was of "modern conveniences," probably looked strange to the outside world. Many visitors said to us: "We'd like to live like this, but . . ." Often the sentence was never finished. What they meant was that some parts of our life were wonderfully compelling (the garden, being outside so much), but other parts (hauling every drop of water, using the outhouse at twenty below) were decidedly not.

But I can *still* say that nothing about our life felt like hardship to me. I had embraced Guy's vision of Barra because it gave me the freedom I needed too. Freedom to create a life, freedom to learn, freedom to be myself. Freedom to share a life with Guy in the only way he could live. This was especially true at the beginning. As Guy's depression deepened I put restraints on myself. And then the way we chose to live at Barra became even more important to me. Our life lived on the land was full and whole. We fit into the seasonal round. What we did there was all of a piece, not fragmented, and we found peace of mind as we performed the daily routines, the rituals of fetching water and working up wood. By placing ourselves in a spot that made us work for our nourishment and comfort, we put ourselves in direct touch with what was elemental. Through our physical work, we eliminated, as it were, the middleman and plugged into a life that more fully embraced the natural world and the land. Without realizing the implications, we had forged a hot-line connection that did as much for our bodily health as it did for the health of our spirits. Guy needed this or Barra never would have happened, and I came to need it too.

Has living with plumbing and electricity now changed my life? Oh, yes! I have lost by gaining these conveniences. I live further now from the essence of things. But a few conveniences fit my circumstances, and I have picked and chosen what I need in my life without Guy, which is a life more about writing and less about working up wood. There is some of that, however, as well as growing vegetables and flowers, blueberries and fruit trees, and reading books — though none aloud.

But in some ways very little has changed. The values I learned by living all those years at Barra will never leave me. "It is good to take care of a piece of land" was how Guy put it. We learned by living on the land how to care for it. We learned to live lightly. We learned to love the land. If future visitors to Barra can take away one thing, I hope it may be that.

If I want to visit Barra today, I put on my boots and make the two-mile walk up through the village, past the church and the library, across the bridge, and onto the dirt road that narrowly twists and turns as it enters the woods. When it reaches the crest it drops steeply and becomes a path leading to a clearing — still its own contained world. Here is the cabin sheltered by the rock ledge hillside on the north, and the garden dreaming in the afternoon sun.

Epilogue

If the last act is not superior to all the rest, you might as well not sing it.

— Maria Callas

In the note he left for me Guy had written, "One part of me will never leave one part of you. But you will build your own life from now on, and I know you will do it well." Even as I read these words on the day he left to kill himself in the cold on Mt. Lafayette, I understood that Guy meant me to know I possessed the power to step across into a life I would make for myself. *He wanted this for me.*

Guy was giving me his blessing, though he would not have used that phrase. He would have thought of it as an encouraging shove. The sort that could happen when we climbed together. Like the first time I led on ice. We had arrived at the base of Willey's Slide in Crawford Notch to discover Guy had forgotten his crampons. He was exceedingly put out by himself, as any climber would be. We were with our friend Louis Cornell, who didn't lead ice then. "So," Guy said, handing me the rope, "it's up to you, Laura." For me, that day on Willey's Slide was an exploration of new terrain, both on the ground and in my head. Guy's encouraging shove worked! As have the words he left in his note to me.

It was black and cast iron and it burned wood. We called it the Barra Cookstove. It took up just the right amount of space in our cabin and sat on stubby legs. The cookstove came up to my waist and had six rimmers — round discs on the top surface that could be removed. I stoked the stove with wood through the rimmers on the left side. I could easily imagine myself as an engineer on a freight train when I ran my stove: building up the heat, keeping it even, especially when I had bread in the oven, decreasing it at the right moment so as not to overcook the loaf or waste fuel. I found it very hands-on and a joy to operate. The Barra Cookstove kept us well fed and warm.

After I moved out of Barra, the stove stayed and served the stewards who continued the homesteading for several more years. But the time came when it was suggested to me that we make a change in the stoves at Barra. Guy and I had two: the other being the Ashley, a sheet-metal powerhouse that delivered full-on winter warmth. The couple at Barra at that time suggested the purchase of one larger cookstove that was also an efficient heater. So the change was made and the Barra Cookstove was moved to the basement: dirt floor, four feet of headroom.

There it remained for several long, lonely years, until I offered it to a young homesteading friend who had been looking to replace his stove. Anders had written me after reading our books and asked if we might correspond. He'd worked on trail crews of the mountain clubs and had opinions and questions based on his own observations. I was more than happy to engage on paper about mountain ethics. Hearing what Anders had to say — his voice from the field — opened another pathway to keeping me current.

Anders arrived at Barra with a burly friend and we wrestled the stove out of the basement and up to his tiny handmade cabin in Vermont's Northeast Kingdom. I didn't have occasion to visit Anders often, but when I did, seeing the Barra Cookstove was like renewing ties with an old and dear friend with whom much history has passed under the bridge.

After another passage of time, after Anders found the perfect mate in Kalyn and bought land in another Vermont village, built a cabin with an attached greenhouse, repaired a small barn for their animals, and began growing astonishingly productive gardens, and, oh, yes, started a family. It was high time for a visit.

The Barra Cookstove was the last thing on my mind as I followed Anders's handwritten directions that involved numerous turns onto progressively narrower and rougher dirt roads. I was about to give up hope when, as is often the case, there I was, at the end, quite literally, with the cabin unmistakably on one side of the dirt track, and a large fenced-in, deer-proof garden on the other. There was Anders, hoe in hand, running to greet me, and Kalyn carrying baby Fay. We were introduced.

Of course I wanted to see everything all at once. We started with the garden, where their ideas were already in practice for the rotation of crops, as was their goal for growing enough winter feed for their cow and sheep. I was introduced to the cow whose name was Gouda and told of the death of their other cow a week ago, exceedingly mourned, but, yes, plans to replace her were in the works. Life on a homestead goes on.

We moved toward their cabin, where an assortment of tools hung in a sheltered alcove near their entrance. None of these tools had motors, none required batteries. I saw no chain saws or battery-driven drills, no weed whackers or brush hogs or buzz saws or table saws. No tractor. What I did see, aside from garden tools, was an assortment of knives for carving, and when I asked Anders if he'd carved that elegant, gracefully curved handle on the scythe hanging from the wall he smiled and nodded. "And the door handle?" I asked. Guy and I had aspired to, but never attained, Anders's level of craftmanship. We'd turned out a door latch or two that over years of constant use had acquired a reasonable patina that lent some distinction. I still used a napkin ring Guy had made from the right-sized limb with a ready-made knothole.

Standing in the midst of Anders's hand tools, each in its proper place, each with its own particular use, threw me back to our days at Barra. The sun, slanting in under the sheltering roof, glanced off the blade of the crosscut saw, defining each tooth that Anders had sharpened to an angled point. We had never mastered that art either, but took our crosscuts to Stanley Oliver, near the village, who patiently answered our questions about the mysteries of sharpening teeth of uneven heights.

Anders held open the door to their cabin and I crossed the threshold. The Barra Cookstove sat in the exact center of the room. I wanted to speak, but couldn't. Tears clogged my throat. The stove looked wonderful, cared for and completely at home. As was I. Its black surface pulled me and I put out my hand, touched the stove lightly and felt a radiating warmth. I looked questioningly at Anders, wondering if he saw that I was surprised by tears. "We cooked our lunch today," he said in his quiet voice. Their cabin smelled of the wood from their land. It smelled of wood they'd used to cook their meals. It smelled like Barra. I felt a great longing and a loss.

On the drive home, as I unwound myself from the maze of dirt roads, I attempted to come to grips with what had just happened. I had not expected to be so deeply affected by Anders and Kalyn's homestead to the point of so acutely missing Barra.

I was quite content with the life I'd been living for the past twenty-five years, focused on writing, gardening, family and friends, and once again mountains. My knees had been replaced in 2004 with triumphal success. I was quite conscious that there were aspects of the homesteading Barra life that I missed and would always miss. Part of that missing was what Guy and I had together. The planning of a life, and then mutually working it out. Anders and Kalyn had that.

It was evident in their shared looks, in the shorthand of their verbal exchanges, in the movement of a hand to assist the other in a small task of daily living.

Another part of the missing was a life lived outside. No longer was I spending four-hour mornings in the garden or in our woodlot, and the afternoons on easier tasks — a simple weeding job or small building project or walk into the village for the mail. This meant I was not so firmly attuned to the bird life, for instance, or so aware of the passage of wind through the upper branches of hardwoods. This meant I was less involved with seasonal changes, particularly with the growing light during our weeks of sugaring in March and April, and then its fading as we scurried to finish wood collection in the fall. Our life was driven by the seasonal work and I would never work such long hours or that hard again. I missed that.

Obviously, the progress of nature's year was not absent from my life, but there was less of it. Walking into Anders and Kalyn's world brought me sharply up against what I no longer had. "That was then," I lectured myself on my drive home. "You've had Barra. Now you are in another life, or another phase of your own life." I asked myself if there was anything I wanted to change in my present life. I still grew a reasonable vegetable garden. I had a root cellar for winter storage. I had more flower beds than I'd ever had at Barra. But then Barra was more about vegetable production than flowers. I heated with wood, but had decided cooking with it was not the way I wanted to spend my time now. "You can be outside more," I instructed myself. Yet I knew that I would not. I had evolved a daily pattern of writing in the mornings; afternoons were free for whatever came up, and that could often keep me indoors. I lived within a half-mile walk of the village that took me through a patch of woodland boasting some sizable sugar maples and ended at the town cemetery, a friendly spot edged with cedars, the grave stones carrying the names of families deeply rooted in the town's history. I often made this walk twice a day. It felt essential to my life — a respite — during which my mind filled with rewriting of my morning's sentences, or thought about nothing more than what I was seeing at ground level, perhaps an imprint of a deer's track that hadn't been there yesterday, or, after a light fall of snow, a fox's perfectly stepped paw print. "Yes, I am in another life," I continued the conversation with myself, "and the life I had at Barra with Guy has shaped it."

What I had lost was a deep connection to land that can only be attained when your life, your livelihood, is centered on gardens or woodlots. Using only hand tools strengthens this connection. We had used our books to write about mountain stewardship, applying what we had learned as homesteaders to trails and, especially, to the care of fragile alpine areas. I could still write about this, and did.

Guy's death opened up the opportunity to do more than write, when a young couple we knew well came to me to express their concern, after reading an article I'd penned, that Guy had felt our books had sunk to the bottom of the pond, leaving few ripples. Not so, they protested: our books had them seeing themselves as stewards, caretakers. They wanted to give back to the mountains they loved. Other close mountain friends said the same, lamenting Guy's regret. Conversations about how to keep our books and our stewardship message alive moved forward, and a small group of us took steps to form the Waterman Fund. But would there be a need for what our new nonprofit had to offer?

We saw that our mission was to support projects in trail maintenance, education, and research. Our targeted area was the Northeast's alpine zones, the land above the trees where errant foot traffic can obliterate the fragile vegetation. These plants are remnants of the Ice Age. Their presence dates back to the retreat of the glaciers thirteen thousand years ago. We envisioned the Fund working at the grassroots level to foster what Guy and I had called the spirit of wildness. By this we meant the imperative — for all of us — to think about the impact of our actions. Is that new hut or shelter, trail or bridge, really necessary? How will such a "convenience" or "improvement," affect the wildness, the wild spirit in that particular location? We hoped restraint would become the watchword for not just the managers, but for anyone who hiked and loved mountains.

Our grants program began in 2002. Our recipients are the trail clubs and public agencies, even individuals, whose responsibilities and concerns stretch from the coast of Maine, across New Hampshire and Vermont to New York's Adirondacks, and extend up to the alpine of Eastern Canada.

The Fund runs an annual essay contest whose goal is to encourage new voices to explore, challenge, and articulate our relationship with wilderness and wildness. The winner is awarded a cash prize and publication in *Appalachia*. In 2017 the Fund published *New Wilderness Voices: Collected Essays from the Waterman Fund Contest*, a milestone, we felt, signifying the success and relevance of the contest. A number of our winners have gone on to publish their own books on environmental and wilderness issues, which has been our fervent hope from the outset.

The Guy Waterman Alpine Steward Award is given out annually to recognize the dedication and significant contributions by an individual who furthers the cause of stewardship across the Northeast's alpine landscape. This award was first made in 2003. It has been followed by an Emerging Steward Award with the younger generation in mind.

From the beginning the Fund recognized the importance of the mountain clubs and public agencies coming together to talk about region-wide concerns as well as their own local issues. These biennial gatherings are much looked for-ward to. It's a chance to renew friendships and hike in a different location. The hosting organization has the opportunity to ask opinions of the "experts" for trouble spots, especially how best to communicate to newcomers to the alpine zone the importance of staying on trails — or rock hopping if leaving the trail.

The Fund holds field trips to view a project to which our grant money has con-tributed. We open this day to our supporters, though, of course, we are limited in group size. Our field trips have taken us, among other places, to the coastal mountains of Maine, Mount Washington's Alpine Gardens, Mount Monadnock's subalpine in southern New Hampshire, Vermont's Mount Mansfield's ridgeline crest, and Cascade Mountain's tiny alpine summit in the Adirondacks.

We are happy to say there was indeed a need for what the Waterman Fund envisioned nearly twenty-five years ago!

I could not forget what Guy had said a few days before he walked out the door for the last time: "I want to get out of your way." He was sitting on the ash log putting on his boots to go out and get the 7:00 p.m. temperatures.

I was finishing the washing up from supper. I turned toward him. "You're not in my way, Guy." How could he think this? It made me sad. And he must have been thinking it for some time. I had no idea. What he said shocked me. It seemed so at odds with how we worked, how we were, together.

I had been living in a paradoxical world for the last eighteen months, know-ing Guy would commit suicide, yet being unable to believe it would happen. He was resistant to my suggestions to "get help." Conversations that went in that direction could end in tears on my part, and his, too, even as I sensed him dig-ging in his feet.

So I lived in a seesaw world. We could be working in the garden mutually enjoying the task at hand of, say, setting out the tomato seedlings. We would harvest this crop together. Except this was the last planting and harvesting of tomatoes we would do together. This was the last garden. This thought could sneak up on me when we were engaged in Barra tasks: the last wood cord, the last sugaring, the last canning of beans, the last, the last . . . I never got used to this. I was always blindsided by it.

After Guy's death, friends asked how did I live with knowing that Guy planned to commit suicide? Part of the answer, it seems to me, is that I was granted an enormous lead time. Guy had set the date for the winter of 2000, nearly a year and a half away. There was plenty of time to change his mind. Life at Barra went along day by day as it always had. Those blindsiding moments would attack and pass. Guy was living his life, which was going to end in his suicide. I was living my life, which would continue after he was gone. The seesaw was very real: he might change his mind, yet I knew that he would not. As the months, the weeks, then days flew off the calendar into the wind, the motion of the seesaw speeded up, faster and faster, yet somehow, even then, I lived with it, and the work at Barra, both of us as full participants, went on. It must have been the work that allowed me to live both happily and unhappily in this world that I knew would end with my husband's deliberate, well-planned death.

There have not been many times since Guy's death that I have wished him alive. I can explain. I'm thinking of political events or the threats we are facing to our planet with climate change and the wholesale dismemberment of protective environmental legislation. He had told me he was very glad to be sidestepping the presidential election coming up. As a loyal Republican with Jeffersonian ideals, Guy carried a profound sadness for what he saw happening to the Republican Party. He wanted to avoid hearing the discussion around these candidates that was only going to plunge him into gloom.

Yet there are close-to-home events, moments when I catch myself thinking: *Guy would be glad of this.* For instance, he would be delighted with the work of the Fund. Ironically, of course, there would be no fund if it were not for Guy's death. The biennial Alpine Stewardship Gatherings were his idea and three were held in the early 1990s. But since there was no presiding group in charge, the Gatherings tapered off. Back then, there was little to no interaction between managers of the mountain clubs or the public agencies. Baxter State Park and Katahdin in Maine were a long way from the Adirondacks. Each club or agency had more than enough work in the field season to keep them in their home territory. Yet Guy had felt that these managers could learn a lot from each other. One of the first efforts of the Fund was to start up these Alpine Gatherings again.

Guy would be glad to know our books are still in print and out in new editions. But what would please him most is that the children of our trail-working and mountain friends, to whom we dedicated our book *Wilderness Ethics*, are now involved with their own environmental causes. At a recent Alpine Gathering, the parents of two of these children asked me to sign copies of the book for their now-grown offspring we'd named in our dedication. Another trail-worker parent described for me how his daughter, also named in our dedication, gained inspiration from our chapter, "Why the Lorax Lost," for her current work encouraging Latin American palm oil companies to improve their environmental and labor practices. It's times like these when I'm sorry he's not around.

Do I miss him? He is never far from my mind, but that doesn't mean I miss him. I'm too aware of how much he wanted to get out of life. I often feel his thought processes moving through my own, his planning, his ability to break down a task that seemed much too big. I've discovered that my way of working and processing is very different from Guy's. But that does not stop me from working thoughtfully through, not what he might have done, but what I will do. So he continues to be both model and touchstone in my life. This cannot be unusual. It must be the case for others who experience in life close connections. The absent person is forever gone, but in so many ways absolutely present.

With the knee replacements, I could return to the mountains. Neither of us foresaw that possibility or how different my approach to mountains is now from what we had together. For Guy and me, mountains were more about the challenge: the difficulty of the terrain, the long days, multiple winter nights camped out, before dawn starts, a hard objective — not always met — but strived for. Then, overtopping the challenge was the seduction of the mountains themselves. Their never-failing beauty, their elemental nature of solid rock, of snow-and-ice-laden trees, of deep, steep, ledgy ravines, of the song of the white-throated sparrow, of wind-whipped cloud shadows, of alpine ridges, and, for us, finally, that land above the trees, where tundra plants carry on their life cycles in wind and storm and intense cold, conditions that can kill us humans. Here can be found wildness.

Now, for me, one day a week is committed to local walks, or a drive to New Hampshire or the mountains in Vermont — with fewer four-thousand footers now. We — my friends and I, few of whom knew Guy — watch the weather as Guy and I never did, amending the plan for rain or snow. We do no camping. No wild bushwhacks. But we have certain peaks we love and return to over and over. I've expanded my mountain travels to England, trips of many days of walking, staying in inns or bed and breakfasts, accommodations Guy, who needed a certain amount of discomfort, of independence, would never have considered, yet I know he would be extremely glad I have mountains again.

Pulling away from Barra was eased for me by the stewards who, especially in the early years, lived there for short-term stays. My help was often needed for planting the garden, wood collection, sugaring, as well as useful tips on how to be comfortable in a cabin with no central heating, plumbing, electricity, or road access. By the time the stewards were coming for longer periods, I was ready to step aside. I had my own garden to take care of, my own life to lead. From the beginning the stewards themselves had made some very useful changes: solar power being a major one that was consistent with living lightly on the land. Hauling water to the garden was eased by a gravity feed system from the stream. The cabin was tightened up, cutting in half the amount of wood needed to heat it. A master carpenter affixed a greenhouse to the south-facing wall that provided winter greens and warm sunlight. Guy and I had learned from the Nearings' books, accepting some parts of their practice and not others. In this way we learned what worked for us. What would delight Guy, as it does me, is when those young stewards have told me that those months or even years spent at Barra led them to see a direction for their own lives.

As our days at Barra wound down, I was concerned that so much of my own identity was bound up with our Barra life. My life was going to change. Who would I be now, on my own without Guy and not living at Barra?

I should have known that a gardener does not stop being a gardener, or a writer a writer, or a hiker a hiker. These parts of me easily carried on, though amended to how I was living now. Amending as I grew older.

I was living my own life. *My* life. Not our life, or my life with Guy. This was the change. This was the new Identity. I was ready for it.

I had loved that decade I'd lived in New York, but I had not found work that really meant something to me. Work that called for a true, unstinting, heartfelt commitment. I was drifting, not driven. When I met Guy, it was easy to step into the vision of this man I loved and wanted to spend my life with.

My family, when I was small, had called me a late bloomer. I understood what that meant; I thought of myself in those terms. And not such a bad thing either, I'd told myself.

"I want to get out of your way," Guy had said. He knew I would flourish without him. He saw, in his discerning way, that I wasn't seeing that he blocked me.

We get one chance at life. The signposts are sparse. The trail often overgrown and stony. Clouds, mists, and fog can obscure the landmarks, especially in that sought-after, hard-to-reach world above the trees. I've grown accustomed to low visibility and keep on walking. I know how the path feels under my boots, and if I lose it, I'll pick it up a little farther on. I could not be what I've become without the life Guy and I had lived together. I see that now.

Acknowledgments

Part of the pleasure of writing, as well as the pain, is involved in pouring into that thing which is being created all of what [I] cannot understand, cannot say, cannot deal with or cannot even admit in any other way.

— Ralph Ellison, quoted in Jill Krementz, *The Writer's Desk*

I couldn't have written this book without being able to refer to the careful notes Guy kept on so many aspects of our life together. This accretion of statistics was impressive, to my mind, for the small amount of space it consumes on my bookshelf. Legible and compact, always informative, never superfluous, the Barra Archives, as I've come to call it, not only revealed forgotten facts but fleshed out fading memory.

Guy's unpublished memoir, which he titled "Prospero's Options," gave me what I needed to know about his life before I met him. Another useful source was the memoir called "The Farm," written by Guy's sisters about the family's growing-up years in North Haven, Connecticut. For keeping me accurate on Waterman family lore, my deep gratitude goes to Anne Waterman Cooley and to the late Barbara Waterman Carney.

My own daily journal, begun on the day we moved to Barra, June 9, 1973, proved a reassuring tool, holding me to the line about the course of events and keeping me straight about dates.

I extend my boundless thanks to the following quintet: Helen Whybrow inherited our *Ethics* books after she became editor in chief at the Countryman Press and made a point of walking into Barra to meet us. This was, we thought, an unusually friendly gesture to backlist authors. She kept *Wilderness Ethics* in print by bringing out a special edition after Guy died. When I told Helen I intended to write a memoir she offered to read the chapters, and I became the fortunate beneficiary of her clarity of mind, her innate sensitivity and discerning guidance, and her steadfast friendship.

Annie Barry, constant friend from my youth, played the hardest role of all. She found the unflagging courage to beam the searchlight on the truly troublesome questions, and I was sustained by her desire that I find the answers. For both of us it was often a rocky road, but to Annie's friendship and loyalty I owe my profoundest thanks.

Brad Snyder became our friend through his climbing partnership with Guy's son Johnny. When we began writing books Brad acted as our first line-of-defense editor. Guy said Brad had the best mind of anyone he knew. Once again, I have drawn in generous portions on Brad's intelligence and wit and devotion to the accurate use of language.

Chip Brown came into my life after Guy had died, when he got in touch about writing his own book on Guy. It was a good match. Guy would have liked Chip, and his generosity to me with his own insights gleaned from his outsider's perspective, along with his skill at asking penetrating questions, drove me deeper into my own territory.

Sue Foster, valiant friend and neighbor, transferred my manually typed drafts to her computer more times than I care to admit, and always with facility and grace.

My deep gratitude to the generosity of Kate Botham, Eleanor Kohlsaat, Rebecca Oreskes, Louis D. Rubin Jr., Sally Tomlinson, and Lisa Troy, who read drafts and offered insight along with their encouragement. Annie Bellerose, Carl Demrow, Marie Kirn, Jon Martinson, Doug Mayer, Chuck Wooster, and Nick Zandstra, dear friends all, listened to me go on about my "discoveries," and through the process of walks and talks and endless cups of tea, led me to see more. The book's title comes from formidable combined inspiration of Doug Mayer and Rebecca Oreskes. I thank Deborah Jones, a therapist I consulted when I was well into this project. For permission to quote from letters and from material read at Guy's memorial service I would like to acknowledge with thanks Louis Cornell, Gil Murray, Annie Barry, Doug Mayer, Sue and Bill Parmenter, Douglas Teschner, Alice Tufel, and the late Earlyn Dean.

My agent, Christina Ward, did a fabulous job in championing my manuscript and arranging the perfect match. Jack Shoemaker and Trish Hoard raise their books like precious children. Under Trish's dedicated care and sensitive guidance, my story blossomed into a lucky book.

Acknowledgments for the Second Edition

For this new edition I have had the incomparable support of my agent Craig Kayser. Together we began a journey of finding a publisher for a book that had been orphaned. That happened when Shoemaker & Hoard, the original publisher, was acquired by Counterpoint. So *Losing the Garden* had been out of print for nearly twenty years. After many twists and turns we landed on the doorstep of the SUNY Press, familiar to us since James Peltz, editorial director, had already released, in 2019, the Thirtieth Anniversary edition of *Forest and Crag*, a history of the Northeast mountains that I had written with my husband Guy Waterman. In 2024 James Peltz had published my *Calling Wild Places Home*, half anthology, half memoir, a sequel of sorts to *Losing the Garden*. At least that's how Craig and I saw it. Evidently James did too! When that happened there was much cheering on the part of Craig and me.

Losing the Garden, however, would have gone nowhere without the responses of six wonderfully generous people who wrote endorsements for a book that had first seen daylight in 2005. Now I have the opportunity to thank those six people from the bottom of my heart: Jeffrey Berman, George Howe Colt, Karen Green, Reeve Lindbergh, Alison Osius, and Christine Woodside.

I also thank Bill McKibben and Mary Margaret Sloan who had offered endorsements for the first edition of *Losing the Garden*. It is with greatest pleasure to carry on their words in this second edition.

Charles Johnson contributed the Foreword that fits the book like a well-broken-in pair of hiking boots. Thank you, Charles! We had not met when I wrote you about writing a foreword, but I knew our lives had touched in both painful and joyous ways.

I want to single out Jeffrey Berman and Darryl McGrath. James had asked them to review the manuscript to see if it was worth bringing back into print. It was, they chorused. In the aftermath of that, Jeffrey and Darryl became champions of the book, easing its way toward publication.

The cover image was snapped by our good friend Ned Therrien, whose photographs taken at Barra and in the mountains are housed with our pagers at the Dartmouth College Library. I thank Morgan Swan and Samantha Milnes of Dartmouth College Library, Special Collections, for their work in helping me locate in our papers the perfect photograph of our homestead for the frontispiece. And a warm thanks to my illustrator for *Calling Wild Places Home*, Nancy Kittridge, with her assist with last-minute technological issues.

At crucial moments my amanuensis, Sue Foster, stepped in. Craig and I were aware that her timing was always impeccable. I want to thank her for the role she played in the whole long process of securing a new publisher.

I close with a hearty thank you to James Peltz and his staff at SUNY Press for bringing my *Losing the Garden* back to life. Out of the ashes it blooms again, a lucky book indeed!

❀ ❁ ❀

About the Author

Laura Waterman has coauthored books on hiking, climbing, and environmental issues with her husband, Guy Waterman. For nearly twenty years, the couple maintained trails in the alpine areas of New Hampshire's White Mountains, notably the Franconia Ridge. In 2000, after Guy's death, Laura and friends who cared deeply about Guy and what he stood for in the mountains started the Waterman Fund, a nonprofit that supports education, research, and stewardship in the alpine zones of Northeastern North America. The American Alpine Club awarded Laura and posthumously Guy their David Brower Conservation Award in 2012. Laura and Guy combined a life of climbing with homesteading and living self-sufficiently on the land, which they sustained up to Guy's death. Laura wrote about this twenty-eight-year experiment in her memoir, *Losing the Garden: The Story of a Marriage* (2005), which was a *Boston Globe* Editor's Pick. That was followed in 2019 by *Starvation Shore*, a novel about a historical Arctic expedition in the 1880s, and in 2024 by *Calling Wild Places Home: A Memoir in Essays*. She has published her writing in various literary magazines, journals, and anthologies, including *Alpinist, Yankee, Appalachia, Vermont Life*, and *Climbing*. She is currently writing a novel about Maria Callas. She lives in Vermont.